A Key
to Charismatic
Renewal in the
Catholic Church

Maria Genovese

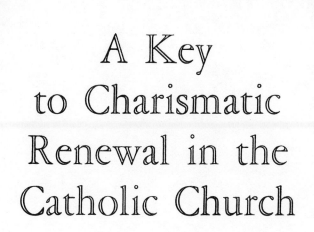

A Key to Charismatic Renewal in the Catholic Church

BY

REV. VINCENT M. WALSH

Abbey Press
St. Meinrad, IN 47577
1975

First Published, 1974
Second Printing, February 1975
Third Printing, June 1975

Nihil obstat: James McGrath
          Censor Librorum
Imprimatur: ✠ John Cardinal Krol
          Archbishop of Philadelphia

The *Nihil obstat* and *Imprimatur* are official declarations that a book or pamphlet
is free of doctrinal or moral error. No implication is contained therein that those
who have granted the *Nihil obstat* and *Imprimatur* agree with the contents, opin-
ions, or statements expressed.

Library of Congress Catalog Card Number: 74-82238
ISBN: 0-87029-033-9
© 1974 by Rev. Vincent M. Walsh
All rights reserved.
Abbey Press
St. Meinrad, Indiana 47577

Printed in the United States of America

To my parents, Joseph and Mary, who first awakened me to the Life in the Spirit.

Contents

Contents

PREFACE

ON FRIDAY OF EASTER WEEK, 1970, ANOTHER PRIEST and I, as if by chance, participated in a mass held at St. Boniface Charismatic Prayer Group. Afterwards, I met Brother Pancratius Boudreau, C.SS.R., who would teach me much of what is contained in this book. Since I was a chancery official, he was just a little uptight about the visit. Afterwards he told me that I really hadn't experienced a prayer meeting and urged me to return. The furthest thing from my mind that night was a return.

During the next few months a number of events occurred. My brother questioned me about the movement, since his wife had become involved with a charismatic group. I, myself, spent more than a month, January, 1971, recovering from a serious cold and infection. But most of all, during these months, a sense was coming over me of the great changes in the world and the new problems of the Church in the face of growing world powers. My part-time work in the Newman Apostolate grew more difficult with fewer results and less response to my ministry.

On Palm Sunday, 1971, my sister-in-law took a few minutes to witness to me about all the changes that had occurred in her own life because of her involvement in the prayer group. Suddenly the lights went back on and the growing darkness in my life was immediately lifted.

A few days later, I went to the bookstore and bought numerous books on Pentecostalism. The next Friday I called Brother Pancratius to ask about the time of the prayer meeting. At the end of the conversation, he remarked, "Weren't you here about a year ago, Father?" "Oh, no, Brother," I responded. "It was only about six months."

After putting down the phone, I tried to recall when that chance attendance occurred, and came to realize that my first meeting was precisely one year before—Easter Friday, 1970.

As I stood in front of the Church, I could not get over the coincidence of having been there exactly one year previously. My thoughts were this: "What a difference one year makes. A year ago I was here and it meant almost nothing. Now, one year later, I am back and I realize that everything I am, or was or will be—my whole past, future and eternity—my whole priesthood—everything— is tied up with what is behind those doors."

I have passed through those doors and the three subsequent years have easily been the most satisfying, holy, fruitful years of my entire life. The thousands of words that follow have been written that many others might also walk through those doors into a deeper life in the Spirit.

> *To the presiding Spirit of the Church*
> *in Philadelphia, write this:*
>   *The holy One, the true,*
>   *Who wields David's key,*
>   *Who opens and no one can close,*
>   *Who closes and no one can open.*
>   *(Rev. 3:7)*

EXPLANATION OF THE TITLE

The title has been deliberately chosen from the message to the Church of Philadelphia, since I naturally drew upon the experiences of the Philadelphia Charismatic Groups.

The word "a" was used, as opposed to "the," to avoid any idea that other books could not also be keys to the door of Charismatic Renewal.

By *Charismatic Renewal* is understood not only the reappearance of charismatic gifts, but the total unfolding of the action of the Holy Spirit in our time, most of which is still hidden.

Particularly important is an explanation of the phrase *"in the Catholic Church."* In no way do I wish to hurt the sensitivities of those who are not Catholic. The phrase "in the Catholic Church" is used for the following reasons:

1. It is the tradition with which I am most acquainted.

2. My purpose is that innumerable Catholics, who have not as yet heard of or understood Charismatic Renewal, would be able to see this movement in the light of the Catholic tradition.

3. I am unable, due to the lack of experience or of theological background, to explain Charismatic Renewal in any other tradition.

I, therefore, beg the pardon of those who are not of the Catholic tradition, when using phrases such as "the Catholic Church has always thought" or "the Catholic tradition is." I do not, by this, intend to slight other ecclesiastical denominations, but hope that those of other traditions benefit by the work.

ON THE WRITING

For almost three years now *A Key to Charismatic Renewal in the Catholic Church* has been a large part of my life. Originally, this work was conceived as a small pamphlet—the hundred questions most frequently asked about Pentecostalism. As the writing began, the work grew and only then did the scope of this burden become clear.

Hopefully, although touching on many aspects of this renewal, the writing has remained simple. There are no claims to great insights and no pretense to being the last word on Charismatic Renewal. Throughout the writing I have tried to keep in mind the many who have never even participated in a charismatic prayer meeting and are yet to know what this movement is all about; and the many who pray regularly with a group and need a clear and simple explanation of what the Lord is doing among them.

Much criticism can surround this work—claiming it is too superficial, the scope too large and the advice too pretentious. This book, however, has not been written to be acclaimed, but to be a help to many people reaching out desperately for a deeper life in the Spirit.

ACKNOWLEDGEMENTS

To Brother Pancratius Boudreau, C.SS.R., God's messenger to the Church of Philadelphia; to Sister Barbara Ann Beck, O.S.F. and Sister Judith Marie Shambo, O.S.F. for their help in preparing the text; and to Sister Maria Rosita, R.S.M., for her insistence on the simplicity of the message.

Chapter One

Understanding the Charismatic Renewal Movement

*It is what Joel the prophet spoke of:
"It shall come to pass in the last
days, says God, that I will pour out
a portion of my spirit on all mankind."*

(Acts 2:16-17)

INTRODUCTION

CHARISMATIC RENEWAL, OR CATHOLIC PENTECOSTALISM, has become a household word in the Church. Its continued growth means that all will soon become aware of the phrase, if not the reality.

Many renewals have preceded this charismatic one—liturgical, scriptural, and patristic, among others. All of these have been a return to the sources, a stripping away of cultural additions and a return to the beginning. Charismatic Renewal, however, is something very special, for the return is to the first Pentecost, the very beginning of the Church itself, in search of a new Pentecost in our day.

Events in Charismatic Renewal have moved extremely quickly from the early days of 1967 to the tremendous gathering in June 1974 at Notre Dame. This chapter proposes to be an overview, a stepping back, an historical look at what has taken place and a prognosis of what will happen. The following insights will be provided:

1) An understanding of those elements termed "Pentecostal."
2) The place of this movement in the Catholic Church.
3) A grasp of how the word "movement" is used.

In a true sense the Lord has surprised us all. When everything seemed bleak, with the large numbers of priests and sisters leaving because of problems in the Church, with widespread disassociation from the Church among the young and with a struggle to renew the Church taking place, the Lord began to pour forth His Spirit in outstanding ways. Suddenly, a new surge of power was felt in Christ's Mystical Body. Large numbers began to experience prayer, use spiritual gifts, and come together regularly to praise God. The powers of the early Church, long covered over, were released suddenly for large numbers. Hopefully this work will help many to realize what God's Spirit is doing and how all can share in this rich outpouring, promised many years ago by Peter on Pentecost Day.

This particular chapter has three sections, examining

the three terms, "Pentecostalism," "Catholic," and "movement."

UNDERSTANDING PENTECOSTALISM

A) *Definition and History*

1. WHAT IS MEANT BY PENTECOSTALISM?

The term refers to certain elements of the Christian life, usually associated with the feast of Pentecost and Christ's gifts of the Spirit.

These elements would include:

a) A prayer experience whereby the Holy Spirit becomes not just an object of faith but also of experience. This is associated with consolations in prayer, a sense of God's presence, or what traditional teaching would call "fervor." This prayer experience is called the "Baptism of the Spirit" and is intimately connected to a personal commitment to Jesus as Lord.

b) The gift of praying in tongues described in Acts 2:4, and Acts 11:46.

c) The charismatic ministries of the Spirit manifested in the Acts of the Apostles and outlined by St. Paul in 1 Cor. 12, 14.

It would also include an attempt to pattern Church life according to the Scriptural model of the Acts of the Apostles so that the power evident in the early Church would be manifest in our times—or, as Pope John prayed, that we would experience a new Pentecost in our day.

2. HOW DID THESE ELEMENTS COME TO BE IDENTIFIED AS "PENTECOSTALISM"?

These elements of prayer experience, charismatic gifts and patterns of Church community are identified as "Pentecostal" for two reasons:

a) They are described extensively in the Acts of the Apostles, which begins with the Pentecost narration.

b) They also "dropped out" of normal Church life as

the Church moved further away in time from the
Pentecostal outpouring.

It is natural that, as these elements reappear and renew
the Church according to the model of the Acts of the
Apostles, they would be termed "Pentecostal."

Although the above could be called the main elements of
Pentecostalism, what God seems to be working through
the Catholic Pentecostal Movement is, in fact, a very complex phenomenon, not easily analyzed or dissected.

3. IN A SENSE, WAS NOT EVERYBODY IN THE EARLY CHURCH A "PENTECOSTAL"?

According to the Acts of the Apostes, early preaching
certainly led up to the full reception of the Spirit in a
prayer experience. Also in the Acts, charismatic activity
was abundant and patterns of Church life were dynamic.
The "pentecostal experience" and charismatic gifts were
available to all, according to the prophecy of Joel, that
the Spirit would be poured forth on all flesh (Acts 2:16).

As Charismatic Renewal spreads and is accepted, hopefully once more the Church will be renewed in the Spirit
of a Second Pentecost according to the patterns of the
Acts.

4. WHAT HAPPENED TO THIS STRESS ON THE "PENTE-COSTAL EXPERIENCE"?

For many reasons the full activity of the Holy Spirit
in the Church became obscure and limited. The manifestations and workings of the Holy Spirit, as outlined in the
New Testament, seemed for the most part to cease. As a
result, many theologians spoke of the apostolic age as
unique, and felt that these special graces were meant only
for the Early Church. Church preaching then turned to
other elements of Church life—such as Creed, Sacraments
and Commandments.

5. WAS THERE A COMPLETE LOSS OF PENTECOSTAL ELE-MENTS IN THE CATHOLIC CHURCH?

There was never a complete loss and these elements have
always been in the life of the Catholic Church and accepted
by spiritual writers. In fact, traditional Catholic spirit-

uality has always stressed the value of a growth in prayer and the Church has always had mystics. Abundant charismatic activity is present in the lives of the saints, and occasional manifestations of God's power are known to a great number of laity. The history of the Church is replete with "enthusiast" groups, who in spite of difficulties, added a devotional richness.

6. WHAT LOSS DID OCCUR IN CHURCH LIFE?

There was an obscuring of the total life of the Spirit in the average Catholic. Church preaching stressed a reception of sacraments and a living according to a certain moral code. In a sense, the Church did not realize the extent of its own powers to bring all the faithful to a personal commitment to Christ, to a deep personal, prayerful life, and into charismatic ministries.

B) *History of Modern Pentecostalism*

7. DID MODERN PENTECOSTALISM BEGIN WITH CATHOLICS?

Far from it. This renewal began among non-Catholic groups and, rather than renewing the Churches, led to the formation of Pentecostal Churches and to what has been called a "third force" in Christianity.

Since its small beginning in the early 1900s, Pentecostalism has literally swept the world. Within the last few decades, however, its power has been manifest within traditional Churches as well as outside of them.

8. WHAT WOULD BE THE GENERAL CHARACTERISTICS OF "MODERN DAY PENTECOSTALS"?

Although there is diversity, the following could characterize "modern day Pentecostals":

a) The belief that the Baptism of the Spirit bestowed on the disciples of Jesus on the first Pentecost Day is meant to be bestowed on all Christians.

b) The belief that the charismatic manifestations, present after Pentecost, were not meant to "die out," e.g., that praying in tongues and the other charismatic gifts are meant to be experienced and used by every Christian.

c) Doctrinally, "Pentecostals" are usually orthodox, subscribing to a traditional understanding of the Apostles Creed. Catholic Pentecostals would also accept other Catholic doctrines contained only implicitly in the Creed itself.

d) In practice, stress is placed on private and group prayer (prayer meeting), faith in the Lordship of Jesus, and the attempt to live according to gospel maxims.

UNDERSTANDING PENTECOSTALISM IN THE CATHOLIC CHURCH

C) *History of Catholic Pentecostal Movement*

9. WHEN DID THIS MOVEMENT BEGIN IN THE CATHOLIC CHURCH?

In 1967, some concerned Catholics at Duquesne University met and prayed regularly. They were upset by the obvious decline of religious practice, both on the campus and throughout the whole Church, and were led to the conclusion that a true renewal in the Church was dependent upon a new Pentecost.

Since Vatican II mentioned that Catholics could learn from the Spirit's action in other Churches, they were led to pray with a Pentecostal group in Pittsburgh.

Eventually they asked to be prayed with for the Baptism of the Holy Spirit. After this, they began to manifest the charismatic gifts and to possess within themselves a prayerful new relationship to Jesus of Nazareth.

(The ideas of the Baptism of the Spirit and the charismatic gifts are treated extensively in later chapters).

This initial opening by Catholics to Pentecostal powers was the beginning of the phenomenon of widespread Charismatic Renewal in the Catholic Church.

10. HOW LARGE IS THE CATHOLIC PENTECOSTAL MOVEMENT?

The National Directory currently lists hundreds of charismatic prayer communities. Many others share in Charismatic Renewal in an unofficial way. Every indication (sizes of conferences, sales of books, number of weekly prayer meetings) witnesses to growing numbers.

When compared with the total numbers in other movements, the growth has been extremely rapid. When compared with the total number of American Catholics, however, the size is still small.

The key in Charismatic Renewal, however, is not in its size but in its message and its power. There is no reason why every Catholic should not experience this new Pentecost as the Church grasps and assimilates the features of Charismatic Renewal into normal Church life.

D) *Relationship of the Charismatic Movement to the Entire Church.*

11. WHAT HAS BEEN THE REACTION OF THE CATHOLIC HIERARCHY TO THE PENTECOSTAL MOVEMENT?

The Catholic hierarchy has assumed the attitude which Gamaliel (Acts 5:34-39) took toward the new movement of Christianity itself, namely, that if this is truly of God, then it will continue and bear fruit.

A statement on Catholic Pentecostalism was issued in 1969 by the Theological Committee of the American Bishops. It stated the following:

a) The movement has a sound Scriptural foundation.

b) The effect on the participants is good, often leading them back to abandoned religious practices.

c) Prudent priests should be involved in the movement so as to assure sound guidance in the use of the charismatic gifts.

In April 1972, the American bishops reaffirmed this statement at their national meeting. Individual bishops have sometimes gone further, with high praise for this movement.

12. WHAT HAS BEEN THE REACTION OF PRIESTS AND LAITY?

Among priests and laity, the reaction to the movement has varied. The great majority have merely heard of the movement without ever having experienced a prayer group. Others are very wary of Catholic Pentecostalism, having theological or personal objections to it. Still others are somewhat attracted to the results they see or hear. Finally, for some, it has meant a great deal, and is a constant source of spiritual strength in the modern world.

13. WHAT IS THE ATTITUDE OF THIS "MOVEMENT" TO THE HIERARCHY?

The Catholic Pentecostal Movement believes in the Catholic Church and in the authority given to the Church by Christ. From the very beginning (and probably more than anywhere else in the Church) there has been obedience and respect to the hierarchy.

Charismatic leaders believe that God has placed authority within His Church. Leaders accept the discipline of obedience to hierarchy, realizing that this is the only way Pentecostalism can benefit the Church.

14. WHY HAS THE CATHOLIC CHURCH BEEN SO OPEN TO THIS MOVEMENT?

The Catholic Church has always esteemed the "Pentecostal" elements, such as a prayer experience and divine interventions. Basically, much of the Pentecostal teaching rediscovers overlooked or neglected parts of our own tradition.

Even the charismatic gifts, as taught in "Pentecostal" literature, are listed by Adolph Tanquerey in his *Spiritual Life* (a text well-known to priests and religious). He explains the nine charismatic gifts and expects them to be manifested as the soul makes its way to God.

15. COULD YOU ELABORATE ON THIS?

The Church's traditional spiritual writers outline the

way to God through three stages: purgative, illuminative and unitive. They presuppose that the soul makes progress in prayer and, by following God's inspirations, comes into a deep personal knowledge of Christ. These, and other effects, are the main fruits of the "Pentecostal experience."

The Church has always taught the presence of the charismatic gifts, for example, in the lives of the saints. Also, the Church has upheld Lourdes and Fatima as places of appearances of Our Lady and a legitimate source of a healing ministry. It has demanded miracles prior to canonization. Its mystical theology is replete with teachings on the charisms, how they are to be used and the dangers involved.

16. HOW IMPORTANT IS THIS MOVEMENT FOR THE CHURCH?

Certainly, this movement contains a *power* and *dynamism*, capable of being extended to all, and of renewing every aspect of the Church's life. Many see the Church's effectiveness in the modern world as intimately connected with this spiritual outpouring.

At this time, when problems of mass attendance, a vocation crisis, Catholic school financial difficulties, a religious education crisis and a host of other difficulties beset the Catholic Church, a movement of this kind is frequently seen as the Church's main hope.

Also, when many others in the Church seem to be losing hope, Catholic Pentecostals are praising the Lord for all that He is doing, and as in the Early Church, they are adding to their numbers day by day.

E) *Objections to Pentecostalism in the Catholic Church*

17. IS IT NOT A CONTRADICTION TO CALL SOMEONE A "CATHOLIC PENTECOSTAL"? HOW DOES THAT DIFFER FROM CALLING ONESELF A "CATHOLIC LUTHERAN" OR A "CATHOLIC BAPTIST"?

There is a great deal of difference between "Pentecostalism" and "Lutheranism," or any other denominational belief. The difference is that "Pentecostalism" is a spiritual way of life, whereas "Lutheranism" is a doctrinal teaching. Luther's break with the Catholic Church (and other such religious divisions) occurred over doctrine that the Church found incompatible with its traditional understanding of revelation. Pentecostalism does not present a new doctrine, but merely stresses the belief that what happened at the First Pentecost is meant to happen to all Christians until the Lord returns. Therefore, it is compatible with any Christian tradition, so that there can be, and are, Lutheran Pentecostals, Baptist Pentecostals, etc.

18. ARE NOT SOME TEACHINGS OF "PENTECOSTAL-ISM" AGAINST THE TEACHING OF THE CATHOLIC CHURCH?

Here, a distinction has to be made between the basic teachings of "Pentecostalism" (which will be outlined later) and those teachings which have been added to "Pentecostalism" because of its contact with a given Protestant tradition.

At any prayer community, the teachings that are given would include "Pentecostal" teaching (such as a correct use of the gifts) and also "Christian" teaching (such as a theology of sacramental Baptism or of forgiveness of sin or of the role of Scripture). Naturally, these Christian teachings will be influenced by the denominational background of the speaker or of the whole community. The Catholic groups have learned from the Protestant Pentecostal groups about the full life in the Spirit and of the charismatic gifts (as Vatican II said we could learn), and yet have not accepted the denominational teachings at variance with Catholic doctrine.

F) *Catholic Pentecostalism and the Catholic Ecumenical Movement.*

19. DO NOT SOME HAVE THE IDEA THAT THIS IS AN ECUMENICAL MOVEMENT?

Because Catholics share with other Christians the basic

"Pentecostal" beliefs, many do think of Charismatic Renewal as an ecumenical movement. However, the goals of the movement are not primarily ecumenical.

The primary purpose of Charismatic Renewal is for the Catholic Church to experience, in every part of its life, the power of the Holy Spirit and charismatic gifts.

However, the Spirit is moving within all denominations, as many churches are experiencing this renewal. Since the Spirit bestows unity, this latest outpouring will have ecumenical effects, resulting in the closer union of the Churches.

The Charismatic Renewal Movement is certainly not ecumenical in the sense of leadership attempting to form a new church, based solely on the Pentecostal experience and charismatic gifts.

20. HOW WOULD A CATHOLIC PENTECOSTAL GROUP DIFFER FROM A PROTESTANT OF INTERDENOMINATIONAL GROUP?

Differences could be examined from a doctrinal or a cultural aspect. Doctrinally, the Catholic group would:

a) Accept the mass as the prime means of worshipping God. Therefore, the weekly prayer meeting would never serve as a substitute for mass attendance.

b) Accept those doctrines authoritatively taught by the Catholic Church and, therefore, would reject any Protestant Pentecostal teachings which were not in conformity with Church doctrine.

c) Be obedient to the commands of the local bishop and would accept the teaching role of priests (in fact, most groups welcome a priest for spiritual guidance).

Culturally, a Catholic prayer group differs from its Protestant counterpart in the following ways. It:

a) Would probably not sing as much and would use different hymns.

b) Would not put as much accent on the charism of healing.

c) Would be somewhat less expressive emotionally.

d) Would possibly use the charismatic word "gift"
   more.

(It should be noted that the author is speaking out of
a Philadelphia tradition of both Catholic and Protestant
prayer groups).

SUMMARY

21. IN SUMMARY, HOW CAN THE MOVEMENT BE CALLED
    "CATHOLIC"?

First, the Eucharist is seen as the center of all prayer
and praise of the Father.

Second, the Pentecostal experience reawakens in the individual an appreciation of traditional practices, such as
participating in mass, confession, the rosary, etc. These
practices, in the lives of some, had been discarded.

Third, it cherishes and is nourished by the traditional
teaching of the Church, especially the traditions of ascetical and mystical theology as outlined by respected authors
and saints.

Fourth, it places itself totally under the bishops.

Fifth, hopefully, with proper leadership, it can avoid
the pitfalls of past "enthusiast" movements and be a
source of true renewal within the Church.

A list such as this could be greatly expanded.

UNDERSTANDING
CHARISMATIC RENEWAL
AS A MOVEMENT

H) *Is It Truly a Movement?*

22. IN WHAT SENSE IS THIS A "MOVEMENT IN THE
    CHURCH"?

It is certainly not a movement in the usual sense. Usually a movement arises from the brilliant ideas of its founder
or from the clever organization of large groups of people,
or from some other humanly explainable, sociological factors.

The history of Catholic Pentecostalism, its origins, spontaneous growth, spiritual powers and scriptural basis, indicate that this movement is not the work of men but of God, truly renewing His Church in a very special hour of crisis.

23. CAN IT BE CALLED A "MOVEMENT" IN ANY SENSE?

It can be called a "movement" in two senses. First, a large group of people share, value, and use the riches of Pentecostalism for their own good and the good of the Church.

Secondly, some (or even many) are attempting to work out human means which would make sure that this charismatic outpouring by God will not go to waste or become ineffectual within the Church.

24. IS "MOVEMENT" THEN THE BEST WORD?

The word "movement" is used reluctantly by all. Perhaps a better phrase would be "Spiritual way of life." An ever-increasing number of people view a Pentecostal spirituality as dynamic, suited to modern needs, and consonant with traditional spiritual principles. These people join together in prayer communities to help one another with this spirituality and to help others who might want to join.

25. HOW DOES THIS "SPIRITUAL WAY OF LIFE" DIFFER FROM OTHER WAYS ALREADY SANCTIONED BY THE CHURCH?

Various spiritual ways have always existed throughout the history of the Church and large numbers of people have been attracted to a given spiritual way of life. The Church has sanctioned spiritualities such as the Franciscan or Dominican or Carmelite. The model of Pentecostal spirituality, however, is not a great saint but the events in the Acts of the Apostles. A spiritual way of life based on Pentecost encompasses all other spiritualities.

I) *Nature of the Movement*

26. IS THIS A LIBERAL OR A CONSERVATIVE MOVEMENT?

In a real sense, it is neither. Liberal Catholics frequently view Pentecostal Catholics as "copping-out" on the issues of changes in the Church, social justice, ecology and the whole list of concerns usually upheld by the liberal Catholic movement. Pentecostal Catholics are seen as avoiding all these issues and escaping into prayer communities.

Conservative Catholics, on the other hand, are somewhat taken back by the freedom, spontaneity and enthusiasm of the Catholic Pentecostal prayer meetings. They seem to have difficulty with the charismatic gifts and are slow to believe that Catholics could learn anything from Protestant groups.

27. WHAT ISSUES ARE IMPORTANT TO THE CATHOLIC PENTECOSTAL MOVEMENT?

The movement has one primary issue; namely, that God be praised and that His Kingdom come. The "kingdom" obviously includes the removal of suffering, the drying of every tear, and the healing of mankind, especially of the internal, psychological wounds which all of us carry.

In a sense, it is a "prayer movement" based on the belief that if man comes into a personal relationship with Jesus Christ then a healing will begin to take place within the individual, which will gradually change the world in which he lives.

28. DOES THE MOVEMENT, THEN, AVOID "ISSUES"?

The movement, as such, avoids being drawn into other issues, although often the members, strengthened by their life of prayer, do concern themselves with religious and social concerns.

The Catholic Pentecostal Movement (or Charismatic Renewal) has a very important message to teach the Catholic faithful. If it begins to get involved directly in issues such as war or peace or social justice, people will surely become confused about the movement and, in many cases, be unable to identify with it. However, a maturing in the

Spirit does seem to bear fruit in true social concern, either by the individual or the group.

J) *Permanence and Extent of the Movement*
29. WILL THIS MOVEMENT LAST?

It is felt by all that Charismatic Renewal will last. It is foreseen that it will cease as a movement, in the sense that some Catholics belong and some don't. Hopefully, some day, experiencing the Baptism of the Spirit, exercising charismatic gifts and praying together in a community will be the normal experience of every Catholic and the pattern of life of every parish.

30. WHAT REASON CAN BE OFFERED FOR THIS CONCLUSION?

The following could be listed:

a) The renewal brought about by the Catholic Pentecostal Movement is not based on concepts conjured up by the theologian or religious sociologist, but rather it is a renewal of the Church according to the Acts of the Apostles.

b) The dynamism of the movement is not provided by any external force or pressure, or even by the power of a brilliant idea. Rather, the dynamism is the very biblical concept of the Baptism of the Spirit. The movement is filled with very ordinary people who have experienced the power of this Baptism of the Holy Spirit.

c) The effects, especially if the person is supported by a prayer community, appear to be long-term. A striking feature of the movement is the depth of change brought about within the person and the fidelity of the people to the prayer community.

d) If the movement is really from the Lord, He Himself will not let it fail. This renewal started with just a handful and now thousands of people are devoted to and interested in Charismatic Renewal within the Catholic Church.

31. IS THIS RENEWAL MEANT FOR EVERYONE?

Two reasons can be given why this renewal is meant for every Catholic.

First, the theory behind Pentecostalism is an attempt to understand what a full life in the Spirit really is. If the powers of the Baptism of the Holy Spirit and of the charismatic gifts are normal workings of the Spirit, then certainly everyone who has received sacramental Baptism would have a call to a full life in the Spirit. "Be ye perfect even as my heavenly Father is perfect" was said to all.

Second, in practice, there is no reason that anyone should be excluded. Participation in charismatic groups comes from every age bracket, social class and personality type. Very ordinary and stable people have found a deeper religious life in this movement. People have been touched and changed who are very normal, not previously over-pious, and from no given social or religious background. The people involved, therefore, represent a true cross-section of Catholic life.

Chapter Two

Jesus Is Lord

*At Jesus' name
every knee must bend
in the heavens, on the earth,
and under the earth,
and every tongue proclaim
to the glory of God the Father:
Jesus Christ is Lord!*
(Phil. 2:10-11)

INTRODUCTION

BESIDES "PRAISE THE LORD" BEING A FAMILIAR GREET-
ing among all involved in Charismatic Renewal, the
word "Lord" itself seems to be interspersed everywhere
in conversation. "The Lord is doing great things"; "The
Lord is teaching us this or that"; "The Lord has led us
to this"; are phrases frequently on the lips of those involved in the renewal. For the most part, the conversation is balanced and betrays a familiarity with the Lord,
taken for granted by those already part of a charismatic
group. Newcomers, while taken aback by the number of
times the word is used, are attracted by this familiarity
which seems to exist between the persons and the Lord.

Although many involved in Charismatic Renewal do
not understand all that is summed up in the phrase "Jesus is Lord," they do realize that the Lord is the center
of this renewal. They understand that the heart of this
renewal is not to encourage religious experiences, although the Lord seems to be doing just that; nor to release charismatic gifts, even though that too seems to
be happening; nor to rediscover this power of prayer together or the wisdom in God's plan for the Early Church.
Rather, the purpose of this movement is to reestablish
Jesus as the Lord of all mankind in whom the Father
reconciles all.

"Jesus is Lord" means so many things—a source of
hope in world events, a claim upon our total being, the
total purpose of our Christian lives.

Unless this whole role of Jesus as Lord is grasped and
renewed in the hearts of all, then this outpouring of
the Spirit will be just another "charismatic outburst,"
having no lasting effect on Church life. Only as Jesus
becomes our personal Lord and the Lord of the Church
will all who call themseves Christians be witnesses to
the world, clothed with power from on high that was
promised to us and bestowed on us at the First Pentecost.

These questions are written so the Lordship of Jesus

may bestow unity and power upon this movement, upon the Church, and upon all mankind.

JESUS IS LORD

A) *Understanding the Title "Lord"*

    1. WHAT DOES THE TITLE "LORD" MEAN, AS APPLIED TO JESUS?

There are a number of facets to the title:

a) That He is equal to the Father.

b) That He is head of all creation.

c) That He is owed complete obedience.

    2. COULD EACH OF THESE BE EXPLAINED IN MORE DETAIL?

Jesus is Lord means:

a) He is equal to the Father in the sense that He shares the same divine nature, is worthy of the same adoration, has the same power and is distinct from the Father only in the relationships within the bosom of the Trinity.

b) He is head of all creation in the sense that the Father created all things through Him and in His image, that all creation and all history finds its purpose in Him, and that all men are meant to be reconciled to the Father in Him.

c) He is owed complete obedience because of man's complete dependence on Him, because He is the only way to the Father and to man's fulfillment.

    3. ARE THERE ANY CONNOTATIONS TO THE TERM "LORD"?

To call Jesus "Lord" implies a number of personal beliefs, such as:

a) His loving care for all peoples.

b) His complete control of events and history.

c) The Christian's total union with Him.

    4. COULD EACH OF THESE BE EXPLAINED?

The personal confessing of Jesus the Lord, as found

among those involved in Charismatic Renewal is fed and
nourished by the following deeply-felt beliefs:

a) Jesus knows each and every person, calling them
   by name, constantly attempting to draw them to
   the Father and to save them from harmful elements. This loving care was shown during His life
   and death and by the many favors bestowed
   through His Spirit. "Lord" indicates a total care
   in our total helplessness.

b) Jesus controls all events and every aspect of history: including every event in the life of the Christian. In difficulties, He asks us to have faith, not
   understanding His purpose in our suffering. He
   assures us that with His help we can handle these
   events and not be crushed by them. He acts both
   outside of the Christian in shaping events and
   within the person, strengthening and consoling him
   in the middle of events.

c) Jesus is close to everyone, both individually and as
   they gather in groups to praise Him. He pours
   forth His Spirit to console the person, to help him
   to pray, to enlighten him.

B) Doctrinal Source for the Title

5. HOW DID JESUS BECOME LORD?

He was Lord from the very first moment of His con-
ception. However, only after His resurrection did the
primitive community confess Him as Lord in the senses
listed above.

The Early Church saw the resurrection as installing
Jesus at the right hand of the Father with heavenly
power to save. His role as Lord, therefore, comes from
two sources—His equality with the Father and His resurrection and Ascension.

C) Scriptural Understanding of the Title "Lord"

6. WHAT IS THE OLD TESTAMENT UNDERSTANDING OF THE WORD "LORD"?

The Old Testament writers used the word as a divine epithet, referring to the ultimate Lord of all creations. (*cf.* Isaias 1:24; Psalm 117:1; Joshua 3:11).

7. WHAT IS THE NEW TESTAMENT UNDERSTANDING OF THE TERM AS APPLIED TO CHRIST?

In the New Testament, a distinction must be made between its use before and after the resurrection. In many of the gospel stories, Jesus is addressed as Lord, without those using the title fully grasping all that was involved.

After the resurrection, Jesus was given the title of Lord in the fullness of its meaning, namely, equal to the Father and the source of salvation for all men.

8. WHAT ARE THE OUTSTANDING SCRIPTURAL "CONFESSIONS" OF JESUS AS LORD?

The following are the highpoints of this title:

John's gospel culminates in the open proclamation of Thomas: "My Lord and My God" (20: 28).

St. Paul sums up the total theology of the Lordship of Jesus, basing it on the equality with the Father and the resurrection: "Although he was in the form of God, he did not deem equality with God something to be grasped at (Phil. 2:6) and "because of this (his obedient death) God highly exalted Him and bestowed on him the name above every other name, so that at Jesus' name every knee must bend, in the heavens, on the earth and under the earth, and every tongue proclaim to the glory of God, the Father, Jesus Christ is Lord" (Verses 9-11).

Peter culminates his Pentecost speech, "Therefore, let the whole house of Israel know beyond any doubt that God has made both Lord and Messiah, this Jesus whom you crucified" (Acts 2:36).

9. HOW DOES SCRIPTURE DESCRIBE THE ROLE OF JESUS AS LORD?

The Scriptures outline clearly the role of Jesus as Lord:

a) He is the object of preaching—"It is not ourselves

we preach but Jesus Christ as Lord" (2 Cor. 4:5).

b) He is the purpose of Christian service—"He whom you serve is the Lord" (Rom. 12:11).

c) He is to be obeyed—"Each of them doing only what the Lord assigned him" (1 Cor. 3:5).

d) He bestows authority—"Authority the Lord has given me" (2 Cor. 10:8).

e) He totally owns the Christian—"When we live we are responsible to the Lord, and when we die, we die as his servants. Both in life and in death, we are the Lord's" (Rom. 14:8).

f) He is Lord of all men—"Here there is no difference between Jew and Greek; all have the same Lord" (Rom. 10:12).

g) He will judge all men when He comes in glory— "The Lord is the one to judge me, so stop passing judgment before the time of his return" (1 Cor. 4:4-5).

D) *Church's Teaching on Jesus as Lord*

10. What is the Church's official teaching on Jesus as Lord?

The title of "Lord" has been given to Jesus from the earliest formulations of Church creeds.

Over a long period of time, in controversy over various heresies, the Church has outlined the mystery of Jesus as Lord in the Incarnation (God becoming man). The doctrine would include the following:

a) The eternal Son, the second Person of the Trinity, has united with His Person a human nature.

b) This union of divine and human natures is true, substantial and definitive.

c) And the Virgin Mary is His true mother.

d) Therefore, Jesus Christ is the Eternal Word of the Father, to whom belong two natures, human and divine, which are truly joined without being mixed.

e) Because of this mystery, the qualities of each nature (God and man) can be predicated of the one Person. Therefore, Jesus can be called God, creator of all things, and Lord: and at the same time can be called man, our brother, human and capable of suffering (before His Resurrection).

E) *Role of Jesus as Lord in Charismatic Renewal*

11. WHAT ROLE DOES THE DOCTRINE OF JESUS AS LORD HAVE IN THE CHARISMATIC RENEWAL?

Jesus as Lord is the center of this movement, with every other part enlightening and exalting Jesus as Lord. The Baptism of the Spirit is the Lord's gift to the person, helping him to actually make Jesus His personal Lord. Charismatic ministries are powers given by the Lord so that others can be brought to Him. People come together in prayer groups to confess Jesus as Lord.

12. WHAT IS THE RELATIONSHIP OF THE BAPTISM OF THE SPIRIT TO THE LORDSHIP OF JESUS?

The following outlines the relationship:

a) To accept and to open oneself to Jesus as Lord is the condition for the reception of this gift.

b) As the person experiences the power of the Baptism of the Spirit, he comes to realize in a personal way that Jesus is His Lord.

c) As he continues to be led by the Spirit, the person submits every part of his life to Jesus as Lord.

d) The power of the Spirit leads the person to praise the Lord in every situation.

e) He fulfills the command of the Lord to be His witness to all the nations.

13. WHAT IS THE RELATIONSHIP OF THE CHARISMATIC GIFTS TO THE LORDSHIP OF JESUS?

Through these gifts, Jesus, the Lord, manifests His loving concern and power for His people. He is enabled to concretely help His people, as through the gifts the ministry of Jesus is continued.

The gifts are the renewal of the Lord's power among us, and the full flowering of His gift of the Spirit. Paul prefaces his teaching on spiritual gifts with their connection to the Lord. "And no one can say 'Jesus is Lord' except in the Holy Spirit" (1 Cor. 12:3).

F) *Praising the Lord*

14. WHAT VALUE IS THERE TO PEOPLE GREETING ONE ANOTHER WITH "PRAISE THE LORD"? DOES THIS NOT SET THEM APART FROM OTHER MEMBERS OF THE CHURCH?

First, the greeting is a simple one, easy to say (usually with a laugh the first time) even by those not involved in the movement.

Secondly, the phrase is a natural one, especially among people who talk so much and so openly about the Lord.

Thirdly, since Jesus should be the Lord of all lives, this simple greeting establishes Jesus as the center of human relationships.

Fourthly, the familiar greeting is an important external expression of inner sentiments.

15. HOW CAN PEOPLE SPEND SO MUCH TIME "PRAISING THE LORD"?

First, by the power of the Baptism of the Spirit, a person is led to prayers of praise and to a true devotion to Jesus as Lord.

Secondly the supportive relations of the prayer group help and teach the person to grow in prayers of praise.

Thirdly, praising God is not seen as a waste of time but the first and most important task of all creation.

16. HOW CAN A PERSON PRAISE THE LORD FOR EVERYTHING, AS SEEMS TO BE TAUGHT IN CHARISMATIC RENEWAL?

The person can only praise the Lord in every situation if he is living by faith, trying to see all things in light of the Lordship of Jesus and believing that all events and all of history are in His power.

Although a person should not praise the Lord for evil, he can praise the Lord in every situation, even a difficult or painful one. The person can and should believe that the Lord intends to draw good out of every situation, even trials.

17. WHAT DOES IT MEAN "TO COME TO THE LORD" OR "TO BRING SOMEONE TO THE LORD"?

Both phrases indicate certain steps being taken. In a sense, an adult who is attracted to religion and becomes a convert has "come to the Lord" and the priest who instructed him has "brought him to the Lord." Parents regularly "bring their children to the Lord" as they see to their sacramental life and to their religious education.

Usually, however, these phrases refer to further steps in the Christian life. "Coming to the Lord" means that the person makes Jesus truly the Lord of his life. Before this happens, the person has to see that Jesus is not really the center of his thought and desires. As he "reaches out" and asks Jesus to come and be his Lord, a certain breakthrough occurs. Changes come about in the person's prayer life, values, life-style and desires. A transformation occurs in some parts of his life immediately, and in other parts only gradually. The person fulfills the command of Paul, "Do not conform yourselves to this age, but be transformed by the renewal of your mind, so that you may judge what is God's will, what is good, pleasing and perfect" (Rom. 12:2).

18. WHAT BRINGS A PERSON TO THE LORD?

A variety of causes have brought people to the Lord. Many have reached out to Him privately, in the quiet of a retreat or in the midst of despair. The saints provide a variety of conversion stories, whether from a life of basic innocence or from a life of sin. The Lord brings people to Himself in a variety of ways.

However, a regular way is meant to exist and should be the door by which most come to the Lord. That basic way is the preaching of the Church.

The heart of this renewal, then, is not that the Baptism of the Spirit or charismatic ministries be restored to Church life, although that is extremely vital. The purpose of the Spirit is that the Church see "bringing people to the Lord" as its basic mission, learn how to bring this about in pastoral care, and direct its preaching to accomplishing this goal.

G) *Church's Pastoral Care*

19. WHAT CHANGES WILL OCCUR IN THE CHURCH'S PASTORAL CARE AS "BRINGING PEOPLE TO THE LORD" BECOMES A PRIMARY GOAL?

A new horizon of pastoral care will emerge which will unite the other pastoral concerns and even facilitate them.

Currently, the Church has many legitimate pastoral concerns, which should in no way be discarded. These concerns would be:

a) A flourishing sacramental life.

b) A complete religious education system.

c) Works of charity.

However, little understanding exists of how to "bring people to the Lord," and sometimes even lack of belief that "coming to the Lord" is for everybody. As a result, the Church is having difficulty fulfilling those pastoral goals to which it is totally dedicated.

As the Church "steps out in faith" in its apostolate, the full release of the powers of Baptism will occur in many, so-called "normal" Catholics and they will "come to the Lord." The fervor of the parish life will increase and the charismatic ministries will emerge.

20. WHAT CONCRETE CHANGES CAN OCCUR IN NORMAL PARISH LIFE SO THAT JESUS TRULY BECOMES THE LORD?

The following would have to happen:

a) Opportunities be provided that everyone understand a full life in the Spirit.

b) A conscious effort be made that every aspect of parish life confess openly that Jesus is Lord—the liturgy, the rectory, the convent, the school, the various organizations, apostolic and charitable.
c) Sunday preaching concern itself chiefly with bringing people to the Lord.
d) The mass schedule and the way this time is used be adapted to provide a suitable atmosphere to bring people to the Lord.
e) The ministries present in the parish be allowed to develop.

H) *Religions in Which Jesus Is Not Lord*

21. WHAT OF OTHER RELIGIONS THAT DO NOT CONFESS JESUS AS LORD?

Concerning them, the following can be said:
a) They contain elements of salvation truly placed there by God.
b) Often, they are more culturally adapted to the people than Christianity.
c) They will find their completion only in the Lordship of Jesus.
d) Because He is not explicity confessed, they do not share totally in His Light and His power over elements that can lead to destruction.

22. WHAT ELEMENTS OF SALVATION ARE CONTAINED IN THEM?

This varies according to the religion but would include:
a) The confession of the one God, the role of Jesus as prophet and Mary as His Mother, the belief in life after death and the importance of a moral life, as among the Moslems.
b) The Old Testament beliefs of the Jewish people.
c) The spiritual teachings of the Eastern religions.

23. WHY ARE THEY INCOMPLETE?

Just as all Catholic doctrine would be incomplete and disunified except for belief in Jesus as Lord, so those religions that do not explicitly confess Him in His total role cannot offer a complete and satisfying view of man's life and history.

If many Catholics are turning to these others religions for a more complete religious outlook, it is mainly because they themselves have never "come to the Lord," or lived and experienced the Lordship of Jesus. Usually when a person is "brought to the Lord" the attraction of Eastern religions fades.

24. WHY DO THESE OTHER RELIGIONS SHARE IN SOME ELEMENTS OF DESTRUCTION?

Because Jesus is not the center, the Eastern religions especially are open to many elements, some harmless and others mixed with the occult.

Jesus, as Lord, is the light of the world and victor over darkness. Especially in the Eastern religions where He is not confessed as Lord, many doctrines which are incompatible with divinely revealed religion, and actually harmful to man's relationship with God, have entered.

This openness to harmful or even occult practices is present in any system that claims to deal in spiritual powers but ignorantly or deliberately excludes the Lordship of Jesus Christ.

Chapter Three

Baptism of the Spirit

"John baptized with water,
but within a few days
you will be baptized
with the Holy Spirit."
(Acts 1:5)

INTRODUCTION

FOR MOST CATHOLICS, THE BAPTISM OF THE HOLY SPIRIT
is a new term. Even for Catholics involved in Charismatic Renewal, the phrase often eludes definition and description. In fact, a correct understanding of the Baptism
of the Spirit and of the reality it signifies is extremely
critical for the true development of Charismatic Renewal
and for the total outpouring of God's Spirit.

Concurrent with this debate over a term, some definite
events are happening—many people have actually received
this deep personal experience of Jesus Christ which the
Baptism of the Spirit signifies, and enjoy a new power
in overcoming the bondage of sin. Even more than that,
God has provided regular means for bringing people into
this prayer experience and into the more powerful Christian life which follows.

The Baptism of the Spirit represents a power, given by
Christ to His Church, which for many centuries has not
been part of the daily preaching and faith of the Church,
but which has always been a part of the Church's ascetical and mystical teaching. In a sense, the term represents
a recovery of the theology of sacramental Baptism which
prevailed in the Early Church. Now, through an understanding of the Baptism of the Spirit, the power has been
uncovered and released to many.

An extremely critical question concerning the Baptism
of the Spirit is the relationship of this prayer experience
to the basic initiation rites of the Church. If this prayer
experience is part of Christian initiation—the basic equipping of the Christian to live a complete life in Christ—
then the pastoral care of the Church has to be directed to
having every Christian accept Jesus as his personal Lord
and experience the divine touch of the Baptism of the
Holy Spirit.

In this section I hope to explain, both doctrinally and
practically, what seems to be happening at the heart of
Charismatic Renewal, and bringing about this total pastoral care in the Church.

THE BAPTISM OF THE HOLY SPIRIT

(Various prepositions are used—"with," "in" and "of." Here we will use the latter.)

A) *Definition and Explanation*

1. WHAT IS THE BAPTISM OF THE HOLY SPIRIT?

The Baptism of the Holy Spirit, as used in Pentecostalism, is an internal religious experience (or a prayer experience) whereby the individual experiences the risen Christ in a personal way.

This experience results from a certain "release" of the power of the Holy Spirit, usually already present within the individual by Baptism and Confirmation. It usually leads to a deep devotional life, an attraction to prayer, Sacred Scripture and the sacraments, and marks the beginning of a closer union with God.

By the Baptism of the Spirit, the individual begins to know, love and serve Christ in a personal way.

Although the "Baptism of the Spirit" is a new term for Catholics, the prayer experience itself has been well described by Catholic spiritual writers.

2. WHAT IS MEANT BY THE TERM "RELIGIOUS EXPERIENCE"?

Religious experience means that the person's imagination, memory and feelings, as well as his intellect and will, are touched by God's action. This experience is different from, but based upon, a religious faith which generally affects only the intellectual faculties.

Signs of a religious experience—like consolation in prayer, the gift of tears, feeling of a deep love for Christ, or of repentance and conversion—might, but need not, accompany the Baptism of the Holy Spirit.

3. WHAT IS MEANT BY THE PHRASE "RELEASE OF THE POWER OF THE HOLY SPIRIT" WITHIN US?

Sacramental Baptism and Confirmation bestow the gift of the Spirit dwelling within the Christian. However, many powers associated with this indwelling are bound up, untapped so to speak. A "release of the power of the Spirit" means that the full effects of the sacraments are actually realized, as the Spirit leads the Christian into a new life of prayer, of outlook and of behavior.

It is evident that many Christians never experience a devout life. For some, even the idea that they should have a personal, religious experience of Christ is new. Others have had an experience of this religious fervor at some period in life, but then have lost this sense of prayer. The power of the Baptism of the Spirit is meant to bring every Christian into a personal knowledge of Christ and a new experience of the Christian life.

4. WHAT IS THE ORIGIN OF THE PHRASE "BAPTISM OF THE HOLY SPIRIT," SINCE THIS TERM NEVER APPEARED IN THE "BALTIMORE CATECHISM"?

The "Baptism of the Spirit" is a scriptural term and comes from the following six texts:

Each of the four gospels records the words of John the Baptist pointing out Our Lord, saying that while he baptized in water, the Lord would baptize in the Holy Spirit and fire (Matthew 3:11; Mark 1:8; Luke 3:16; John 1:33).

Our Lord Himself used the phrase in the Acts of the Apostles, as He commissioned His Apostles to wait in Jerusalem. "John baptized with water, but in a few days you will be baptized with the Holy Spirit" (Acts 1:5).

St. Peter used the phrase when describing the events of Gentile conversion—"Then I remembered what the Lord had said: 'John baptized with water but you will be baptized with the Holy Spirit'" (Acts 11:16).

5. DOES THE TERM "BAPTISM OF THE SPIRIT," AS USED IN PENTECOSTALISM, HAVE THE SAME MEANING AS ITS SCRIPTURAL USE?

The use is not exactly the same, for the following reasons:

In Pentecostalism, the term has a very specialized use, referring to an internal religious experience, which usually initiates a life of fervor and results in the gift of prayer tongues.

In Scripture the phrase refers to the total gift of the Holy Spirit and not merely this one aspect of religious experience.

6. IS THE TERM "BAPTISM OF THE HOLY SPIRIT" IMPORTANT, OR COULD NOT A PHRASE SUCH AS "RENEWAL OF BAPTISM" BE USED INSTEAD?

The term, "Baptism of the Spirit" is important for the following reasons:

a) Although not used in Pentecostalism exactly as employed in Scripture, it probably has more Scriptural basis than any other term to describe God's inner action on the soul.

b) The proof of the validity of the term "Baptism of the Holy Spirit" is not from Scripture but from the living witness of thousands who have experienced the Baptism of the Spirit, pray in tongues and manifest the charismatic ministries.

c) The term is important if the faith and teaching of the Catholic Church is to be renewed.

7. HOW IS THIS TERM IMPORTANT FOR THE RENEWAL OF THE FAITH AND PREACHING OF THE CHURCH?

The term is important in order to restore the full teaching on Baptism that was present in the Early Church. In a sense, the Early Church did not need such a special term because it possessed a full teaching on Baptism, which included what are called here the effects of the Baptism of the Holy Spirit.

However, many of these faith elements concerning Baptism dropped out of the Church's understanding, faith and preaching on the sacrament. It seems that a new term is needed, at least at this time, to call attention to these lost elements.

B) *Scriptural and Traditional Understanding of the Baptism of the Spirit.*

8. WHAT IS THE SCRIPTURAL BACKGROUND FOR UNDER-
STANDING THE BAPTISM OF THE SPIRIT?

A basic Scriptural understanding would be:
First, Christ himself described Pentecost as being baptized in the Spirit (Acts 1:5). The feast itself was definitely a religious experience, for the Apostles rejoiced,
became bold and expressed their joy in prayer tongues.

Second, Peter's preaching indicated that all who re-
pented and were baptized would receive the same gift
(Acts 2:38).

Third, this special religious experience of the Holy
Spirit could be received at a later time than the moment of
sacramental Baptism as happened to the disciples in Samaria (Acts 8:14-17). On this occasion the Spirit produced something visible, at least enough to attract Simon
Magus (Verse 18).

Fourth, a religious experience exactly like Pentecost occurred to the Gentile Cornelius and his family (Acts 10:
44-48) and is equated with the first Pentecost by Peter,
who uses the term "baptize with the Holy Spirit" (Acts
11:16-17).

9. WHAT IS THE PAULINE TEACHING ON THE SPIRIT'S
ROLE?

St. Paul taught that Christ offered to men new life and
the Spirit communicated this dynamic, vital principle to
men.

Paul's explanation of the Spirit's activity is very much
in the realm of experience:

a) He is the Spirit of Power (1 Cor. 2:4; Rom. 15:
13; Thes. 1:5).

b) He helps us to pray (Rom. 8:26).

c) He frees from the law and the bondage of the flesh
(Rom. 8:2-11).

d) He reveals God's wisdom to men (1 Cor. 2:10; John
14:26).

10. WHAT IS THE CHURCH'S TRADITIONAL TEACHING
CONCERNING THE ROLE OF THE SPIRIT IN PRAYER
EXPERIENCE?

The role of the Holy Spirit in bestowing the gift of prayer upon many Christians is firmly founded in ascetical and mystical literature. Authors, as well as many saints, describe the realm of prayer experience from beginner to mystic. The Holy Spirit is the Mover and Director in these experiences.

11. WHAT IN THE CHURCH'S TRADITIONAL TEACHING CORRESPONDS TO THE "BAPTISM OF THE SPIRIT"?

The effects of the Baptism of the Spirit seem to correspond to the sensible consolations of beginners, usually called "first fervor." Tanquerey describes these as "tender emotions that effect our sensibility and cause us to experience a feeling of spiritual joy." Most writers describe a breakthrough in prayer as the individual comes to know Christ in a personal and affective way.

C) *Effects of the Baptism of the Holy Spirit*

12. WHAT ARE THE EFFECTS OF THE BAPTISM OF THE HOLY SPIRIT?

The power of this experience is evident in a number of ways. The person:

a) Has a new awareness of Christ's presence in his own life and in the Eucharist.

b) Is drawn into a deeper life of prayer.

c) Finds a new attraction in the Scriptures.

d) Discovers new help in trying to live up to the moral demands of Christianity.

e) Finds a new ease in practicing the fruits of the Spirit.

In general, a spiritual reawakening takes place and a taste for spiritual things becomes evident. Many of these effects are evident as the person continues to pray with the community. Besides these effects, the person usually begins to pray in tongues after the reception of the Baptism of the Spirit.

13. COULD THESE EFFECTS BE EXPLAINED IN DEPTH?

A complete list of these effects is impossible. Some of the more important ones are:

a) A deep hunger and thirst for mental prayers. The person feels drawn to prayer, looks forward to finding time when he can be alone with the Lord, and tends to spend periods in fervent prayer.

b) A desire to read Scripture. The person has a new attraction to Christ's words and looks to the inspired Word for guidance and light.

c) Power over sin and evil habits. Frequently, the person has struggled for years, attempting by his own effort to conquer sin in his life. This infilling of the Holy Spirit often provides a new inner power over sinful elements.

d) Detachment from material goods. The prayer experience helps the person to be detached. Many witness to a new simplicity of life which helps them toward a more intimate union with God.

e) Growth in union with God. God, who seemed so abstract and far away, is suddenly experienced as close. The prayer experience leads the individual into a relationship with all the Persons of the Trinity.

14. HOW DEEP AND SIGNIFICANT ARE THESE CHANGES?

That depends on the following:

a) The person's religious background.

b) His age and spiritual needs.

c) The generosity that has gone into the person's preparation for the Baptism.

d) The amount of cooperation with grace which follows the Baptism of the Holy Spirit.

In general, it can safely be said, a person's entering fully and deeply into the Pentecostal experience, especially if supported by a strong prayer community, marks a significant beginning to a deeper, more personal Christian life.

D) *Conditions for the Reception of the Baptism of the Holy Spirit*

   15. ARE THERE ANY CONDITIONS FOR THE RECEPTION OF THE GIFT OF THE BAPTISM OF THE HOLY SPIRIT?

The basic conditions are:
a) A knowledge of the Baptism of the Spirit.
b) Faith in the promise of Jesus to baptize in His Spirit.
c) Repentance, sorrow for sin and a desire to do better.
d) Some "reaching out for," "desire for" and "openness" to this fuller life in the Spirit.
e) Praying and sharing regularly with others who have received this gift of the Spirit.
f) Being prayed with by others for the Baptism of the Spirit.

   16. HOW DOES THE CHARISMATIC RENEWAL MOVEMENT FOSTER THESE CONDITIONS FOR THE BAPTISM OF THE HOLY SPIRIT?

Within Charismatic Renewal the following factors are present:
a) A faith that this religious experience is available to all who seek it.
b) A clear teaching on the conditions for its reception.
c) A prayerful atmosphere so that God's Spirit can be active.
d) A regular set of teachings entitled "Life in the Spirit Seminars" which helps newcomers into this new life.
e) A communal prayer by leaders with the person for this gift.

E) *Ways of Receiving the Baptism of the Holy Spirit*

   17. HOW DOES A PERSON RECEIVE THE "BAPTISM OF THE SPIRIT"?

People have received the "Baptism of the Holy Spirit" in just about every conceivable way or situation. Two general ways, however, can be listed—privately (hidden) or publicly (manifest).

18. What is meant by experiencing the Baptism of the Spirit privately?

A person experiences the Baptism of the Holy Spirit privately when, under the influence of God's grace, he is led to reach out to God and seek a deeper life with Him. At this time of private prayer, God touches the person spiritually and he begins to experience what is called "fervor." This divine touch is usually accompanied by sensible consolations and spiritual delight in prayer.

Even if a person has received the Baptism of the Spirit privately, there seem to be many additional effects from being prayed with for the full release of the Spirit publicly.

19. Has this Baptism of the Holy Spirit been privately experienced by many?

The religious experience, called Baptism of the Holy Spirit, seems to have been received privately by quite a few people. In all honesty, however, it does not seem to have been experienced by *most* Catholics. A possible cause of this situation is that the Baptism of the Spirit is not part of the Church's regular preaching. For a long time the Church has not taught the idea of religious experience, except for those who were called to religious vocations.

On the other hand, this Baptism of the Spirit seems to have been experienced by most of the people involved in charismatic prayer communities, since the preaching and faith of the community centers around a personal experience of the committal to Jesus as Lord.

20. When does a person receive the Baptism of the Spirit publicly?

A person receives the Baptism of the Holy Spirit publicly when, having learned about and begun to have faith in the Baptism of the Spirit, he asks those who also believe to pray with him for the Baptism of the Holy Spirit. This fraternal prayer in faith is meant to release the powers of sacramental Baptism. In practice, it seems to have great effects.

21. HOW ARE PEOPLE PREPARED FOR THIS PUBLIC RE-
    CEPTION OF THE BAPTISM OF THE HOLY SPIRIT?

Newcomers to Charismatic Renewal are prepared by the
"Life in the Spirit" seminars for the Baptism of the Holy
Spirit. These talks, plus the sharing in the community's
prayer life, awaken a faith in Baptism of the Spirit. When
the individual feels prepared, and when the leaders discern
that he is ready, he is prayed with for the Baptism of the
Holy Spirit.

22. HOW IS A PERSON "PRAYED WITH FOR THE BAPTISM
    OF THE HOLY SPIRIT"?

Members of the prayer community usually impose hands
upon him as a fraternal gesture (although this is not absolutely necessary). The leader says a prayer of deliverance, followed by a petition that Jesus baptize the person
in His Spirit and that the person realize all the effects, devotional and charismatic.

F) *Problem of Not Receiving the Baptism of the Holy
   Spirit*

23. IF A PERSON DOES NOT "PRAY IN TONGUES," HAS HE
    THEN NOT RECEIVED THE BAPTISM OF THE SPIRIT?

Catholics have never demanded "praying in tongues" as
a sign of the reception of the Baptism of the Spirit, even
though most, in practice, do yield to tongues at this time.
This prayer experience has many effects, personal and
charismatic, which begin to be manifest as the person continues with the prayer community. "Praying in tongues"
should not be seen as the exclusive and universal sign of
this internal release.

24. DOES IT EVER HAPPEN THAT A PERSON WHO HAS
    BEEN "PRAYED WITH FOR THE BAPTISM OF THE
    HOLY SPIRIT" DOES NOT ACTUALLY RECEIVE THIS
    "RELEASE OF THE SPIRIT"?

Yes, this might happen for a number of reasons:
a) If serious obstacles have not been removed by basic
   repentance.

b) If the person approached the prayer community too early, with little understanding of the Baptism of the Holy Spirit or the condition for its reception.
c) If the community's faith in the prayer for the Baptism of the Holy Spirit was weak. This sometimes happens in prayer communities that are just beginning.

25. WHAT IF THE FAULT LIES WITH THE PRAYER COMMUNITY?

The following remedies are suggested:
a) Interviewing and screening those who are prayed with for the Baptism of the Spirit.
b) Strongly suggesting sacramental confession for Catholics.
c) Establishment of solid teaching seminars to prepare newcomers.
d) Allowing only mature members to pray with people for the Baptism of the Spirit.

Sometimes, though, a person has truly been baptized in the Holy Spirit but has just not yet yielded to the gift of prayer tongues. (This problem is handled in the section on prayer tongues). This lack of the gift of praying in tongues is sometimes misjudged as a lack of the Baptism of the Holy Spirit.

26. WHAT IF THE FAULT LIES WITH THE PERSON HIMSELF?

Then the source of the obstacle should be identified and removed. If the problem was merely lack of knowledge, then a few teaching sessions should remedy the situation. If some emotional or spiritual block exists, then it must be recognized and removed.

If, however, the problem involves serious moral difficulties, as unrepented bitterness or hatred or involvement with the occult or drugs, then there is need for personal ministry, i.e., prayers for psychological healing or deliverance and sacramental confession.

27. CAN THE PERSON EVER BE "PRAYED WITH AGAIN" FOR THE BAPTISM OF THE HOLY SPIRIT?

Strictly speaking, we should believe in faith that, if the person was properly disposed, he did receive the Baptism of the Holy Spirit and need not be prayed for again. However, since the Baptism of the Holy Spirit is not a sacrament but essentially an internal religious experience, if it were discerned that some obstacle prevented the reception of the Baptism of the Holy Spirit on the first occasion, then the person could be prayed with again.

28. WILL THE POWER OF THE BAPTISM OF THE SPIRIT EVER BE EXPERIENCED BY MOST OF THE CATHOLIC CHURCH?

As long as Charismatic Renewal remains a movement (not totally integrated into the mainstream of normal Church life), it will never engage a large percentage of Catholics. Only as the teachings of Charismatic Renewal become integrated into the Church's faith, Sunday preaching, catechetical teaching, and Sunday worship, will the vast majority of Catholics ever share or experience the full action of the Spirit.

G) *Relationship of the Baptism of the Holy Spirit with the Sacraments of Baptism and Confirmation.*

29. IS THERE ANY CLEAR RELATIONSHIP BETWEEN THE BAPTISM OF THE SPIRIT AND THE SACRAMENTS OF BAPTISM AND CONFIRMATION?

The relationship is not as clear as other parts of the Church's doctrinal teaching for the following reasons:

a) The exact relationship of Baptism to Confirmation is not clear.

b) It is difficult to have clear-cut categories when dealing with religious experiences.

c) Scriptural accounts give varied pictures of the relationship of these sacraments with the religious experience.

30. WHAT SEEMS TO BE THE CLEAREST WAY OF RELATING THE BAPTISM OF THE SPIRIT WITH SACRAMENTAL BAPTISM AND CONFIRMATION?

The following theological teaching seems to integrate the Scriptural model, the Church's teaching and actual experience:

  a) Baptism and Confirmation (and the Eucharist) are the sacramental parts of Christian initiation.
  b) The Baptism of the Spirit can also be considered part of Christian initiation and would be seen as the religious experience aspect of that initiation.
  c) Both the sacramental rite and the religious experience are complementary parts of basic Christian initiation.

The Church's preaching on Christian initiation should teach both sacramental and experiential aspects of the total gift of the Spirit. Although a theological outline should be as clear as possible, it is more important that the full power of the Spirit be made available to Catholics by the Church's preaching.

31. IS NOT THIS A DRASTICALLY NEW TEACHING, NAMELY, THAT A RELIGIOUS EXPERIENCE IS PART OF CHRISTIAN INITIATION?

It is new in the sense that this part of Christian teaching was dropped out of the Church's life. It is not new if compared with the Scriptural patterns nor with the preaching of the patristic period.

32. WHAT IF THE PERSON HAS EXPERIENCED THE BAPTISM OF THE SPIRIT AND HAS NEVER RECEIVED SACRAMENTAL BAPTISM?

This sometimes occurs and should, sooner or later, lead the person to be baptized sacramentally. When the Gentile Cornelius and his family experienced the full outpouring of the Spirit, Peter immediately baptized them into the Christian community. "These people have received the Holy Spirit just as we did. Can anyone, then, stop them from being baptized with water?" (Acts 10:47).

33. WHAT DOES THE TERM "BAPTISM OF THE HOLY SPIRIT" ADD TO THE TERMS "BAPTISM" AND "CONFIRMATION"? IN OTHER WORDS, WHY DOES A PERSON HAVE TO EXPERIENCE THE BAPTISM OF THE

HOLY SPIRIT IF HE HAS ALREADY BEEN BAPTIZED
AND CONFIRMED?

"Baptism of the Spirit" is a term which contains a belief
that every Christian, to some extent, is meant to experience the same powers as were evident in the early Church.
This is the basic belief of Pentecostalism. Obviously, the
full effects of Baptism and Confirmation are just not being
experienced in the lives of many, and yet these effects *are*
meant to be part of normal Christian life.

The term "Baptism of the Spirit" brings home to Catholics that the sacramental rites are meant to be powerful,
and the source of spiritual and psychological changes. This
truth is best taught by a new term, distinct from, yet
linked to, these sacraments.

34. COULD NOT THE TERM "RENEWAL OF BAPTISM" BE
BETTER INTEGRATED INTO CATHOLIC THINKING
THAN THE TERM "BAPTISM OF THE HOLY SPIRIT"?

Objections to replacing the phrase "Baptism of the Holy
Spirit" with the phrase "renewal of Baptism" are the following:

a) "Renewal" indicates a refurbishing of something
that is already present, yet "religious experience" is
not present in the lives of many—at least not as a
daily, vital, religious force in their lives.

b) The term "renewal of Baptism" is so vague that people would not bother inquiring into what is meant.

c) In practice, to receive the Baptism of the Spirit, the
person needs a simpler, more personal faith in God
than is required for sacramental Baptism.

Chapter Four

Praying in
Tongues

*All were filled with the Holy Spirit.
They began to express themselves
in foreign tongues and make bold
proclamation as the Spirit prompted
them.*

(Acts 2:4)

INTRODUCTION

WHEN PEOPLE HEAR OF THE PENTECOSTAL MOVEMENT, nothing so quickly comes to their minds as "praying in tongues."

In a real sense, "praying in tongues" has become either an attractive sign or a very difficult obstacle to Charismatic Renewal. For those attending a Charismatic prayer meeting for the first time, the most strikingly new experience is that of hearing the community pray or sing in tongues.

The gift often arouses many fears and touches deep feelings within them. Often, a newcomer can think to himself, "I won't get that gift" or "I don't see the value of that gift" or "I just aim at love for that is the highest of the gifts." These feelings often reflect fears, anxieties or worry about this wonderful manifestation of God's power.

Others already in the movement, even if already praying in tongues, do not always understand the power involved in this gift and, above all, find difficulty in explaining the gift to others.

A very important distinction is often overlooked between the power to pray in tongues, which seems to be enjoyed by almost everyone, and the charismatic ministry of "speaking in tongues," which is used only by some mature members of the community.

Hopefully, this section will mean that prayer tongues will no longer be an obstacle to many sincere people who are attracted to Charismatic Renewal. May it help newcomers to understand this gift. Also, may those who already praise God in this way use this gift with deeper power in their life and be better able to explain this manifestation of the Spirit to others.

PRAYING IN TONGUES

A) *Understanding the Gift*

    1. WHAT IS "PRAYING IN TONGUES"?

Praying in tongues is a gift whereby the person prays to God in a language which he does not know, by simply "yielding" to the action of the Spirit.

When "praying in tongues," the person does not use his rational powers of memory or intellect which are usually employed in speaking or praying. He does use the other faculties associated with speech—the lips, the tongue and the larynx.

2. WHAT DOES "PRAYING IN TONGUES" SOUND LIKE?

Praying in tongues, when first yielded to, usually sounds like five or six words repeated in various ways. This praying in tongues begins and continues as long as the person wills. As time goes on, the prayer tongues usually lengthen or change and, on occasion, a different language is used.

3. WHAT CONTROL DOES THE PERSON HAVE OVER THE GIFT OF "PRAYING IN TONGUES"?

"Praying in tongues" is totally under the person's control. The person decides when he wishes to pray in tongues and when he wishes to stop. The person, however, has no control over what words will be spoken since, as St. Paul says, "If I pray in a tongue my spirit is at prayer but my mind contributes nothing" (1 Cor. 14:14). The mind has no control over the words used in this prayer.

4. DOES THE GIFT OF PRAYER TONGUES COME AND GO, OR IS IT PERMANENT?

The gift is a permanent one, i.e., whenever a person has yielded to the gift, the power to pray in tongues remains with him. After this first yielding, the person then prays in tongues whenever he wishes.

Sometimes, when a person has only recently begun to pray in tongues, fear, self-consciousness, doubts or some other obstacle begins to interfere with the use of this gift. The person even begins to think he has lost his gift. Usually these obstacles are removed by praying with others.

5. WHEN DOES A PERSON BEGIN TO PRAY IN TONGUES?

It can happen anytime. Sometimes a person prays in tongues even before attending a charismatic prayer community. Frequently, a person begins to pray in tongues during the course of instruction provided by the prayer community. Usually, the person begins to pray in tongues when he is prayed with by the community for the Baptism of the Spirit.

This gift usually is the first bestowed by the Holy Spirit and is the doorway to the other gifts.

6. WHY IS PRAYER TONGUES DIFFERENT FROM THE GIFT OF TONGUES AND OTHER CHARISMATIC MINISTRIES?

It is different for the following reasons:
a) It is meant primarily for the individual's life of prayer.
b) It can be considered part of the Church's initiation rites.
c) It seems to be quasi-universal, so that, in general, it can be said that all should be encouraged to yield to prayer tongues.
d) It usually appears very early in a person's life in the Spirit.

The charismatic ministries, in contrast:
a) Are meant for the good of others.
b) Require another infilling of the Spirit beyond that associated with the initiation rites of the Church.
c) As St. Paul states, are spread throughout the Mystical Body, with different ministries given to each.
d) Usually begin to emerge when there is some maturity in the life of the Spirit.

In fact, praying in tongues is deliberately treated in this separate section, distinct from the nine charismatic ministries, to specifically set it apart doctrinally from those ministries, with which it is usually grouped and confused.

B) *Scriptural Basis for the Gift*

7. MOST PEOPLE THINK THAT THE "GIFT OF TONGUES" AT PENTECOST WAS USED BY THE APOSTLES TO TEACH. IS PRAYING IN TONGUES DIFFERENT FROM WHAT THE APOSTLES DID AT PENTECOST?

On the contrary, praying in tongues is what the Apostles really did on the first Pentecost.

Most people do not realize that *two distinct* manifestations of the Holy Spirit occurred on Pentecost, the first was the gift of prayer tongues and the second was really a "miracle of hearing."

a) Acts 2:4 reads: "All were filled with the Holy Spirit. They began to express themselves in foreign tongues and make bold proclamation as the Spirit prompted them." At this point, the gift of tongues was not used to teach, but to praise God, since no one was present to hear.

b) The second manifestation at Pentecost occurred when the large crowd gathered. "They were much confused because each one heard these men speaking in his own language" (Acts 2:6). This could either have been a "miracle of hearing" or, perhaps, the disciples were speaking in tongues that the bystanders happened to know.

This second manifestation, namely, people hearing the Apostles speaking in their own language, does not occur anywhere else in Scripture. However, praying in tongues, that is, Christians praising God in unknown languages, is repeated throughout the New Testament.

8. DID CHRIST EVER SPEAK ABOUT "PRAYING IN TONGUES"?

In Mark 16:17-18, Christ makes the following allusion to tongues: "Signs like these will accompany those who have professed their faith: they will use my name to expel demons, they will speak entirely new languages, they will be able to drink deadly poison without harm, and the sick upon whom they lay their hands will recover."

Scripture scholars seem to believe that these words reflected the experience of the post-Pentecostal Church rather than a personal teaching of Jesus. The passage, though, is still considered inspired.

9. WHAT OTHER SCRIPTURAL REFERENCES ARE THERE TO PRAYING IN TONGUES?

The following are the outstanding ones:

a) The Gentiles pray in tongues (Acts 10:46) : "Whom they heard speaking in tongues and glorifying God."

b) At Ephesus (Acts 19:6) : "As Paul laid his hands on them, the Holy Spirit came down on them and they began to speak in tongues and to utter prophecies."

c) Some references are made to prayer tongues in 1 Corinthians (14:28), in the instruction on tongues and interpretation: "But if there is no one to interpret, there should be silence in the assembly, each one speaking only to himself and to God."

There are other Scriptural passages which probably refer to praying in tongues, but they are not as explicit as the above.

C) *The Gift of Prayer Tongues and Reason*

10. DOES NOT THIS PRAYING IN TONGUES OFFEND REASON, SINCE A PERSON SHOULD KNOW WHAT HE IS SAYING?

It is true that this praying in tongues does not have any rational purpose, in the sense of being used to communicate ideas to other minds. It is a prayer and is based on the faith that the religious powers described in the New Testament are still available in our day.

The gift does not offend reason although, like all of God's mysterious actions, it does ask reason to submit itself to a mystery it cannot adequately grasp.

It should also be noted that speech is a very unique faculty—whereby sense organs common to the animal (tongues, lips, etc.) are used for rational activity, i.e., the communication of ideas. It seems fitting that God should "touch" this unique faculty where mind and matter converge and bestow a powerful sign of His presence.

11. WHEN A PERSON PRAYS IN TONGUES, IS HE ACTUALLY SPEAKING A LANGUAGE?

Concerning this question, the following can be said:

a) Prayer tongues are not gibberish as some believe,

that is, noises unrelated to a language. When someone hears another or himself praying in tongues for
the first time, he usually asks what language it was
or says that it sounded like such and such a language. The acoustic experience is the same as hearing a foreign language.

b) Prayer tongues have all the qualities usually associated with a language—accents, patterns, cadence,
etc.

c) The person praying in tongues has a subjective experience of speaking a language.

d) It is not necessary for prayer tongues to be actually
a language. It is enough for it to be a new way of
praying to God, bestowed by the Spirit of God, and
to be identified with the praying in tongues as described in Scripture.

Our claim, therefore, is that modern-day "praying in
tongues" is the same religious activity described in Acts
2:4; 10:46; 19:6; and in 1 Cor. 14.

12. HAS THERE EVER BEEN A TRANSLATION OF THE
PRAYING IN TONGUES SO THAT PEOPLE KNEW WHAT
WAS BEING SAID?

The following are experiences that have happened within our Philadelphia area:

a) A Jewish nurse translated the Yiddish prayer of an
Irish school teacher.

b) A Mother Provincial from Ireland, visiting Philadelphia, was sceptical of the Charismatic Movement
until she heard an Italian boy praying in Gaelic.

c) A Greek-rite priest told an Irish layman that his
prayer tongue was Greek and was the canon of the
Greek-rite Mass.

d) A five-year old prayed in Hindu and a student, who
was studying that language, gave the translation.
It was a Hindu prayer praising God.

e) Two different people in the prayer community
prayed in Latin and have had the prayer translated
by a priest.

f) An Italian woman praised God in Polish, translated by a leader in the community.

Practically all prayer communities have had similar experiences.

Isolated experiences do not prove, one way or the other, that tongues is "language." The phenomenon often is that the normal prayer in tongues changed to a known language at that moment for the sake of someone's faith.

13. DOES THE PERSON UNDERSTAND WHAT HE IS SAYING WHEN "PRAYING IN TONGUES"?

Usually not, unless, as mentioned above, someone who knows the language has translated it. Scripture does not give any indication that the disciples "knew" what they were saying. They seemed to have had a general sense that they were praising God. In fact, the later Scriptural explanation of the gift in Paul's letters indicates that the person did not know what he was saying. "A man who speaks in a tongue is talking not to men but to God. No one understands him, because he utters mysteries in the Spirit" (1 Cor. 14:2).

D) *The Purpose of Praying in Tongues*

14. HOW DOES PRAYING IN TONGUES BENEFIT THE INDIVIDUAL?

Even with years of experience, all of the effects of this gift have not been uncovered. However, the following could be listed:

a) It helps the individual to fulfill Christ's command to pray always.

b) It is an aid to recollection and leads to more fervent mental prayer.

c) It is the doorway to charismatic ministries—the use of prayer tongues somehow sensitizes the person to yield to other charismatic activity of the Holy Spirit.

d) It is a personal, concrete sign of God's action within.

e) It is a powerful weapon against Satan.

f) It is an effective means of intercessory prayer, especially when the person does not know exactly for what to pray.

15. IS PRAYING IN TONGUES IMPORTANT FOR THE CHARISMATIC RENEWAL MOVEMENT?

Although praying in tongues is by no means the center of the movement (Christ is), nor is it the most important gift of the Spirit (a prayerful awareness of Christ's presence is that), still it would be hard to conceive of the dynamism of the movement without prayer tongues. The following would be the roles the gift plays in the movement:

a) It is a striking "manifestation" of God's action and leads many people to look into the movement.
b) It is an integral part of a charismatic prayer meeting.
c) It helps people to place more faith in the concept of "Baptism of the Holy Spirit," since prayer tongues is a concrete, external manifestation of God's action within.

E) *Universality of Prayer Tongues*

16. DOES EVERYONE IN THE MOVEMENT PRAY IN TONGUES?

Not everyone involved in Charismatic Renewal prays in tongues, although certainly a very high percentage do. Many prayer communities with solid teaching and a favorable attitude toward prayer tongues do have all their members praying in tongues. From experience, it seems that almost everyone can easily be helped to pray in tongues.

Sometimes Pentecostal prayer groups are accused of "overstressing" prayer tongues, but really, through experience, it has been found that the gift is not exceptional but normal and quasi-universal.

17. ARE THERE NOT SOME COMMUNITIES IN WHICH MANY OF THE PEOPLE DO NOT PRAY IN TONGUES?

If this occurs, it is probably due to any of the following reasons:

a) The community misinterprets St. Paul's letter to
the Corinthians and believes that only some are supposed to have "the ability to speak in strange
tongues." Here the community is confusing praying
in tongues with the gift of tongues.
b) The community does not stress the gift nor does it
urge its members "to step out in faith."
c) The community does not know how to help its members to "yield to tongues."

F) *Yielding to Tongues*

18. WHAT IS MEANT BY "HELPING TO YIELD TO
TONGUES"?

A practice exists among charismatic groups, especially
those which stress the importance of praying in tongues,
to help the person who has just been prayed with for the
Baptism of the Holy Spirit, to yield to prayer tongues.
This is accomplished by having someone who already prays
in tongues pray aloud, with the other person attempting
"to imitate" him. What happens is this: By coming out
with the first few strange syllables, the person yields to
the gift of prayer tongues and discovers himself praising
God in an entirely different language than that of the person who helped him yield to this gift.

19. IF A PERSON HAS NOT "YIELDED TO TONGUES" AT
THE TIME OF THE BAPTISM OF THE HOLY SPIRIT,
WHAT SHOULD HE DO?

Usually within each prayer community there is a particular person or a number of people who have the ministry of helping others to "yield to tongues." They are
people in whom these others have great faith, with whom
they are relaxed, and who themselves are open to the gifts.

The person who has not yielded to prayer tongues should
ask one of these to help him. This ministry is usually accomplished by a prayer over the individual, asking God to
remove any psychological barriers that are blocking prayer
tongues and to grant a new infilling of the Holy Spirit.

The person performing this ministry then begins to pray in tongues. The person attempting to yield to tongues is told to leave English aside, to leave behind any rational activity of the intellect and memory—and to open his mouth like a little child "imitating" the prayer tongues of the other person.

20. IS NOT THIS A "MECHANICAL" OR "GIMMICK" APPROACH TO A MYSTERIOUS POWER?

Quite the contrary. It is a childlike step whereby the person confounds the wisdom of the world by leaving his natural powers of intellect and memory behind, and steps out in faith.

21. COULD YOU EXPLAIN WHY THIS PROCEDURE IS USED?

God bestows the gift of tongues in many ways, and many do receive this gift without being helped to yield. However, many people do have psychological barriers or just plainly do not know how to yield to this gift.

In bestowing this gift, God does not force a person's mouth open. The normal procedure is for the person to take the first steps in faith by moving his lips and allowing God to fill it with prayer tongues. This is most easily done in the presence of others who are praying in tongues.

22. CAN A PERSON EVER "LOSE THE GIFT"?

It sometimes happens that a person who has "yielded to tongues" will come up the next day and say that he has "lost the gift." It is much like the little child who rides a bike and later says he "forgot how to do it."

If this happens, the person should be helped again to yield. He should also be encouraged to pray frequently in tongues so that he gains confidence in using the gift.

G) *Reasons for Renewal of This Gift*

23. WHY HAS IT NOT BEEN UNTIL RECENTLY (1900 WITH ORIGINAL PENTECOSTALS AND SINCE 1967 WITH CATHOLIC PENTECOSTALS) THAT THE PRAY-

ING IN TONGUES HAS BECOME APPARENT AND WIDESPREAD?

The widespread renewal of praying in tongues is due mainly to two factors.

First, more people, especially among the educated, have accepted "praying in tongues" as a real spiritual power. Formerly it was thought of as "gibberish" or the result of emotionalism. It was sometimes even seen as a result of demonic activity. Now, however, it is accepted among educated people and can no longer be pushed aside. Obviously, before this gift could become widespread, the scepticism and disbelief had to be dispelled.

Secondly, the experience gained by charismatic communities in helping people to yield to this gift has been instrumental in bringing about its abundant presence. For most people, praying in tongues is one of the effects of participation in a Charismatic community. Without the teaching, practical and theoretical, which is available in the prayer communities, this gift could never have become so widespread.

25. DID NOT SOME WRITERS THINK OF PRAYING IN TONGUES AS "ECSTATIC UTTERANCE"?

Many are still under that impression. In the past, theologians clearly admitted that the charismatic gift of prayer tongues was present in the Early Church. However, they associated it with the mystical experiences of the saints, whereby under a transitory divine "touch," the person would find himself uttering unknown words to try to express his delight in the experience. All of these writers, however, were denied the actual experience of prayer tongues.

Now that praying in tongues is widespread, it is obvious that the theological explanation was wrong and that praying in tongues is not the transitory expression of an ecstatic experience but a permanent power meant to be given abundantly to many.

H) *Difference between Prayer Tongues and the Gift of Tongues*

26. WHAT IS THE DIFFERENCE BETWEEN "PRAYER TONGUES" AND THE "GIFT OF TONGUES"?

Praying in tongues is a permanent ability given to a person as an outward manifestation of the Baptism of the Holy Spirit, whereby the person, at any time, can pray to God in a language which he does not know and which is not the result of his intellectual powers.

The gift of tongues is a passing manifestation of the Holy Spirit whereby an individual is prompted to "give a message in tongues," i.e., speak aloud, by himself, usually at a prayer meeting. As mentioned, this manifestation should be followed by the charismatic gift of interpretation. The gift of tongues followed by interpretation is very close to prophecy.

27. IS THIS DISTINCTION FREQUENTLY OVERLOOKED?

Yes, and this causes some problems, especially in trying to explain the Pentecostal Movement to others and to newcomers. Most people seem to be aware of St. Paul's admonition, "If any are going to talk in tongues let it be at most two or three, each in turn, with another to interpret what they are saying" (1 Cor. 14:27).

They are also aware of Paul's words in 1 Cor. 12:10, "One receives the gift of tongues," and do not realize that the ministry of tongues which is given only to some is different than praying in tongues which seems to be offered to all.

28. DURING THE COURSE OF A CATHOLIC CHARISMATIC PRAYER MEETING, ARE THERE NOT TIMES WHEN EVERYONE DOES START PRAYING IN STRANGE TONGUES TOGETHER?

Yes, and this is not against St. Paul's admonition that the gift of tongues should be used in turn, because praying in tongues and giving a message in tongues are two distinct charismatic manifestations. What really occurs is not many giving a message in tongues at once but the "collective use of prayer tongues," that is, the community begins to praise God out loud, with those who pray in tongues using that gift to praise God. Anyone who has heard and/or participated in this form of praying or singing usually experiences a deep sense of peace and the presence of Christ.

29. WHAT IS "SINGING IN PRAYER TONGUES"?

As the community begins to praise God aloud in prayer tongues, it begins to sense that it would be even more beautiful to sing God's praises. One by one the members go from "praying in tongues" to "singing in tongues." At this point, the Holy Spirit leads the group into harmony and the individual finds himself being led to sing with the others on a given note. (Any musician could probably chart the singing on a scale.) Another impressive phenomenon about both praying and singing in tongues is that the entire community is led to stop almost simultaneously.

30. WHAT IS MEANT BY SAYING THAT "PRAYER TONGUES" IS A SIGN OF CHRIST'S SPIRIT?

It is so designated because the gift of "prayer tongues" did not appear until Pentecost Day. There were many manifestations of God's power and activity in the Old Testament. There were healings, miracles, people raised from the dead, etc. These same manifestations were also evident in Christ's life.

However, the phenomena of people "praying in tongues" is first recorded at Pentecost, and was a clear sign of the gift of the Spirit promised by Christ.

31. WAS NOT "PRAYING IN TONGUES" IMPORTANT IN THE CONVERSION OF THE GENTILES?

This role of "being a sign of Christ's Spirit" was extremely important in the conversion of the Gentiles. Only with great reluctance did Peter go to Cornelius in the first place and only after the vision recorded in Acts, Chapter 10. During his sermon to Cornelius's family, the Holy Spirit descended on them and they began to pray in tongues.

"The circumcised believers who had accompanied Peter

were surprised that the gift of the Holy Spirit should have been poured out on the Gentiles also, whom they could hear speaking in tongues and glorifying God" (Acts 10: 45-46).

This praying in tongues was seen as proof that they had received the same Spirit of Christ as the disciples on Pentecost. Peter then went far beyond the original intention of his visit and accepted these Gentiles for sacramental baptism.

"Peter put the question at that point, 'What can stop these people who have received the Holy Spirit, even as we have, from being baptized with water?' So he gave orders that they be baptized in the name of Jesus Christ. After this was done, they asked him to stay with them for a few days" (Acts 10:47-48).

Chapter Five

Understanding Charismatic Gifts

*Now, brothers, I do not want
to leave you in ignorance
about spiritual gifts.*
(1 Cor. 12:1)

INTRODUCTION

THE CHURCH TODAY IS LOOKING FOR POWER TO SANCTIFY
and to change peoples' lives in the face of growing
world powers and the power of evil. It has encouraged
various renewals which have uncovered the sanctifying
power of liturgy, scripture, etc. Before many realized
what had happened, the Church discovered herself immersed in a Charismatic Renewal Movement. Spiritual
gifts were suddenly abundant in Church life and many
who felt the Church could in no way be a true spiritual
force in the modern world were drawn to the power of
charismatic prayer and spirituality.

The variety of books and cassettes published by this
movement testify to the fact that Charismatic Renewal
has gone far beyond a mere preoccupation with spiritual
gifts. Nevertheless, the charismatic gifts and ministries
are, and will remain, very key, dynamic elements in this
latest outpouring of God's Spirit. Hopefully, the miscon-
ception that these gifts were meant to pass away after
the period of the Early Church has itself been once and
for all swept away by the widespread phenomenon of
Pentecostalism.

People today are hearing stories of strange tongues,
healings and prophecies. They hear the stories from
people whom they know are stable, credible and cannot
be written off. They see the changes in the peoples' lives
and themselves are led to investigate the phenomenon of
the reappearance of the charismatic ministries, so identified with the Corinthian model of Church life. In a sense,
"charismatic" has become a household word in the Roman
Catholic Church.

This section will provide a general background to understanding charismatic gifts in the Church. Later sections will describe each gift, according to St. Paul's list
in 1 Corinthians, Chapter 12.

Our attitude toward the gifts and ministries is important. While many would want to circumvent the gifts and
have a charismatic movement without them, and others

would spectacularize them, St. Paul would have us understand them, grow in them and use them for the building up of Christ's Body, the Church. "Now, brothers, I do not want to leave you in ignorance about spiritual gifts" (1 Cor. 12:1).

CHARISMATIC GIFTS IN GENERAL

A) *Understanding the Gifts*

1. WHAT IS MEANT BY A CHARISMATIC GIFT?

A charismatic gift is a manifestation of God's power and presence given freely for God's honor and glory and for the service of others.

Specifically the term refers to manifestations of the power of the Holy Spirit mentioned in the Scriptures, especially after Pentecost, and which have always remained with the Church in both her teaching and practice.

2. HOW MANY CHARISMATIC GIFTS ARE THERE?

Since the charismatic gifts are manifestations of the Holy Spirit, it is impossible to say how many there are. Scripture provides a number of lists of offices and ministries. The classical list, used by most, is St. Paul's in 1 Corinthians (12:8-10), where nine gifts are described. These nine seem to be normal ministries that should be present in every local church.

The text of 1 Corinthians on these gifts is:

"To one the Spirit gives wisdom in discourse, to another the power to express knowledge. Through the Spirit one receives faith; by the same Spirit another is given the gift of healing and still another miraculous powers. Prophecy is given to one; to another power to distinguish one spirit from another. One receives the gift of tongues, another that of interpreting the tongues."

3. PLEASE LIST AND DESCRIBE THESE NINE GIFTS.

The nine gifts, according to the usual threefold division are:

A. The Word Gifts (The Power to Say)

a) *The Gift of Tongues*—whereby the person gives God's message, in a language unknown to him, for the community present.

b) *The Gift of Interpretation*—whereby a person, after the use of the gift of tongues, gives the general meaning of what the person has said, or a response to what has been said. Interpretation can also be used privately in conjunction with the gift of prayer tongues.

c) *The Gift of Prophecy*—whereby the person gives God's message in the vernacular for the community or for an individual.

B. The Sign Gifts (The Power to Do)

a) *The Gift of Faith*—which enables the person at a given moment to believe, and to call upon God's power with a certainty that excludes all doubt.

b) *The Gift of Healing*—which enables the person to be God's instrument in bringing about the well-being of another, on one or more levels, spiritual, psychological or physical.

c) *The Gift of Miracles*—which enables a person to be God's instrument in either an instant healing or in some other powerful manifestation of God's power.

C. The Intellectual Gifts (The Power to Know)

a) *The Word of Wisdom*—whereby a person is granted an insight into God's plan in a given situation and is enabled to put this into words of advice or of direction.

b) *The Word of Knowledge*—whereby a person is granted an insight into a divine mystery or facet of man's relation to God and is enabled to put this into a word that helps others to grasp the mystery.

c) *The Gift of Discernment*—whereby a person is enabled to know the source of an inspiration or action, whether it came from the Holy Spirit, his own human spirit or from the evil spirit.

4. ARE THERE MORE THAN NINE CHARISMATIC GIFTS?

Since a charismatic gift is defined as a manifestation of God's power, obviously there are more than nine ways in which God can act. In 1 Corinthians, Chapter 12, St. Paul was speaking from experience, both his own and that of the early Church. He realized that the Holy Spirit *regularly* manifested Himself in these nine ways. St. Paul wanted the Early Christians to be familiar with these *regular* manifestations, to learn about them, to expect them and to yield to them all. In fact, he expected all nine gifts to be present in each Christian community. The absence of these gifts would signify some weakness in the Church's power.

5. ARE THERE NOT OTHER GIFTS OF THE HOLY SPIRIT? WHAT IS THEIR RELATION TO THESE CHARISMATIC GIFTS?

There are two sets of "gifts of the Holy Spirit." One set is *personal* and the other is *charismatic*. The personal gifts sanctify the individual while the charismatic gifts are meant for the good of the community. It was the personal gifts of the Spirit which were listed in the *Baltimore Catechism* as the results of Confirmation.

In our discussion, gifts will be used as "charismatic gifts" and not the personal or sanctifying gifts.

B) *The Gifts in the History of the Church*

6. SINCE MANY OF THESE CHARISMATIC GIFTS SEEM TO BE MISSING FROM NORMAL CATHOLIC LIFE, WOULD THE CATHOLIC CHURCH THEN BE REGARDED AS WEAKER THAN GOD INTENDED?

In a certain sense, yes. The power of the Baptism of the Holy Spirit, the manifestations of the charismatic gifts, and the service of ministries, are meant to be regular parts of Church life. When these are not operative, the Church is not all that Christ meant it to be. In calling for renewal, the Church freely admits that she is not all that she could be.

7. HOW LONG DID THE CHURCH REMAIN CHARISMATIC, I.E., WHEN THE CHARISMS WERE REGULAR PARTS OF ITS LIFE?

The charisms seemed to die out in the second century. The stress in the Scriptures moved from charismatic activity in the Acts of the Apostles and the early epistles, to the importance of office and order in the later pastoral letters (Titus and Timothy). The abuses of the gifts in the Montanist heresy (2nd century) hurried the demise of these signs and wonders which had helped the Christian message to spread quickly throughout the world.

8. HOW DID THEOLOGIANS EXPLAIN THE LOSS OF THE CHARISMATIC GIFTS IN THE CHURCH?

The loss of charismatic powers was always an embarrassing question for theologians in defending the apostolic nature of the Church. Their main defense was to claim that the gifts were meant by God to die out of the Church's life.

Theologians saw the gifts as extraordinary means given to the Early Church so that the Church would spread quickly throughout the world. Since the purpose of these gifts was supposed to be the diffusion of the Church, the theologians explained away their loss by saying the gifts were supposed to cease when their purpose was fulfilled. Thus, Fr. Karl Rahner in *Sacramentum Mundi* calls the gifts the "peculiar privileges of the Apostolic Church."

9. WHY DID THESE CHARISMATIC MANIFESTATIONS DROP OUT OF THE CHURCH?

A number of reasons are offered by Church historians:
a) The growth of the contemplative spirit (which seems to be a valid fruit of the charismatic prayer life).
b) Abuses in the use of charismatic gifts causing the Church to institute safeguards, which unfortunately led to a loss of the gifts themselves.
c) Loss of the dynamic faith of the Early Church.
d) The union of the Church and State under Constantine and the beginning of mass conversions.

10. WERE THEY ACTUALLY SUPPOSED TO "DIE OUT"?

There is no Scriptural basis for saying that God meant the charisms to cease in the Church. If anything, the

Church of the New Testament saw charisms as an integral part of the Christian life.

The abundance of the charismatic gifts in the modern Pentecostal prayer communities witnesses to the fact that the theologians were wrong in calling these gifts the prerogatives of the Primitive Church.

11. DID THESE GIFTS SURVIVE AT ALL?

Naturally, something so vital to the Church as charismatic powers could never entirely cease. They continued to be manifested in the lives of the saints and in some cases were communicated to those associated with the saint, as in the Benedictine or Franciscan renewals. However, they have been conspicuously absent from the mainstream of Church life until the present Charismatic Renewal.

12. ARE THERE CHARISMS WHICH ALL CATHOLICS ARE FAMILIAR WITH?

Catholics are familiar with a number of charisms:
a) The infallibility and indefectibility of the Church are collective charisms, i.e., God's special intervention in history to safeguard the body of believers.
b) The infallibility of the Pope is a personal charism attached to the Office, whereby God intervenes to safeguard the unity of the Church.
c) Offices in the Church are "structural" charisms (*cf. Catholic Encyclopedia*).
d) Many confessors, teachers and parents have been influenced at times by the teaching charisms in explaining truths to others.
e) The sacraments of Penance and the Anointing of the Sick should be regular means of the charism of healing.

13. IF SOME CHARISMATIC ACTIVITY HAS ALWAYS BEEN PART OF CHURCH LIFE, WHAT IS NEW ABOUT CHARISMATIC RENEWAL?

Concerning charismatic gifts the following appear to be new phenomena:
a) Large numbers of people who pray in tongues.

b) A familiarity with and an ever-increasing use of the nine charismatic ministries listed by St. Paul. Some of these ministries are extremely new, such as the ministries of tongues, interpretation and prophecy. Other charismatic ministries are new in their abundance—such as healing, Words of Wisdom and Knowledge.

14. WHY AND HOW IS THIS CHARISMATIC ABUNDANCE OCCURRING?

There seems to be a number of keys to this abundant activity:

a) An attitude of acceptance of charismatic gifts in the normal life of the Church.

b) An ever-deepening knowledge and experience in these gifts.

c) The wide-scale communication of these gifts to others, especially through the prayer communities.

Behind all this appears to be an extraordinary pouring forth of God's Spirit in our day.

15. WHY ARE THESE EVENTS HAPPENING NOW IN THE CATHOLIC CHURCH?

The following seem to be the doors (or windows) that opened the Church to the gifts:

a) Pope John, and the rest of the Church with him, prayed for a new Pentecost.

b) Vatican II committed the Church to an investigation of charismatic activity (Speech of Cardinal Suenens and Chapter Two of the *Constitution on the Church*).

c) The Church realized that it could learn about the Spirit's activity from the other Churches in bringing about this second Pentecost.

d) The Church needs the power of the charismatic ministries to effectively combat the rising tide of evil and confusion.

C) *The Gifts in the Life of the Individual*

16. WHAT IS THE RELATIONSHIP BETWEEN "MANI-
    FESTING THE GIFTS" AND GOODNESS OF LIFE?

On this, two things could be said:

First, charismatic gifts, even if of a powerful and sen-
sational nature, should not be equated with holiness of
life. These gifts are quite distinct from sanctifying grace
and are no indication of a person's holiness.

On the other hand, however, the use of the charismatic
gifts can be a concrete manifestation of a very deep love
and concern for the community. The correct use of the
gifts should lead to the fruits of the Spirit, which are a
true sign of holiness of life.

17. WHEN DOES A PERSON BEGIN TO YIELD TO THESE
    CHARISMATIC GIFTS?

A distinction has to be made between an occasional,
almost accidental, manifestation of charismatic gifts and
a regular and powerful use of these gifts. Probably every
Catholic, at some time, has been used by God to further
His Kingdom by doing or saying something that was a
charismatic manifestation of the Holy Spirit.

A regular and powerful use of these gifts usually
emerges after the person:

a) Has come to experience Christ in a personal way,
   called by Pentecostals "The Baptism of the Spirit."
b) Has begun to pray in tongues.
c) Has been praying privately for some period.
d) Has been praying regularly in a charismatic prayer
   community.

18. WHAT IS THE ROLE OF THE PERSON'S FREE WILL
    IN "CHARISMATIC MANIFESTATIONS"?

The person's will remains free, even in the extraordinary manifestations of a charism. The gifts, therefore,
are subject to the individual's will, in the sense that he
freely chooses whether or not to yield to God's activity.
In fact, the will is very active in leading the various faculties to cooperate with God in yielding to the gifts.

At times, however, the charismatic manifestation is so
important to the life of the community that the individual

is almost forced to yield. The pain experienced by the Old Testament prophets when they refused to deliver God's message is an example. This unique manner of God's action is found among newcomers who have to be "pushed" to use the gifts and among the very mature in whom God's activity is deep.

19. WHAT IS THE ROLE OF THE INTELLECTUAL FACULTIES IN CHARISMATIC MANIFESTATION?

First, the person must know about the gifts. Many people, because they are unaware of the gifts, do not use or manifest them to the degree expected by God. St. Paul stresses the intellect's role when he wrote, "I want you to know the truth about the spiritual gifts." A detailed knowledge and experience of the gifts is a necessary condition for growth.

Secondly, the imagination, memory and intellect are extremely active in all of the gifts, since these are the faculties directly touched by God's action. The Spirit prepares these powers of man to be used by Him, and gradually teaches the individual to recognize and yield to His promptings.

20. DOES THIS COOPERATION OF THE INTELLECT EVER CAUSE PEOPLE TO FEEL THAT "IT IS JUST THEM" AND NOT THE HOLY SPIRIT?

That doubt is frequently present with every individual who yields to the charismatic gifts. For newcomers, this doubt is very common, and they need the help of the prayer community to reassure them that it really is the Spirit's action. As the person gets through this initial stage of doubts, he is better able to discern when it is truly God's prompting and when it is merely himself.

Constant trial, error, and discernment, both by the person and by the community, bring a confidence in the gifts. With experience the person matures and grows in discernment so that these doubts pass.

21. WHAT SHOULD A PERSON DO TO GROW IN THESE GIFTS?

It would be helpful if the person:

a) Led a deep life of prayer and a life in close union with God's will.
b) Studied the gifts and shared regularly with those who also exercise them.
c) Acted like a little child, walking wherever the Lord led and not being afraid of honest mistakes.

If these things are done, the Lord, for His part, will do great things for the person and for the community.

22. WHAT IF THE PERSON DOES NOT GROW IN THE GIFTS?

Then the community definitely suffers, since the Lord wants to lead all prayer communities into a deeper life in the Spirit. He wants the people to sense that they are "getting somewhere" and that the group is growing in prayer. Also, the person might get discouraged with Charismatic Renewal, not realizing that he is missing out on an important aspect of this movement.

In a sense, growth of a prayer community depends very much on using the gifts, allowing the Holy Spirit to freely manifest Himself and lead the group where He wants it to go. Communities that are gifted with balanced leaders who are charismatically oriented do this best.

D) *Having a Charismatic Ministry*

23. WHAT DOES IT MEAN TO HAVE A "MINISTRY IN A CERTAIN GIFT"—SUCH AS PROPHECY OR HEALING?

To understand a "ministry in a certain gift," the following should be kept in mind:

a) "Charismatic gifts" are not something we possess (so, in a sense, "gifts" is not the best word to express God's action here), but rather they are "ways" in which God regularly manifests Himself through an individual.

By charismatic gifts, we do not possess God as much as God possesses us and uses us for His people. Therefore, a person "yields" to a gift rather than "has" a gift.

b) As a person is more and more faithful to God, recognizing and being sensitive to the activity of God's Spirit, he yields more regularly to God's action. In this way, God is able to use that person more frequently.

c) The person, although perhaps yielding to many of God's charismatic gifts, tends to become sensitive and responsive to a particular one—as the gift of interpretation, or of prophecy or of discernment or of healing. The person then is said to exercise a "ministry."

A ministry is a regular and frequent yielding to God's action through a given charismatic gift.

24. WHAT, FOR EXAMPLE, WOULD BE A "PROPHETIC MINISTRY"?

To have a "prophetic ministry" simply means that God uses an individual on a regular basis for prophetic utterances. The person has learned to cooperate with God and has willingly "yielded" to this gentle prompting of the Spirit.

As the person becomes "trustworthy" with the prophetic gift, using it responsibly for the building up of the community, God uses that person more and more. Prophecy becomes an almost permanent gift, manifested regularly. It is also manifested, at times, in rather extraordinary ways.

The "prophet" is different from someone who experiences prophecy only from time to time, and then usually only in "ordinary ways."

25. ARE THERE ANY DANGERS IN HAVING A "MINISTRY"?

There are two general dangers:

a) The person feels that he is an "expert" in the field and refuses to submit to the judgment or discernment of other leaders, whom the person judges are not "experts" in his field.

b) The person "specializes" in that ministry and does not develop the other gifts.

E) *Correct Attitude Toward the Gifts*

26. WHAT IS THE DIFFERENCE BETWEEN "OPENNESS
TO THE GIFTS" AND "CHARISMANIA"?

Being "open to the gifts" means that the person sees
charismatic gifts as normal activities of the Holy Spirit,
to which he yields in a childlike way. This correct attitude is based on the simple faith that God does intervene in our lives through charisms.

Charismania, on the other hand, presents a twisted use
of God's gifts, often asking God to become subject to man.
Some aspects of charismania would be:

a) Expecting God to intervene in a charismatic way,
when natural powers would be enough to handle the
situation.

b) A refusal to do normal work, such as study or
preparation, with the idea that God would provide
through His gifts.

c) Seeing charismatic activity as an end in itself rather
than as a means to personal and community growth.

27. WHAT, THEN, IS A CORRECT ATTITUDE TOWARD
THE GIFTS?

First, the person should learn about them and pray
for them.

Secondly, he should not be afraid of them, since these
are ways the Holy Spirit wants to act.

Thirdly, he should not hinder the Holy Spirit by creating a lot of human rules for their use.

Fourthly, he should actively seek them and yield to
them with childlike faith.

28. WHAT IS MEANT BY "NOT BEING AFRAID OF THE
GIFTS"?

"Not being afraid" means to step out in faith in the
use of the gifts and to trust the Lord, who will take care
of any honest mistakes in their use.

With the gifts, there has to be a certain "boldness,"
a "being at home" feeling. Otherwise, the gifts will become objects of discussion and a source of tension. In
addition, leadership must not stress the dangers involved

in charismatic gifts to the degree that people are afraid
to seek or use them.

29. SHOULD NOT A PRAYER COMMUNITY STRESS A GROWTH IN LOVE MORE THAN A GROWTH IN THE GIFTS?

Certainly love is the most important aspect of any
prayer community. However, two things should be noted:

First, these gifts are means God gives to us to grow in
love. They are the tools for the garden, which if used
correctly, will certainly bring forth good fruit.

Secondly, a community which plays down the gifts,
with the idea of aiming at love, might be guilty of a subtle pride, presupposing that it can arrive at love without
using the normal ministries established by God.

30. WHAT ROLE DOES "LOVE" PLAY IN THE GROWTH OF THE GIFTS?

Since charismatic gifts are given to a person for the
benefit of the community, love for others is the only atmosphere in which the gifts will grow. Also, the secret of
growth in the gifts is a love for the Lord and for the
brethren, and not a love for the gifts themselves.

Chapter Six

The Gifts of Tongues and Interpretation

One receives the gift of tongues, another that of interpreting the tongues.

(1 Cor. 12:10)

INTRODUCTION

ST. PAUL WRITES QUITE CALMLY IN 1 CORINTHIANS, Chapter 12, Verse 10, "one receives the gift of tongues, another that of interpreting the tongues." With that sentence, Paul adds these two charismatic ministries, which appeared only after Pentecost, to those which had previously been manifested in both the Old and New Testaments. With tongues, a new power was given to man to release God's message and by interpretation to listen to His word.

St. Paul seemed to be worried about an abuse of these gifts. In a sense we have to be thankful for these abuses, for they occasioned the extensive teachings on these gifts recorded in 1 Corinthians, Chapters 12 and 14. None of the other charismatic gifts received such an orderly and complete Pauline teaching.

Our own experience is that the gifts of tongues and interpretation are not used as extensively as they should be. The gift of prayer tongues is common, as is the beauty of the community praying and singing in tongues. However, the gifts of tongues and interpretation are lost in the shuffle. These companion gifts provide a beautiful variety to a prayer meeting. To lose them, or to willfully neglect their use in favor of communal use of tongues, would be to lose an important power contained in Charismatic Renewal. The lack of use can be traced to faulty knowledge of the distinction between prayer tongues and the gift of tongues. Many who have yielded to prayer tongues are often unaware that God might want to use them in a distinctive way through the gift of tongues.

St. Paul wrote often about the power of prophecy to edify and to strengthen the Church. Yet, he also wrote that tongues, followed by interpretation, was equal to prophecy. This section is written with the hope that these powerful gifts will not be overlooked or fall into neglect but rather that the full power of this renewal will be unleashed within the Church.

THE GIFTS OF TONGUES AND INTERPRETATION

A) *Understanding the Gift of Tongues*

1. WHAT IS THE GIFT OF TONGUES?

The gift of tongues is a passing manifestation of the Holy Spirit to an individual (usually a mature member) during a charismatic prayer meeting, whereby the person is prompted to speak aloud in tongues, which must be followed by use of the companion gift of interpretation. This use of the gifts of tongues and interpretation is very akin to the gift of prophecy.

A previous section treated of prayer tongues.

2. WHAT IS THE DIFFERENCE, THEREFORE, BETWEEN PRAYING IN TONGUES AND THE GIFT OF TONGUES?

There are quite a number of differences.

Prayer tongues:

a) Are a permanent gift.

b) Seem to be given to all.

c) Need not be followed by interpretation.

d) Can be used in communal praying or singing.

e) Are usually a prayer of praise and thanksgiving.

f) Are meant primarily for the person's own spiritual growth.

On the other hand, the gift of tongues:

a) Is a passing manifestation of God's power.

b) Seems to be given only to those with a ministry of tongues.

c) Should always be followed by interpretation.

d) Should be used alone, and not in common with others.

e) Is not limited to a prayer of praise, but can take diverse forms.

f) Is meant primarily to release God's message to the community.

3. WHY IS THIS DISTINCTION IMPORTANT?

Unless the distinction is clear, a number of misunderstandings arise concerning both prayer tongues and the gift of tongues. Three mistakes seem prevalent:

a) First, 1 Corinthians, Chapter 12, Verse 10 ("One receives the gift of tongues"), which refers to the gift of tongues, is frequently misunderstood to refer to prayer tongues. Thus many feel that only a few are meant to pray in tongues.

b) Secondly, the rules for interpretation following the gift of tongues in 1 Corinthians, Chapter 14 can mistakenly be applied to prayer tongues and to the false conclusion that interpretation must follow the community's prayer in tongues.

c) Thirdly, a person who is truly being moved by God to the gift of tongues might be unaware that God wants to use him in this way and thus be inhibited in yielding to the gift.

B) Understanding the Gift of Interpretation

4. WHAT IS THE GIFT OF INTERPRETATION?

The gift of interpretation is the power given to an individual to speak, in the vernacular, the general meaning of whatever was said aloud in the gift of tongues.

5. WHAT FORM DOES THE "INTERPRETATION" TAKE?

There are two general forms. The first is a prayer of praise of God. In a sense, this is probably the purest form of interpretation. The second is the form of a message from God to the community. In this form, interpretation is very close to prophecy.

C) Scriptural Basis for the Gift of Tongues

6. WHAT IS THE SCRIPTURAL BACKGROUND FOR THE TONGUES?

The biblical basis for this gift is found in 1 Corinthians, Chapters 12 and 14. Chapter 12, Verse 10 lists this gift as one of nine charismatic ministries, while Verse 28 gives speaking in tongues in a second list of ministries in the Church.

In Chapter 14, St. Paul provides a rather lengthy teaching on this gift:

a) Tongues does not have the power of prophecy, unless it is followed by interpretation (Verse 5).

b) Tongues can be confusing if misused (Verse 6-12).

c) Tongues is frequently a prayer of praise or thanksgiving (Verse 16).

d) Tongues is a sign for those who do not believe (Verse 22).

e) If misused, tongues can confuse the unbeliever or the uninitiated (Verse 23).

f) When tongues are used it should be in good order (Verse 26-27).

g) Tongues should not be forbidden (Verse 39).

7. WHY, IN OUTLINING THE SCRIPTURAL BASIS FOR THE GIFT OF TONGUES, WERE THE EVENTS AT PENTECOST AND OF OTHER PARTS OF THE ACTS OF THE APOSTLES OVERLOOKED?

These texts were not used since they seem to refer to the ability to pray in tongues rather than the gift of tongues.

Acts, Chapter 2, Verse 6, "They were much confused because each one hears these men speaking in his own language" is a unique experience, recorded only at Pentecost. This seems to be a very special "miracle of hearing" and not the gift of tongues and interpretation as described by St. Paul in 1 Corinthians, Chapter 14.

D) *Scriptural Basis for the Gift of Interpretation*

8. WHAT IS THE SCRIPTURAL BASIS AND TEACHING ON THE GIFT OF INTERPRETATION?

Being a companion gift to tongues, the teaching on the gift of interpretation is also contained in 1 Corinthians, Chapters 12 and 14.

Chapter 12, Verse 10 reads, "One receives the gift of

tongues, another that of interpreting the tongues." In Verse 30, St. Paul lists interpretation as a charismatic ministry given only to some. "Do all speak in tongues, all have the gift of interpretation of tongues?" In Chapter 14, St. Paul gives an extended teaching on the gifts:

  a) Interpretation is for the upbuilding of the Church and is equal to prophecy (Verse 5).

  b) One who speaks in tongues should pray for the gift of interpretation (Verse 13).

  c) The gift of tongues should be followed by interpretation (Verse 27).

  d) If no interpreter is present, then the gift of tongues should not be used aloud (Verse 28).

    9. How DOES SCRIPTURE DESCRIBE THE USE OF THE GIFTS OF TONGUES AND INTERPRETATION AT A PRAYER MEETING?

Three cases are given in 1 Corinthians, Chapter 14 about a person yielding to the gift of tongues.

  a) Being his own interpreter:
    "This means that the man who speaks in a tongue should pray for the gift of interpretation" (Verse 13).

  b) Having others as interpreters:
    "If any are going to talk in tongues let it be at most two or three, each in turn, with another to interpret what they are saying" (Verse 27).

  c) No interpreters present:
    "But if there is no one to interpret, there should be silence in the assembly, each one speaking only to himself and to God" (Verse 28).

E) *Using These Gifts*

    10. How, IN PRACTICE, ARE THESE GIFTS MANIFESTED?

Their use follows closely the Scriptural teaching:

During a charismatic prayer meeting, a mature member of the community is moved by God to speak aloud by himself in tongues. This is generally followed by a message from God in the vernacular. Used together, the gifts are very close to the charismatic gift of prophecy (1 Cor. 14:5).

11. How Does the Person Know That God Is Moving Him to Speak in Tongues?

Usually the person is a mature member of the community who has become sensitive to God's movements. The sensitivity takes into account the circumstances of the prayer meeting and an internal touch or anointing. As the person recognizes God's movement, he yields to it by an act of the will, speaking aloud, by himself, in tongues.

12. Is There Any Time When the Gift of Tongues Should Not Be Used?

There are definite times when the gift of tongues should not be used, since all must be in order. Thus, if something else is occurring—a hymn, scripture reading or talk—it should not be interrupted by tongues speaking.

On the other hand, a mature member moved to speak in tongues will sense the moment and the situation in which God wishes to use him. The gift of tongues will fit in with what is happening and will lead to a deeper use of the gift.

13. How Does a Person "Yield To" the Gift of Interpretation?

First, after the use of the gift of tongues, the person should make an act of childlike faith, that God will speak to him.

Secondly, each member should "pray for" an interpretation. This does not mean to "make up" appropriate words, but rather to remain quiet and prayerful to see if words begin to come to mind. Often, as the words come together in a sentence, the person will be "urged" to speak it forth for the good of the community.

After a while, the person becomes quite experienced in this "yielding" and begins to exercise a ministry of interpretation.

14. COULD THIS YIELDING TO "INTERPRETATION" BE
    EXPLAINED A LITTLE MORE IN DEPTH?

What seems to occur in a prayer meeting, after the
use of the gift of tongues, is that a certain stillness and
quiet sets in (and should be deliberately fostered). During this period, the people ask God to speak to them.
Frequently, members experience the charismatic activity
of phrases or sentences coming to mind. These thoughts
must be tested to see if they really are from God. If the
person feels they are, then the words should be spoken
aloud.

15. HOW CAN ANYONE OR ANY GROUP BE CERTAIN
    THAT THESE WORDS ARE TRULY FROM GOD?

A number of ways exist:
a) If other members with the gift have the same interpretation, the group can be certain that God has
   spoken to them.
b) If the words are given by an experienced member
   and contain great power, bringing joy and peace to
   the group, then some certainty exists that the words
   are from God.
c) If neither of these first two is present, then the
   group might suspend judgment on whether or not
   God has truly spoken.

16. WHY ARE THESE GIFTS IMPORTANT TO THE PRAYER
    MEETING? WHAT IS THE PURPOSE OF THESE
    GIFTS?

These gifts seem to have the following purposes:
a) They add a variety of charismatic manifestations
   to a prayer meeting.
b) They are often the source of an important message from God to the community.
c) They can unleash other charismatic gifts that are
   not being used.

17. IS NOT THE USE OF TONGUES AND INTERPRETATION
    A STRANGE WAY FOR GOD TO SPEAK TO HIS
    PEOPLE?

For those involved in charismatic prayer groups, it

has become a very natural and beautiful way of listening to God's message.

For those not involved, an explanation should be sought in Scripture, for man does not choose how God is to work and speak to His people. In Scripture, this charismatic way of tongues and interpretation was a regular means of listening to God, accepted both by the Corinthian community and St. Paul.

F) *Growth in these Gifts*

18. HOW DOES A PERSON GROW IN THE GIFT OF INTERPRETATION?

First, he must overcome the self-consciousness associated with speaking God's message. There is always fear that an interpretation is just of our own making.

Secondly, he must realize that the Holy Spirit is gentle and seeks the person's cooperation with this gift, in no way compelling the person to speak out.

Thirdly, the person should not wait for perfect certitude that his words are from the Spirit. A stepping out in faith is always an important element in growing in the gifts.

Therefore, if while a person is speaking in tongues, the Spirit seems to prompt the individual with a thought, the person, after a short period of prayerful discernment, should speak those words for the community, later accepting the community's discernment on the gift.

19. HOW DOES A COMMUNITY GROW IN THESE GIFTS?

Certain factors foster growth:

a) A clear and practical knowledge of these gifts.
b) A fostering of the prayerful spirit in the meeting. Often these gifts are manifested in the quiet of deep prayer and are easily overlooked in a superficial prayer meeting.
c) An openness to these manifestations as a normal way of God speaking to His people.

G) *Problems with the Gifts*

20. Are there any abuses with these gifts?

Two common problems do exist which leaders should be aware of.

First, people speaking aloud in tongues who are not really being moved to do so by God; secondly, people giving interpretations to tongues which are not a real and true gift. Naturally, the use of these gifts has to be discerned by the leaders and steps taken to remove a wrong use of the gifts.

21. Why do these problems arise:

A person might use the gift of tongues even though not moved for the following reasons:

a) Mistakenly believes he is moved to such.

b) Feels a charismatic ministry is needed for acceptance.

c) Grows anxious when periods of silence occur.

The gift of interpretation is open to misuse, since the charismatic community is usually aware of St. Paul's teaching that interpretation should follow the gift of tongues. A certain pressure can be present to 'force" an interpretation at this time. Obviously, the wrong use of the gift of tongues can easily lead to a similar wrong use of the companion gift of interpretation.

22. What is the counterfeit gift of tongues?

It is a manifestation that occurs rarely. The tongues are uncontrolled, harsh and disturbing. Discernment of false tongues is fairly easy for any experienced leader.

The person who experiences false tongues should review with a priest what in his life opened him up to this activity of a counterfeit gift. Usually it is rooted in the kingdom of darkness.

H) *Practical Questions about Tongues and Interpretation*

23. What is the difference between the gifts of tongues and interpretation, and the ministries of these charismatic manifestations?

In general, a gift is something that is present from

time to time and in what could be called an ordinary way. The ministry means that the power is manifested regularly and in a very powerful way.

Thus a person could use the gift of tongues and interpretation without possessing a ministry in these gifts. A person with the ministry of tongues probably speaks out regularly at prayer meetings.

24. HOW CAN SOMETHING BE CALLED AN "INTERPRE-TATION" WHEN IT IS OBVIOUSLY MUCH LONGER OR MUCH SHORTER THAN THE GIFT OF TONGUES?

Various explanations can be given:
a) The gift of tongues was a petition and the interpretation was God's reply—thus the gift of tongues could be a prayer asking God to speak to the community while the interpretation was God's response to the prayer.
b) The gift of tongues is used to unleash other charismatic gifts, such as a prophecy that someone was afraid to give.

I) *Tongues, Interpretation and Prophecy*

25. WHAT IS THE DIFFERENCE BETWEEN PROPHECY AND THE GIFT OF TONGUES FOLLOWED BY INTER-PRETATION?

Prophecy:
a) Is not necessarily preceded by the speaking in an unknown tongue but can occur at any time.
b) Is always a message from God to someone or some group.

Interpretation of the gift of tongues:
a) Is always preceded by the gift of tongues.
b) Need not be a message to the community but could be a prayer of praise.

26. SOMETIMES, ESPECIALLY IN SMALL AND EXPERI-ENCED GROUPS, A PERSON WILL PRAY IN TONGUES AND ANOTHER WILL INTERPRET. THIS WILL GO ON

FOR A WHILE. IS THIS THE GIFT OF TONGUES AND INTERPRETATION?

It probably is the gift of prophecy which can be more easily yielded to when another prays in tongues.

27. WHY IS THE GIFT OF TONGUES SOMETIMES NEEDED BEFORE PROPHECY IS GIVEN?

A couple of reasons emerge from experience with these gifts:

a) A person frequently is "holding back" from delivering prophecy because of fear or awkwardness or uncertainty. The gift of tongues moves him to deliver God's words.

b) Tongues often touches off the gift of prophecy which was present but unrecognized.

c) Tongues prepares a community to look for and listen to God's message.

28. WHY IS THE DISTINCTION BETWEEN INTERPRETATION AND PROPHECY NOT CLEARER?

a) The charismatic prayer groups are growing in experience and use of the gifts. This growth leads to tentative explanations of what God seems to be doing.

b) Although St. Paul neatly and rightly divides the charismatic gifts, in practice it is sometimes difficult to give the right name to a charismatic manifestation.

c) Since all charismatic activity is rooted in the same Spirit, the use of one gift often helps another person yield to a different gift. With the gifts, members help and encourage one another in their use.

Chapter Seven

The Gift of Prophecy

Set your hearts on spiritual gifts—
above all, the gift of prophecy.
(1 Cor. 14:1)

INTRODUCTION

PROPHECY IS THE POWER TO SPEAK GOD'S MESSAGE AND has emerged as a new and powerful way for God to influence, direct and console His people. This phenomenon of charismatic prophecy comes at a time when the world is taken up with many forms of false prophecy and with strange means of seeking to know future events.

Since the charismatic gift is new to most Catholics, it presents some unique problems. The newcomer to Charismatic Renewal is struck by words spoken in the first person, as if coming from God's mind. For those involved longer in this renewal three aspects of the gift are evident:

1) The need of the power of prophecy for growth in the Christian life.
2) The problem of the human spirit in prophetic utterances.
3) The great danger of false prophecy.

In spite of difficulties, regular attendance at charismatic prayer meetings brings everyone to a moment when he realizes that God has spoken to him in a very definite and powerful way through a prophecy given by another. At that moment, a sense of the tenderness of the Provident Father, or of the thoughtfulness of Jesus or of the power of the Spirit, overwhelms the person as he realizes that Almighty God has revealed His mind.

Since prophecy is an extremely powerful gift, it must be understood, surrounded with safeguards and be subject to leadership. Honest mistakes in its use will be taken care of by God. However, failure to study the gift or to seek needed guidance can only result in problems.

Although this discussion can be only an incomplete guide compared with a community which understands and uses the gift, it is an attempt to say a few basic things about this divine power which will become more powerful and more important in the years ahead.

It takes a two-fold attitude toward the gift, first, encouraging its use and its growth; secondly, demanding safeguards and discernment. In reestablishing this gift in the Church, the Lord has called us to the simplicity of the dove and the cunning of the fox.

THE CHARISMATIC GIFT OF PROPHECY

A) *Understanding the Gift*

1. WHAT IS THE GIFT OF PROPHECY?

It is the gift whereby God manifests to man His own thoughts so that a message may be given for the individual or for a group of individuals, or for the community.

2. WHAT IS THE PURPOSE OF PROPHECY?

Prophecy helps the individual and the community to know God's thoughts in many areas of Christian life and, therefore, helps all to fulfill His will.

Prophecy can enlighten both the individual and the community about the following:

a) Graces to seek from God.
b) Actions to undertake.
c) Attitudes to inculcate or to remove.
d) Events to prepare for.

3. IS IT NOT PRESUMPTUOUS TO SPEAK OF KNOWING GOD'S THOUGHTS?

Catholics presume to know God's thoughts in many areas of Christian life—the infallible doctrines of the Church, its moral teaching and certitude about the state of grace. For the person to advance closer to God, he often must have more sensitive ways of discovering God's will. Especially important is a sensitivity to God's inspirations. The reemerging gift of prophecy is a tremendous help to make us sensitive to God's will. Its importance cannot be overestimated nor can its dangers be overlooked.

4. DOES PROPHECY DEAL ONLY WITH THE FUTURE?

Prophecy deals both with the present (forthtelling) and with the future (foretelling). Forthtelling prophecy is God's message for the community here and now. In this context, it edifies (upbuilding), exhorts (admonition), or comforts (encouragement). Foretelling, on the other hand, is predictive of the future and is usually evidenced only by those in the established office of prophecy.

5. IS PROPHECY FOR THE COMMUNITY OR FOR THE INDIVIDUAL?

Prophecy can be for an individual, a number of people or for the entire community. Prophecy which is for the community is frequently repeated so the community does not miss the message, and, if the prophetic gift is used correctly during a prayer meeting, a theme usually emerges. Some prophecy, even during a prayer meeting, will be directed toward an individual or a given group, such as leadership.

B) *Scriptural Basis for the Gift of Prophecy*

6. WHAT IS THE ROLE OF PROPHECY IN THE OLD TESTAMENT?

The prophetic office played an important role in the history of Israel, beginning especially with Samuel and the establishment of kings. Many prophetic personalities followed, including the three major Old Testament figures of Isaias, Jeremias and Ezechial.

In practice, the strength of the prophetic office caused periods of religious fervor and devotion to Yahweh. The demise of the office initiated a period of religious darkness. Prophecy, therefore, was extremely important to Israel's fidelity to God and to His will.

7. WHAT PICTURE DOES SCRIPTURE GIVE OF CHRIST AND THE PROPHETIC GIFT?

Although Jesus never directly claimed to be a prophet, He saw Himself as a prophet ("No prophet is without honor except in his native place, indeed in his own house" Matt. 13:57), and allowed Himself to be called a prophet by others ("a great prophet has arisen among us" Luke 7:16).

Christ delivered many prophecies, such as Peter's denial, Christ's own passion, death and resurrection, the plight of the apostles when dragged before kings, and the great works they would do in His name.

8. WHAT ARE OTHER EXAMPLES OF PROPHECY IN THE NEW TESTAMENT?

The following should be listed:

a) Zechariah's prophecy about his son, John the Baptist (Luke 1:67-79).

b) Simon's prophecy about Jesus as "a revealing light to the Gentiles, leading to the downfall and rise of many" (Luke 2:32-34) and his prophecy of the sorrow of Mary (Verse 35).

c) Agabus's prophecy of a severe famine over all the world (Acts 11:28), and later his prophecy that Paul would be bound and handed over to the Gentiles (Acts 21:11-14).

d) A prophecy at Antioch stating that Paul and Barnabas were to be sent apart for God's work (Acts 13:3).

e) Timothy was given a charge in accord with the prophecies (1 Tim. 1:18), which was done by the laying on of hands (1 Tim. 4:14).

f) Most of the Book of Revelations is prophecy (*cf.* Rev. 22:6).

9. WHAT IS THE ATTITUDE OF THE NEW TESTAMENT TO PROPHECY?

The New Testament seems to accept and to encourage prophecy as a normal means of God's speaking to His people. Peter sees the Pentecostal outpouring as a fulfillment of Joel's prophecy that prophetic powers would be given to all (Acts 2:17).

Paul in 1 Corinthians gives the most detailed explanation of this gift.

a) It is a charismatic ministry given to some (12:10).

b) Ranks second, after the ministry of the apostles, in importance in the Church (12:29).

c) Is worth nothing without love (13:8).

d) Will cease (although probably referring to heaven

since Paul also talks about knowledge passing away)
(13:8).
e) Is imperfect (13:9).
f) Should be sought more than any other spiritual gift
(14:1).
g) Is used to speak to men for their upbuilding, encouragement and consolation (14:3).
h) Builds up the Church (14:4).
i) Is preferred to speaking in tongues, unless interpretation follows (14:5).
j) Is meant for those already having faith (14:22).
k) Only two or three prophets should speak, while the
rest judge (14:29).
l) All can speak their prophecies, but one by one (14:
31).
m) Is always under the control of the prophet (14:32).
n) Hearts should be set on it (14:39).
A final note would be that, while open to the prophetic
gifts, Scripture also reminds us of Christ's warning about
"false prophets" (Matt. 24:11).

C) *Developing the Gift of Prophecy*

10. HOW DOES AN INDIVIDUAL DEVELOP THE GIFT OF
PROPHECY?

First, he must develop a deep, personal life of prayer.

Secondly, he must be detached from the world—for he
cannot hear God speaking to him if he is overly taken up
with worldly concerns.

Thirdly, the person must have a deep love for the prayer
community, desiring to enrich it by prophecy.

Fourthly, the person must "step out" in faith when he
recognizes God moving him to prophecy.

11. HOW DOES A PERSON "RECOGNIZE" THAT HE IS BE-
ING MOVED TO PROPHECY?

First, he senses that some activity is taking place within him, of which God is the cause and not himself. This
could be a sense of being "filled up," or a special joy or
peace or a feeling of God's presence.

Secondly, the person perceives certain words or phrases going through his mind. Or perhaps a certain picture comes into the imagination seemingly "out of nowhere." In other words, the person perceives God's action and that divine activity results in an intelligible message. The ways this occurs seem to vary greatly. Some receive whole sentences while others seem only to have a word at a time. Others have no words, but the sense of a message. After a while, the person recognizes and understands how God touches them in prophecy. One aspect that seems common is that the use of prayer tongues sensitizes the person to yield to this gift.

12. ARE THERE ANY "FEELINGS" WHILE THE PERSON IS GIVING A TRUE PROPHECY?

There can be definite feelings on the part of both the community and the individual.

The individual often has the feeling of speaking words which are more "coming" to him, rather than making them up. This passivity in yielding also causes consolation and an intense sense of God's presence.

The community has a feeling of respect and gratitude that God has spoken to His people. True prophecy tends to bestow peace and joy, even when it points out the faults of the community.

13. IF THE PERSON PERCEIVES THAT GOD IS WORKING IN THIS WAY, WHAT SHOULD HE DO?

The person should remain deep in prayer, somewhat passive and childlike, asking God to help him cooperate with this grace. He should allow God to influence His intellect, memory and imagination and begin to search out what God wants him to say. As he actively cooperates, he will become somewhat certain that God is moving him to prophecy and will at least be certain of the beginning words. As he speaks these "in faith," the rest are given.

If God's activity begins with a picture, the person should pray for the accompanying words. Sometimes, another person in the prayer meeting is given the words and the person can then relate that God was moving them to the same theme.

14. HOW DOES A COMMUNITY DEVELOP THE GIFT OF PROPHECY?

First, the community must have a childlike faith in prophecy, believing that God does speak to His people.

Secondly, the members must be taught how to recognize God's action as He moves an individual to give a prophecy.

Thirdly, the community must encourage the members to "step out in faith" even if some "non-prophecy" results. Too much discernment can retard the growth of the gift with the result that opportunities for prophecy are lost.

Fourthly, leaders must be aware of the correct and incorrect use of prophecy so that the gift is constantly improved.

15. WHAT IS "CONFIRMATION" OF A PROPHECY?

As a person "steps out in faith" and delivers a prophecy, he is still not perfectly certain that his prophecy is from God. "Confirmation" is necessary so the person and the community obtain the needed certitude.

This happens in a number of ways:

a) If others in the prayer community have received similar prophetic messages. This is one of the ways St. Paul wanted the prophets to test the prophecy.

b) If the prophecy comes true and was important for the fulfilling of God's plan.

c) Sometimes a confirmation for a prophecy comes only later as when the prophecy is a means of grace for an individual.

D) *Discernment of Prophecy*

16. WHEN AN UTTERANCE IS GIVEN IN PROPHETIC FORM, WHAT DISCERNMENT IS NEEDED?

The discernment must be made whether the utterance is true prophecy, non-prophecy or false prophecy.

17. WHAT IS TRUE PROPHECY?

True prophecy is a message from God meant for the

community or for the individual. Although this need not be Scriptural in form, it cannot be contrary to Scripture. When received, the community experiences a great joy that God has spoken to His people.

18. WHAT IS "NON-PROPHECY"?

"Non-prophecy" is a general statement—usually pious or Scriptural in form, which comes from the person's human spirit rather than from God's Holy Spirit. It is usually harmless to the group and differs from true prophecy because it does not come from God and lacks power to build up the community or to encourage the members.

19. HOW DOES NON-PROPHECY OCCUR?

It usually happens when people do not have clear teaching on true prophecy and therefore mistakenly judge that their thoughts, while at a prayer meeting, are prophetic.

Scripture quotes are common non-prophecy, especially among newcomers. Also common is the practice of placing pious thoughts, more suitable as prayers of praise, into prophetic form.

A more difficult discernment is to recognize the difference between prophecy and the Words of Wisdom and Knowledge.

20. WHAT IS "FALSE PROPHECY"?

False prophecy is an utterance which comes from the evil spirit and brings with it many harmful effects, such as disruption of the prayer meeting or confusion among leaders or members of the prayer community. False prophecy is usually very rare and most prayer communities seem to have more of a problem with non-prophecy.

21. HOW DOES FALSE PROPHECY OCCUR?

It occurs in the following ways:
a) The person has areas of his life that are in occult bondage and therefore the person can be used by evil.
b) The group itself is looking for spectacular prophecies.

c) The group has opened itself up to evil by quarreling, bickering, hatred or some other sin.

E) *Criteria for Judging Prophecy*

22. HOW DOES LEADERSHIP DISTINGUISH TRUE PROPHECY, NON-PROPHECY AND FALSE PROPHECY?

The following criteria can be used:

True prophecy edifies and leads to the fruits of the Spirit. When given at a prayer meeting, the group receives a greater sense of Christ's presence. True prophecy touches people's hearts or gives a clearer understanding of God's activity among His people.

Non-prophecy brings forth no fruit—good or bad. Although not disturbing, it does not possess the power of the true charismatic gift. If a prayer meeting is marked by too much non-prophecy, it is sluggish and God's power among the members is smothered.

False prophecy disrupts, causes anxiety and leads the meeting or the community away from God's will. People who should be at peace with God are thrown into turmoil and confusion. The fruits of false prophecy are bad although sometimes this can only be seen after some period of time, as the results of believing the prophecy emerge.

23. HOW SHOULD TRUE PROPHECY BE ACTED UPON?

Acting on prophecy depends on the prophecy itself and the circumstances in which it was given.

If the prophecy is general and confirmed, then the leadership can easily discern that it is true prophecy. If given during a prayer meeting, the moderator might want to manifest this judgment to the group and urge the members to continue to use the gift as they had been doing. He should mention that he feels God has spoken to the community, and that His words should be pondered by all.

If the prophecy is very concrete, or even spectacular, then leadership has to be more careful in discerning. If thought to be truly from God, leadership has to judge how to act on God's word.

24. HOW SHOULD NON-PROPHECY BE HANDLED?

It is important that tact be used so as not to hurt feelings. However, to allow a lot of "non-prophecy" at a prayer meeting would not be good for the individual or the community.

The community leaders should take the following steps:

a) Speak with the person who regularly uses non-prophetic utterances.

b) Give clear teachings on the use of prophecy with examples of non-prophecy and its causes.

c) Show how non-prophecy should really be given in the form of a prayer of praise.

25. HOW SHOULD "FALSE PROPHECY" BE HANDLED?

Sometimes it need not be "handled" at all since the community, especially if well-instructed, will discern prophecy as false and reject it. The prophecy will have no effect except to make the group turn to the Lord and seek His protection.

If, however, the community is not mature or the "false prophecy" is so clever that only leaders realize the source of the prophecy, then something must be done to forestall the harmful effects. Leaders must make the judgment whether to inform the community of their discernment immediately or later.

26. IN DISCERNING PROPHECY, DOES THE LEADERSHIP TAKE INTO ACCOUNT THE PERSON WHO DELIVERED THE PROPHECY?

Certainly, skilled discernment will look carefully at the person who delivered the prophecy. If the person has a deep goodness of life and in the past has been true in prophetic utterances, then the presumption would be that the prophecy is true. If, however, the person is unstable, has a questionable goodness of life, and has, in the past, uttered false prophecies, then the presumption would be that this, too, is false.

Concerning a striking or directive prophecy, even more attention must be given to the person delivering the message. If God is going to give some important message to

His community, He will give it to either a number in the
community or to one who would be easily believed.

27. IS A "PROPHETIC UTTERANCE" EVER CHANGED OR
    MODIFIED BY THE PERSON DELIVERING THE PROPH-
    ECY?

The following elements can easily modify, reverse or
add to a true prophetic utterance and must be considered
in discernment:

a) The person's theological background.
b) His emotional state and problems.
c) The atmosphere in which the prophecy is delivered,
   especially if problems exist in the community.

Just as water passing through a rusty pipe comes out
as rusty water, so in prophecy God's message can be modi-
fied by the person's human condition, even though the person is truly moved by God's charismatic activity.

F) *Prophecy and Prayer Community*

28. IS PROPHECY IMPORTANT TO A PRAYER COMMU-
    NITY?

Prophecy in a charismatic prayer community has an extremely vital role. Its absence signifies superficiality in
prayer and presents an obstacle to any deep walk in the
Spirit. St. Paul told the Corinthians to especially desire
prophecy. "Seek eagerly after love. Set your hearts on
spiritual gifts—above all, the gift of prophecy" (1 Cor.
14:1). He also lists the prophets as of second importance
only to the apostles and ahead of those who teach or work
miracles or heal (1 Cor. 12:28).

29. WHAT ARE THE PURPOSES OF PROPHECY IN THE
    PRAYER COMMUNITY?

Some have already been mentioned:

a) It is a source of joy and peace to the individual and
   to the community.
b) It frequently provides a theme for the prayer meeting. This theme should be pondered by all, since
   God's word, both in Scripture and in charismatic

prophecy, has many effects—healing, consoling, enlightening, etc.

c) It is a source of guidance and direction to the leaders of the community.

Other purposes include:

a) Prophecy is often a source of grace to an individual. Everyone who has attended prayer meetings can recall prophesies which were meant "just for them," opening them up to God's action as nothing else could.

b) Prophecy also can assure a hesitant member of the community that he has a true prophetic gift, i.e., as his prophecy concurs with the others.

30. AS THE GIFT OF PROPHECY DEVELOPS, WHAT CHANGES OCCUR?

Prophecy becomes more powerful, more directive and more frequent, and is, therefore, of greater importance to the community. In the beginning, prophecy is usually general—consoling, chastising, pointing out virtues or vices. Mistakes with the gift of prophecy at this stage are usually not too important and leadership learns to discern. During this period, God is preparing leaders for a more highly developed gift, whereby He will more and more determine the action of the community. Thus, when the more powerful gift of prophecy emerges, the leaders have the necessary background and discernment to use the gift for the upbuilding and not the destruction of the community.

31. ARE THERE ANY "SAFEGUARDS" SO THAT THE GIFT OF PROPHECY IS NOT MISUSED?

The following general "safeguards" should be kept in mind by all leaders:

a) Persons can easily add their own thoughts to true prophecy. Therefore, parts of a prophecy might be from God and some from the person.

b) The "time" element in prophecy is extremely difficult to discern. A prophecy, therefore, could be true but its fulfillment still be many years away.

c) Too much stress should not be placed on a single,

individual prophecy. Usually God reveals His plan slowly, over a lengthy period of time, to a group that meets faithfully.

G) *Personal or Private Prophecy*

32. IS PROPHECY EVER "PRIVATE" OR "PERSONAL"?

Yes, and "private" or "personal" prophecy is extremely important. In these cases, especially when the prophecy predicts the future or gives particular directions, there must be the greatest care in "discerning." Yet, to "discern" prophecy is not to "despise" it, nor to deny its existence. It means merely to proceed cautiously until God's will, with the aid of prophecy, is discerned.

33. WHERE AND HOW IS "PERSONAL" PROPHECY GIVEN?

Personal prophecy is given during a prayer meeting and also in private prayer. During a prayer meeting, the person delivering the prophecy might have no idea for whom it is meant. The person who hears the prophecy, knowing that it "fits his case" or speaks to him about a present opportunity or problem, can be fairly safe, after some discernment, in believing God has used that person to speak to him.

When personal prophecy is received privately, the person who received the prophecy knows for whom it is meant, even though he might not know just what it means. The person for whom the prophecy is meant will know what it means. Again, discernment must be used, but if the person receiving the prophecy has no idea of the problem or decision facing the other person, then more credence would be given to it as coming from God than if the person who received the prophecy were aware, by natural means, of the other's problem.

34. IS THIS LATTER FORM OF "PERSONAL" PROPHECY COMMON?

Usually, this very special type of prophecy is not common but is manifested only by those who are very deep in the Spirit and have been faithful to the inspirations of grace over a long period of time, i.e., a number of years at least.

35. IS PROPHECY EVER USED FOR "PERSONAL GUIDANCE" IN A PARTICULAR DECISION, I.E., WHETHER A PERSON SHOULD ACCEPT A GIVEN JOB OFFER OR ACCEPT AN OPPORTUNITY THAT PRESENTS ITSELF?

People frequently talk about "praying over a decision." In the right sense, this would mean turning to God so that He would help the person to choose rightly. This would be God's grace helping the person to arrive at a decision. In the wrong sense, it would mean God dictating a particular decision by means of the charismatic gift of prophecy.

PERSONAL AND DIRECTIVE PROPHECY

Only with some reluctance is this special section added to the above body of teaching on prophecy. Personal and directive prophecy seem to exist and to have Scriptural basis. Yet, every natural prudence and supernatural sensitivity is needed to avoid serious problems with its use. It is, in a sense, a "new frontier" in which guidelines are often hard to come by. Yet, this chapter on prophecy would stand incomplete if this powerful manifestation of God's power were not mentioned.

A) *Understanding Personal Prophecy*

36. WHAT IS PERSONAL PROPHECY?

Personal prophecy is God's message for a particular person. It can be for the here and now or it can be predictive. Its purpose would be any of those normally listed in Scripture.

37. HOW DOES PERSONAL PROPHECY DIFFER FROM THE USUAL PROPHETIC UTTERANCES GIVEN AT A PRAYER MEETING?

The following seem to be the unique qualities of personal prophecy:

a) The person for whom it is meant is known.

b) Therefore, the prophecy is usually more specific and more powerful.

c) Because of this unique divine action, it is usually also more key and decisive in a person's life than the prophecies he might hear at a charismatic prayer meeting.

38. WHAT IS THE PURPOSE OF PERSONAL PROPHECY?

Personal prophecy can have the following uses:

a) Bring to light certain qualities of the soul or modes of God's action that the person can sense but not identify or verbalize. As such, it is a great help in corresponding with God's grace.

b) Help the person to grasp God's love and provident care that He would reveal His thoughts.

c) Make clear God's plan that in many ways is only vaguely understood.

B) *Understanding Directive Prophecy*

39. WHAT IS DIRECTIVE PROPHECY?

Directive prophecy is personal prophecy, containing directives more or less specific, of how to proceed or what to expect in a given situation.

40. WHAT WOULD BE SOME EXAMPLES OF DIRECTIVE PROPHECY?

Directive prophecy could have the following purposes (many others are possible):

a) To lead to prayers of intercession for someone.

b) To warn of an upcoming problem.

c) To urge to go or to avoid going somewhere.

d) To make explicit a ministry.

e) To clear up or define a confused situation or opportunity.

41. WHAT IS THE PURPOSE OF DIRECTIVE PROPHECY?

Some purposes of directive prophecy are:

a) To confirm a course of action that the person or the group feels it should take, but might "back out of" without the promptings of prophecy.

b) To illumine a course of action which the person or the group would take, but would not exactly know how to proceed. In this area, the charismatic activity of prophecy could very easily be called a Word of Knowledge. The difference between the two seems to be the degree of God's intervention and the degree of the activity of the human intellect. Probably the two gifts are both operative.

c) To lead to a course of action that the person or group would not even have considered without the prophecy. In this latter case, many safeguards must be present and "waiting on the Lord" takes place before going ahead.

42. WHO USUALLY EXERCISES THE GIFTS OF PERSONAL AND DIRECTIVE PROPHECY?

Since this is a powerful, and highly specialized gift of prophecy, only very mature members of the prayer community would experience this. The gift is powerful, although open to many dangers. However, if God so desires to touch people with personal and directive prophecy, this gift must not be rejected. Rather, the group should seek solid teaching and exercise great care so that the power of this gift will build up and not ravage the prayer group.

C) *Scriptural Basis of Personal and Directive Prophecy*

43. WHAT ARE SOME SCRIPTURAL EXAMPLES OF PERSONAL PROPHECY?

Christ delivered a number of personal prophecies:

Some of the examples already given are personal prophecies: His own death and resurrection; Peter's denial of Him; the apostles' being brought before kings for His sake.

Agabus prophesied that Paul would be handed over to the Gentiles (Acts 12:11-14).

A prophecy that Paul seemed to receive in every town he visited (Acts 20:23).

44. WHAT ARE SOME SCRIPTURAL EXAMPLES OF DIREC-
   TIVE PROPHECY?

Scripture has a number of directive prophecies:
In the Old Testament, many directives were given by
God to his servants. Some examples are:
a) Noah to build his ark (Gen. 6).
b) Abraham to sacrifice Isaac (Gen. 22).
c) Moses to go to Pharoah (Exod. 3) and God's directives throughout the Exodus story.
d) Samuel to anoint Saul and later to anoint David (1
   Sam. 16).

In the New Testament, the following are examples of
directive prophecy:
a) The directive of Philip in the conversion of the
   Ethiopian eunuch (Acts 8:20).
b) The directive to Ananias concerning Paul (Acts
   9:10-19).
c) The directive to Paul after his conversion (Acts
   9:6).
d) The prophetic vision of Peter to go to the Gentiles
   (Acts 10:9-23).
e) The prophetic setting apart of Barnabas and Saul
   (Acts 13:2).

D) *Interpreting Personal and Directive Prophecy*

45. WHAT IS MEANT BY INTERPRETING PERSONAL AND
   DIRECTIVE PROPHECY?

An "interpretation" of directive prophecy would mean
arriving at a somewhat clear understanding of what steps
God intends the person to take. Thus, St. Paul received
clear personal prophecy many times that he would be
handed over to the Gentiles, yet his "interpretation" of
this prophecy was that God was preparing him for the
trials, and not telling him to avoid the circumstances that
would lead him into the difficulty.
Therefore, two very important steps are needed in "interpreting" personal and directive prophecies. First, the
people involved must be certain that God has spoken and,

secondly, that they clearly "interpret" what steps they are to take. Since the gift is so powerful, many safeguards must be present.

E) *Interpreting and Safeguarding Directive Prophecy*

46. WHAT SAFEGUARDS SHOULD BE TAKEN CONCERN-
    ING PERSONAL AND DIRECTIVE PROPHECY?

To use the gift correctly, those receiving such prophecy must:

a) Handle this prophecy with the greatest prudence, so that others are not upset or frightened.

b) "Wait on the Lord" until they are certain that God has spoken in this way.

c) Be aware of the possible "adding" to God's message by human thoughts.

d) Be aware of the many elements that were not revealed, e.g., whom to tell, how or when to act.

e) Discern the degree of certitude about the prophecy. For example, if God has spoken frequently, and even confirmed by external events, then a degree of certitude exists that is greater than other prophecies that are not so clear or confirmed.

47. WHAT IS MEANT BY "WAITING ON THE LORD"?

Since the human mind grasps only one part of a truth or one element on a total picture at one time so "waiting on the Lord" means that the person continues to pray until all the elements of God's prophetic activity are completely understood. Even when a "revelation" is made, much remains unknown about just what exactly should be done, or how the prophecy is to be followed up. Often it is not clear, or false conclusions are "jumped at."

48. WHAT IS MEANT BY "ADDING TO GOD'S MESSAGE"?

Solid Church tradition readily admits that God does reveal things to his prophets. It also teaches that, once the mind has begun to receive God's message, it is very possible for those mental processes to continue even though the divine touch has been removed. In this area, great prudence is needed, even though a discernment is made that God has spoken in a personal and directive way.

49. HOW DO THE PEOPLE DISCERN DEGREES OF CERTITUDE?

Certain rules of certitude can be formulated:

a) Certitude is usually greater with more general prophecies and grows less as the prophecies touch on more specific details. Thus, prophecy could confirm a certain task or ministry, but should not necessarily be confirmation of exactly how to proceed in that task. In some of these areas, the charismatic activities involved seem to be a Word of Knowledge more than prophecy.

b) Prophecies which come time and again, and correspond to the external circumstances of the group and the internal promptings of the members, have more certitude than prophecies which do not correspond to those circumstances or promptings. Usually, the latter, if truly prophetic, are somewhat distant in time. Their value is that, later on, as circumstances and inner promptings begin to correspond, the people involved have a great degree of certitude, since the Lord had spoken to them some time before (even years) of what would occur.

c) More certitude exists concerning prophecies that illumine a current problem or clarify God's inner action on the person than those prophecies which do not seem to fit into the person's present internal and external situation.

The former, in a sense, "fits" the person perfectly, causes him to rejoice and enlightens an area of darkness, frees him from a struggle or opens him more to God's grace. The latter does not "fit," in the sense that the person does not know what to do with the prophecy, since it in no way harmonizes with his present mental attitude or external concerns. Regarding the latter, he should feel perfectly free to put it away, so to speak, until its meaning and purpose is clearer.

50. HOW AND WHEN IS PERSONAL AND DIRECTIVE PROPHECY BEST USED?

Certain circumstances are safeguards for this gift:

a) Good personal relationships exist among those exercising the gift.

b) The group is committed to the spread of God's kingdom, in fact, have been given charge of God's people by external circumstances, e.g., confirmed leadership. In this case, directive prophecy can almost be seen as the grace of office.

c) They pray together regularly. Directive prophecy develops slowly, as God confirms time and again what he expects the people to do before asking them to act.

d) Prophecies are taken in context, that is, as part of a whole body of prophetic utterances. As the persons involved pray together regularly and as they regularly exercise the charismatic ministry, God can gradually give to them a sense of His plan.

e) The word of prophecy corresponds to the external responsibilities of the person's state in life.

f) The word of prophecy corresponds to the internal word of what God is doing within the person—in this way God's internal and external activity harmonize.

51. IS EVERY "PROPHETIC UTTERANCE" TO BE ACCEPTED IN THE SAME WAY?

The person has to realize that there is a whole range of God's charismatic activity in speaking to man. Sometimes His Word is clear, definite, and even overpowering. In these cases, because the message is so important, the person's faculties are seized by God in a powerful way and very little room is present for human error or misunderstanding.

At other times, however, God illumines in a gentle or general way—giving only a partial light. Here, the persons have to realize that much is not clear and that error in deducing too much is very possible.

52. WHY ARE ALL THESE SAFEGUARDS AND DIRECTIVES SO IMPORTANT?

Mainly, because the gift of prophecy is so extremely important for the renewal of Church life. In a sense, no other charismatic ministry contains the power to restore Church life as does prophecy. For this reason, Paul places it as the highest charismatic ministry (1 Cor. 14:1) and asks that all yield to its power (1 Cor. 14:5).

The safeguards, then, are needed because of the power of this gift. Without the safeguards, prophecy soon falls into ill repute and causes confusion among those trying to exercise the gift in simple faith.

SUMMARY

The preceding questions on personal and directive prophecy were not written to encourage and urge the use of this gift (as contrasted with the book's attitude to prayer tongues, which are to be encouraged and sought). Rather, the questions try to point out the fact that personal and directive prophecy is manifested in this movement: sometimes validly, with great effects; sometimes invalidly, with very harmful effects. The purpose of the questions, rather, is to establish limits and safeguards for those situations in which such prophecy is present.

Chapter Eight

The Gift of Healing

*By the same Spirit
another is given
the gift of healing.
(1 Cor. 12:9)*

INTRODUCTION

Healing has recently emerged as an important part of Church life and as a definite power contained in Christianity. The renewed liturgy of anointing of the sick gives greater stress to healing. Even those who keep at arms length from the Charismatic Renewal Movement are intrigued by the concepts of "inner healing" which are so widespread in Charismatic Renewal in Latin America, and in the renewed *Power in Penance* as explained by Fr. Michael Scanlon.

Initial involvement in Charismatic Renewal tends to see prayer tongues and prophecy and religious fervor as central to this movement, with healing sort of as an extra—a gift tossed in by a compassionate God. Further involvement, however, reveals the centrality of the healing power and the absolute need for inner healing—both spiritual and emotional—if the individual and the prayer group are to continue to walk in the Spirit. "Wounds" await everyone on the road to perfection and to community growth. Only a constant openness to God's healing action can remove the painful memories and refresh the tired spirit. Without God's constant "healing action," we would all "faint" along the way.

Various attitudes can be discerned toward healing:
  a) Those who deny even the possibility that God would, or even could, heal man.
  b) Those, at the other extreme, who hold that God wants to heal everyone and only lack of faith blocks this divine activity.
  c) Those who believe that God can and does heal, but usually associate such activity with canonized saints or very unusual divine interventions. This could be called the normal Catholic attitude.

Charismatic Renewal would situate itself in the traditional Catholic stance to God's healing power, while understanding that the ways and the times when God's healing power is operative are more common than usually understood by the average Catholic.

The attitude of those involved in Charismatic Renewal

could be described as: believing that God's presence and activity is always healing to man, at least at some level of his being, and yet realizing the mystery and the power of suffering in God's plan to redeem the world.

Many object to Charismatic teaching on healing offering examples of misuse of the gift. Certainly as large numbers of people become more open to God's healing power, there is also opened up a whole host of new problems. The problems are best handled by prudent people, sensitive to the feelings of others, who, while making honest mistakes also take necessary safeguards. The healing gifts, therefore, are best taught and yielded to in a prayer community.

THE GIFT OF HEALING

A) *Understanding the Gift*

1. WHAT IS THE GIFT OF HEALING?

The gift of healing is the manifestation of the Spirit whereby a physical, psychological or spiritual healing or renewal occurs which is due primarily to God's action, although natural causes can be used.

2. WHAT IS MEANT BY "PRIMARILY" TO GOD'S ACTION?

Primarily means that "healing" is not limited only to God's direct action upon the person but also can include His activity in helping the person to take advantage of natural causes that are available.

For example, God's healing action upon an alcoholic might be to move him to take advantage of the natural help available in an Alcoholics Anonymous group. In fact, God's healing activity most of the time moves us to or presupposes the use of available natural means.

3. WHAT KINDS OF HEALING ARE THERE?

Healings are usually divided into three classes:

a) Physical Healing—whereby some disease of the body is remedied and the person, at least in this area, is returned to health. The number of healings which can occur corresponds to the list of possible diseases.

b) Psychological Healing—whereby some emotions or mental problems, usually associated with unhappy memories or unhealthy psychological attitudes, are alleviated. The healings in this area would correspond to the list of possible psychological problems.

c) Spiritual Healing—whereby some habit of sin or temptation is removed. The possible healings in this realm would correspond to the list of spiritual illnesses.

Often, healing occurs in a number of areas, since a spiritual healing could have psychological and even physical effects.

4. ARE HEALINGS IMPORTANT TO CHARISMATIC RENEWAL OR ARE THEY SORT OF AN EXTRA?

Healings are not an extra but have a very important role in Charismatic Renewal. The following reasons could be listed:

a) Everyone needs to be healed—at least on the spiritual and psychological levels (and at times, even in a physical way)—if he is to do God's will. It seems that the very first thing God wishes to do to the person, as he becomes involved in Charismatic Renewal, is to change and to heal him, removing psychological and moral illnesses.

b) These deep changes make the person a better instrument in witnessing to the Lord and in being a part of the prayer community.

c) Healings are a reminder of God's loving presence and a source of joy in the community.

In Charismatic Renewal, healings are *not*:

a) A showpiece to increase numbers (although some investigate the power of the movement because of a healing).

b) To preclude the primary purpose for people coming together: to pray.

c) Meant to substitute for natural ministries of healing exercised by the medical profession.

B) *Scriptural Basis for the Gift of Healing*

5. WHAT IS THE ROLE OF HEALING IN THE OLD TESTAMENT?

Healing played a very small role in the Old Testament, as God's wondrous activity was described more in terms of miracles.

The Psalms pray for healings: "Heal me, O Lord, for my body is in terror." "The Lord will help him in his sick bed. He will take away all his ailment when he is ill" (Ps. 41:4).

Some examples of healings would be:
a) The prophet Isaiah's healing of Hezekiah (2 Kings: 20).
b) Lord's healing of Miriam after seven days, due to the prayer of Moses (Num. 12:9-16).

6. WHAT BASIS EXISTS FOR THE HEALING IN THE NEW TESTAMENT?

Healings are abundant in Christ's ministry and the power to heal is communicated to the Apostles even before Pentecost as a sign that the kingdom is at hand. After Pentecost, healings occur so abundantly that even the shadow of Peter (Acts 5:15) and handkerchiefs touched to Paul (Acts 19:12) are instruments of this power.

Healing is so constant a power with the Early Church that it becomes a regular ministry of the elders. "Is there anyone sick among you, he should ask for the presbyters of the church. They in turn are to pray over him, anointing him with oil in the name of the Lord. This prayer uttered in faith will reclaim the one who is ill, and the Lord will restore him to health. If he has committed any sins, forgiveness will be his" (James 5:14-15).

7. IN SCRIPTURE, WHAT IS THE RELATIONSHIP BETWEEN "HEALING" AND PREACHING THE GOSPEL?

A very important connection exists between the two.

Healings, in the time of Jesus, were a confirmation of His preaching. He discouraged them as "goals" to be sought after, but tried to get the people to see them as "signs" of the kingdom and of the importance of His message. The message was more important than the healing. The apostles, too, tried to show healings as a sign of what people could not see (cf: Acts 3:11-26).

8. WAS THERE ANY OTHER REASON JESUS HEALED OTHER THAN AS A CONFIRMATION OF HIS PREACH-ING?

Jesus felt great compassion for those who were suffering. Therefore, He was happy to relieve them of any ill when their faith was sufficient to do so.

Also, in modern days, He gives the power of the healing ministry to those who are compassionate and sensitive to others. Through their instrumentality Jesus continues to show compassion toward mankind.

C. Theological Basis for the Gift of Healing

9. HOW IS A HEALING MINISTRY JUSTIFIED THEO-LOGICALLY?

That God would heal and would raise up a healing ministry in His Church is a theological conclusion of basic belief and understanding of Christ's preaching about the Kingdom and of Christ's total redemptive act.

10. HOW DOES A BELIEF IN THE KINGDOM JUSTIFY A BELIEF IN THE HEALING MINISTRY?

In the ultimate phase of Christ's Kingdom, all will be totally healed in every way. Although this ultimate phase is still to come, the Kingdom is among us and the Church is the Kingdom already existing, here and now, in mystery (Paragraph 3 of Constitution on the Church of Vatican II). The Church would be expected, therefore, to manifest in some ways the characteristics of this final coming, that is, to make Christ's healing power already operative here and now as a sign of the presence of His Kingdom.

Christ taught us to pray that the Kingdom would come. Vatican II linked healings with the Kingdom stating, "the miracles of Jesus also confirm that the Kingdom has already arrived on earth" (Paragraph 5 of the *Constitution on the Church*).

11. HOW DOES AN UNDERSTANDING OF CHRIST'S REDEMPTIVE ACT LEAD TO A BELIEF IN A HEALING MINISTRY?

The Catholic Church has always taught that Christ did not redeem us by a mere legal change in our status before the Father, but the Redemption involved adoption as sons of God and a share in the power of His risen life. It has also taught that sin brought about an alienation in every part of man's being.

A share in Christ's divine life and power, and salvation from sin that has produced havoc at every level of life, would seem to presume that the effects of Christ's power would be manifest and the overcoming of the effects of sin would occur in some way at every level.

In practice, the healing ministries are central to Church life and are incorporated into the Church's faith in the Eucharist and the special powers of sacramental penance and the anointing of the sick.

D) *Physical Healings*

12. DO PHYSICAL HEALINGS ACTUALLY OCCUR IN CHARISMATIC RENEWAL?

There does seem to be some physical healings associated with many prayer communities. Also, the ministry of healing seems to be emerging among some mature members and is usually associated with the other charismatic gifts which safeguard it.

The presence of some physical healing is expected when large numbers of people come together regularly to praise God. As the group continues in faith, the opportunity for God's activity and intervention increase. Up until now, Catholics associated physical healing with the saints and

extraordinary holiness of life, although the faith usually
associated with novenas did seem open to God's healing.

13. HAS THE CHURCH'S ATTITUDE TOWARD PHYSICAL HEALINGS CHANGED?

The Church has always held to the belief in God's
healing power. Although always cautious in putting
her seal of approval to a healing, she has always taught
the faithful to pray for such divine activity.

A definite change, however, has taken place with Vatican Council II. The Church adopted the name "Anointing
of the Sick" in place of "Extreme Unction" and now urges
priests to anoint at an earlier stage of the illness than
formerly.

Pope Paul changed the words accompanying this anointing giving two new perspectives to the sacrament. First,
the work is attributed explicitly to the Holy Spirit: "May
the Lord assist you by the grace of the Holy Spirit."
Secondly, the anointing is a remedy for soul and body,
replacing the former emphasis on the penitential aspect
of forgiveness of the sins committed by the five senses.
Also, the gesture of the laying on of hands is emphasized,
a practice which symbolizes the healing power.

14. WITH MODERN MEDICINE, IS NOT THE NEED FOR PHYSICAL HEALING GREATLY REDUCED?

God certainly does not do directly what man can do for
himself. Healings, therefore, are very much associated
with physical ills that modern medicine cannot handle as
yet, or with parts of the world where medicine is still
in the primitive stage.

15. WHAT ABOUT THE PRACTICE OF NOT USING A DOCTOR BUT HAVING FAITH IN GOD'S HEALING ACTION?

In sickness, God wants us to turn to Him and to those
gifted with natural healing talents. His activity, when
modern medicine is available, seems to be a quicker healing than usual, or greater ease in the operation or recup-
eration. God's healing action supplements and completes
the natural healing activity which man can carry out
for himself. Not to consult a doctor seems to be a testing

of God and is not recommended as a normal course of faith activity.

E) *Psychological Healing and Healing of Memories*

16. WHAT IS A PSYCHOLOGICAL HEALING?

Psychological healing is a cure of, or at least a relief from, emotional ills. Man's emotional life, subject as it is to so many problems, is an important area of God's activity. Since healings occur wherever man is ill, one of the areas of God's healing spirit is man's emotional life.

17. WHAT IS THE SCRIPTURAL BASIS FOR PSYCHOLOGICAL HEALING?

The following are examples of emotional health in the Scriptures:

a) Christ constantly told the apostles not to be anxious, promising that through the action of His Spirit, they would even stand before kings without fear (Matt. 10:19; Mark 13:11; Luke 21:15).

b) Christ promised peace as His gift to those who believe (John 14:27).

c) Paul tells us to rejoice always (Phil. 4:4) and expects our emotional life to be dominated by the fruits of the Spirit (Gal. 5:22-23).

d) Scripture stresses that, as the power of Christ's Spirit takes hold of a person, a certain emotional well-being ensues, indeed, must occur if spiritual progress is to follow.

18. WHAT ARE THE RESULTS OF A PSYCHOLOGICAL HEALING?

This type of healing has a number of results:

First, the person feels more content with himself, and often, the physical symptoms accompanying the emotional disorder (as upset stomach, headaches, nervous tension) are also removed.

Secondly, the person feels more comfortable in personal relationships within the family or at work.

19. DO PSYCHOLOGICAL HEALINGS RESULT FROM A HEALING PRAYER ALONE?

Emotional healing usually requires time, although a healing prayer can be a source of much help. The prayer for emotional healing seems most effective when it is preceded by a great deal of personal cooperation with God's grace and is followed by continued cooperation.

Much psychological healing occurs within a prayer community and the full effects of God's action might depend on the person continuing to attend prayer meetings. A healing might also be dependent on the person's willingness to face responsibility, as in a marriage or in a family.

Psychological healing occurs over a period of time and requires cooperation throughout. The ministry of healing often includes the natural and charismatic gifts connected with counseling which fosters this continued personal cooperation.

F) *Healing of Memories*

20. WHAT IS THE "HEALING OF MEMORIES"?

"Healing of memories" is a ministry whereby one person, using many charismatic gifts, is used as an instrument by God in freeing another person from problems arising from painful experiences of the past. It is a well-defined and developed part of a psychological healing ministry.

Why is the "healing of memories" important?

Psychology and psychiatry have discovered the effects of memories on behavior, moods and dispositions. Memories, even forgotten ones, are alive within the person and often painful to him. The individual reacts to situations in certain ways and accepts definite limits to his personality, an acceptance which in many ways is really *bondage*. The healing of painful memories removes this bondage, allowing the person to break free of the patterns, react more spontaneously to situations, and establish new and more healthy relationships.

21. THERE SEEMS TO PREVAIL A GREAT CONFIDENCE IN THIS PRAYER FOR "HEALING OF THE MEMORIES." WHY IS THIS SO?

As mentioned previously, a theological basis for the healing ministry is the understanding of Redemption as removing not only the legal effects of sin but actually restoring divine life and dealing with sin directly.

Confidence in this prayer for healing of memories is so great because painful memories are very closely connected with sin. These memories include the person's own sin— the memories of guilt, of having failed, or of having let others down. Also, the memories are often due to the sins of others—the selfishness of parents, of siblings, of teachers, of spouses or of companions. Because painful memories or psychological problems are closely connected with sin, a great confidence exists that Jesus wants to heal these painful memories.

Another reason for this confidence is that psychological difficulties seem to be much more a hindrance to spiritual growth than physical problems. They also are more prevalent than physical problems and often unresponsive to professional treatment. In a real sense, everyone needs a psychological healing of memories.

All of these factors lead to a strong belief that Jesus wants to cure painful memories in everyone.

22. CAN CHILDREN BE PRAYED WITH FOR THE HEALING OF MEMORIES?

This prayer is quite effective with children, especially those manifesting signs of unusual emotional stress such as nightmares, bed-wetting, etc. A discussion with the child should precede the prayer and touch on causes of the difficulty and provide an explanation to the child of how he can cooperate.

The reasons the prayer can be effective with children are:

First, many of the harmful memories are still known to the child and not yet forgotten.

Secondly, children appreciate the spiritual world more

than we suspect and frequently pray and cooperate beautifully.

Thirdly, children readily believe that God is good and will help them.

23. WHAT IF THE CAUSES OF THE MEMORIES ARE STILL PRESENT IN THE HOME?

If the causes of the unhappy memories are still present, then some action should be taken to remove them. This would include a discussion with the parents. Parental cooperation and a complete turning to God is absolutely essential, since the child will continue to live under their dominance for years to come and new memories will pile up if family problems are not remedied.

G. Prayer for the Healing of Memories

24. HOW DOES THE PRAYER FOR THE "HEALING OF MEMORIES" USUALLY TAKE PLACE?

The most fruitful way is the following:

a) The prayer is preceded by counseling, or a discussion of the emotional problems facing the individual. The prayer would culminate the counseling relationship and be the final help offered by one human being to another.

b) The prayer itself covers every stage of the person's life up to the present, naturally stressing the unique problem already presented and frequently uncovering, through charismatic prophecy, either probelms or root causes which were still hidden. This revelation of problems by charismatic prophecy shows God's loving concern and builds up faith in His healing power.

c) The prayer is followed by a discussion of the future and of how the person can best yield to God's healing action.

25. IS THERE ANY COOPERATION DEMANDED FROM THE PERSON WHO IS PRAYED FOR?

a) Faith in the prayer itself.

b) Yielding to the Spirit's action during the prayer by allowing painful memories to come to the surface.

c) Forgiving those who caused the memories.

Following this prayer, for some period of time, forgotten memories will continue to come into consciousness and the person will realize that healing effects are taking place.

26. HOW DOES THE PERSON KNOW THAT A "HEALING OF MEMORIES" HAS TRULY TAKEN PLACE?

When the "healing of memories" has truly taken place, the person will discover that these past memories or incidents no longer cause an inner cringing or hurt, nor even a spontaneous urge to repress them. On the contrary, there is a sense of relief and release, even of joy, and when the occasion warrants it, these memories can be used to help others in need.

Again, it must be remembered that although "healing of memories" often seems instantaneous, its complete effects usually take time.

27. IS THERE ANY "FOLLOW UP" TO THIS MINISTRY?

In all of the psychological healing ministries, but especially in the healing of memories, the original sense of release and the ability to use this release are maintained only if the person truly lives a life of prayer and is open to the activity of the Holy Spirit. Obviously, the greatest effect occurs if the person himself is already manifesting the charismatic gifts. If not, an introduction to the full life of the Spirit and charismatic prayer should follow shortly.

28. ONCE A PERSON HAS BEEN PRAYED OVER FOR "HEALING OF MEMORIES," CAN THEY BE PRAYED OVER FOR IT AGAIN?

Some teach that once a person has been prayed over for "healing of memories" by a mature Christian or a group of mature Christians, he should not be prayed over regarding *these* memories again, but believe in faith that the healing has begun in him. Others speak of the need for continued prayer. Really, each case must be discerned. Certainly, as the person progresses in life, other relationships or situations or incidents may arise which cause further hurt in different areas. A healing could and should, then, be prayed for regarding these. Also the person may realize the importance of a certain painful memory in hindering spiritual growth. This could be prayed for.

29. IS THERE ANY RELATIONSHIP BETWEEN "PRAYER FOR DELIVERANCE" AND PRAYERS FOR "HEALING OF MEMORIES"?

In a number of instances, before actual prayer for "healing of memories" is offered, the one praying is led to ask for deliverance from any evil influences or bondage. Sometimes, a mild type of deliverance must take place before the "healing of memories" is effective. This relationship between healing and deliverance is treated later in this chapter.

30. WOULD IT BE A HELP IF THE PERSON PRAYING FOR THE "HEALING OF MEMORIES" WERE A PROFESSIONAL PSYCHOLOGIST?

Obviously, God builds on natural talents, and frequently prepares people by their background for the role in which He will use them.

Professional training would be a help in yielding to the gift of the Word of Knowledge, in understanding underlying problems, and in offering the prayer. However, such professional background could actually hinder a cure if the person depended more on this natural talent for "detecting and solving" problems than on the healing power of God.

H) Healing and Tears

31. WHAT IS THE ROLE OF TEARS IN HEALING?

Tears, when from the Lord, seem to be a part of the gift of healing. The following effects result. Tears can wash away:

a) A refusal to forgive oneself.
b) Hurts and wounds caused by self or others or events.

c) Obstacles to spiritual conversion.
d) Painful memories.
e) Anxieties about oneself or the future.
f) Tension over a given situation.
g) Burdens of an apostolate or responsibility.

32. ARE TEARS PREVALENT IN CHARISMATIC RENEWAL?

They are not prevalent in the sense that most people at a prayer meeting are crying or are led to tears. They are prevalent in the sense that probably all who are involved have experienced tears on various occasions, as opposed to going years without crying.

33. WHY ARE TEARS SO PRESENT WITHIN CHARISMATIC RENEWAL?

A number of factors lead to the presence of tears:
a) The accepting attitude of the group if an individual is led to tears. There is no stigma to a person crying at a prayer meeting, and the others present will not feel that something must be wrong if it happens.
b) Peace and the deep sense of God's presence often provide a stillness and calm in which God can touch the person in this way.
c) There is care and concern, shown especially in prayers, for one another.

These factors then are in sharp contrast to so-called normal American society which:
a) Does not accept tears in public.
b) Is constantly on the move, ruining the atmosphere needed for deep feelings.
c) Often shows little personal concern, but stresses functional relationships.

34. WHAT CAUSES A PERSON TO YIELD TO TEARS?

The following seem to be the most common causes:
a) A Word of Wisdom or Knowledge or the gift of prophecy often touch a person directly, opening them to this gift.

b) A personal sense of prayer and experience of God's presence.
c) A prayer said by others in personal ministry—especially the prayer for the healing of memories.
d) A sense of failure to serve God in the presence of others who seem to delight in Him.
e) A realization of burdens and anxieties that God wants to release.

35. WHAT ATTITUDE SHOULD THE PERSON HAVE TO BE OPEN TO TEARS?

No one should "force" tears, for they should be an outward expression of what God is doing within. The person should, however, be open to tears, putting aside worldly sophistication, allowing others to minister to him, and recognizing the need to be healed in this way from time to time.

There is a simplicity in tears, very similar to the results of deliverance, as the person allows God's power to lift him out of the difficulty. Any "I can handle my own problems" attitude militates against the reception of tears.

I) *Spiritual Healing*

36. WHAT IS A SPIRITUAL HEALING? HOW DOES IT DIFFER FROM A PSYCHOLOGICAL HEALING?

A spiritual healing touches the normal spiritual problems that everyone faces—difficulty in mass attendance, habits of sin, refusal to be reconciled to another, hostility, etc. Although somewhat akin to psychological healing, the person could very well be spiritually ill and emotionally very happy.

Practice has shown that frequently the psychological or even physical healing is withheld until the person yields to a spiritual healing being offered by God.

37. WHAT IS THE RELATIONSHIP OF SPIRITUAL HEALING TO THE SACRAMENT OF PENANCE?

By its teaching on the sacrament, the Church reaffirms

its powers to heal spiritually. In fact the sacrament for the average Catholic should be the ordinary avenue for this healing. Catholic tradition calls the priest "the physician of the soul" and a "spiritual doctor healing wounds."

38. WHY DO NOT CATHOLICS EXPERIENCE MORE SPIRITUAL HEALING IN THIS SACRAMENT?

Mainly because neither priest nor penitent approaches the sacrament "with a definite anticipation of results and with reliance on the power of the Holy Spirit" (*cf. Power in Penance*, page 14, by Fr. Michael Scanlon, T.O.R.).

Besides seeing the sacrament as a source for the forgiveness of sins, the priest and penitent should sincerely seek the causes of sin, spiritual and psychological, identify the difficulties blocking spiritual growth, and following the absolution, pray in faith either for a healing, deliverance or strengthening.

Charismatic powers should be used together with the sacramental powers in bringing about this spiritual healing. If this were done, then the Church would witness a reemergence of the importance of auricular confession rather than the gradual fall into desuetude which is now occurring. This reemergence is already occurring among the prayer communities.

J) *Praying for a Healing*

39. IN WHAT WAY IS THE CHARISMATIC GIFT OF HEALING EXERCISED?

Yielding to this gift usually takes the form of a prayer for healing, either over the individual who is afflicted (as in the sacrament of Anointing of the Sick) or even over someone who acts as a proxy. It can also be done as a private or group intention.

40. HOW IN PRACTICE SHOULD A PERSON PRAY FOR A HEALING?

The prayer should present the problem to God, the loving Father, in a human way, placing before Him the disease to be healed and adding whatever other thoughts the Holy Spirit so directs for the occasion. It should also dispose the person to faith, so as to receive the healing.

Also, the prayer should *not* be a *long* one but a *complete* one. An overly *long* prayer is burdensome, wearying to all and gives the impression that the *prayer* itself is the cause of healing. In a long prayer, the *human spirit* can enter, with the person attempting to see instant results.

41. Is there a special "healing prayer"?

Strangely enough, the most effective way to pray for healing is to praise and thank God for all He has done. The person himself should be introduced to the prayer of praise. In this prayer of praise lies a hidden, powerful source of healing, frequently bypassed by most.

42. Are there any other suggestions for "praying for a healing"?

The following should be kept in mind:

a) The person should be instructed before the prayer so his faith can be released.

b) Prayers of praise to God should precede, accompany and follow any prayer for healing.

c) Prayer for a healing should be made in the name of the Church and of the prayer community.

d) All aspects of the human spirit should be removed— especially any desire to "be in on the action" or "to chalk up another one."

e) Besides praise for God, a sense of compassion for the person affected should predominate. This charismatic gift exists "for others" and is manifested abundantly where love is obvious.

K) *Faith and Healing*

43. What is the role of faith in this prayer of healing?

Faith is an extremely important element in the yielding to God's healing power. However, the *types of faith* should be distinguished.

On the part of the one praying for the healing, there must be a yielding to the charismatic gift of faith. On the part of the one prayed for, there is required only a normal faith (fruit of faith) which believes that God can and does heal.

44. ARE THERE NOT BAD RESULTS IF THE ROLE OF FAITH IS DISTORTED IN THE HEALING PRAYERS?

If the role of faith is distorted in "praying for a healing," then bad results do occur. Sometimes people are told that God always wants to heal and that the reason people are sick is they do not have enough faith in God's action. This teaching has horrendous results and does not respect the divine mystery present in suffering.

A person who believes this teaching begins to blame himself for remaining ill; or else, strains to "work up" enough faith in order to *be* healed. These efforts are in vain, for healing is God's work among us and not our own.

Faith is not the *cause* of healing, but only a condition for a healing to take place. God alone is the cause of a healing.

L) *Prayer for Healing and Other Charismatic Gifts*

45. ARE ANY OF THE OTHER CHARISMATIC GIFTS BROUGHT INTO THIS HEALING PRAYER?

Many other charismatic gifts are used in a healing prayer and the person leading the prayer should be acquainted with all of them, together with much of the literature on the healing ministry.

46. WHAT ARE SOME OF THESE OTHER GIFTS?

Certainly the gift of faith plays a large role in healings and the person should know when and how to distinguish God's activity within himself through the gift of faith.

The gift of the Word of Knowledge frequently can help the person understand what obstacles exist to being healed, or what God expects of him so that His action can occur.

The gift of discernment is needed to distinguish between

the need for healing and the need for deliverance. Lack of discernment can frustrate God's action.

Since many gifts are used in healings, especially psychological and spiritual, a team approach to this prayer is frequently recommended.

47. WHAT IS THE VALUE OF READING WORKS ON THE "HEALING MINISTRY," SINCE THIS SOUNDS LIKE READING A FIRST-AID MANUAL?

There are guidelines and teachings on charismatic activity. If God, through Scripture and the experiences of others before us, has revealed to us these principles and conditions for prayers of healing, then He expects us to be acquainted with them. St. Paul did not want anyone to use the gifts in ignorance.

In practice, God has blessed the ministry of those who have been concerned with learning what He has revealed by Scripture and the ministry of others.

M) *The Ministry of Healing*

48. WHAT IS A "MINISTRY OF HEALING"?

It means that a person is used by God to be an instrument of His healing power. Usually, this ministry is most powerful in a certain area—such as healing of memories, or spiritual healing, although it probably extends in some degree to every area of the healing ministry.

49. IF A PERSON HAS THE "MINISTRY OF HEALING," CAN HE USE THIS MINISTRY AT WILL?

Charismatic ministries are not powers given permanently to a person so that he can use them at will. The "ministry of healing" is not at all like the power of healing which a doctor possesses from a natural study and skill. The doctor's power is his own and he does attempt to cure all. A charismatic power is God's and the person is only an instrument. The "ministry of healing" means that God frequently uses the person as an instrument when He wants to heal.

50. DOES THE PERSON KNOW WHEN TO PRAY FOR A HEALING?

The person to whom the "ministry of healing" is given learns to discern. Through being attentive to the movements of the Spirit, he comes to recognize how and when the Spirit wishes him to pray.

The person might be asked to pray for a certain healing and be led by the Spirit to ask for quite a different grace. The person with a "ministry of healing" usually has some sense of what God's will is in the particular case. This ministry, as others, is usually accompanied by other charismatic gifts (such as the Word of Knowledge) which safeguards its use.

N) *The Community and Healing*

51. WHY IS HEALING IMPORTANT TO THE PRAYER GROUP?

The gift and the ministry of healing are important in the following areas:

a) Individual spiritual growth demands the removal of many obstacles rooted in the memory, personality, disposition and spiritual state. The individual has to receive healing help from the community so these problems can be overcome.

b) Relationships in a prayer group are both powerful and highly sensitive. Leaders constantly experience the need for the healing of these relationships if they are to continue their roles.

c) Healings of any kind are a sign of God's power in the group and an important source of encouragement for continued effort.

52. WHAT IS THE ROLE OF THE COMMUNITY IN BRINGING ABOUT THESE HEALINGS?

The prayer community is extremely important in the healing ministry. The following can be noted:

a) As the community praises God, an atmosphere of God's power is brought about,

b) A person who has experienced a spiritual or psychological healing often needs the continued support of the prayer group.

c) The prayer group is used by God to teach and communicate these ministries.

d) Through the prayer group, God is able to instill a faith in His power and in His desire to heal.

O) *Healing and Deliverance*

53. WHAT IS A PRAYER OF DELIVERANCE?

The prayer of deliverance is a command given in the name of Jesus, said either by the person himself or by another, which demands that any influence which the kingdom of darkness has over the person would depart.

54. HOW DOES A PRAYER OF DELIVERANCE DIFFER FROM A PRAYER OF EXORCISM?

A prayer of deliverance:

a) Is said in a case of obsession.

b) Can be said by any Christian.

c) Can be said in any manner that seems appropriate.

A prayer of exorcism:

a) Is said in a case of possession.

b) Can only be said by a priest duly authorized by a bishop.

c) Must be said according to the prayers in the Roman Ritual.

55. WHAT IS THE SPECIFIC DIFFERENCE BETWEEN OBSESSION AND POSSESSION?

Obsession is:

a) Much lighter than possession.

b) Is probably experienced by every Christian at some time.

c) Affects only a given part of personality.

Possession is:

a) A very serious diabolical problem.

b) Is experienced only in the most rare circumstances.

c) Can extend to bodily organs and lower spiritual faculties.

56. WHAT IS THE DIFFERENCE RETWEEN A PRAYER OF HEALING AND A PRAYER OF DELIVERANCE?

They differ according to the problem involved. If the person is merely ill, then healing prayers should be offered. If, however, an obsession is present, then prayers of deliverance should be said.

It is important for the person to correctly discern the problem before offering the prayer and not be saying a prayer for healing when deliverance is called for and vice versa.

57. WHY SHOULD NOT THE PERSON JUST PRAY IN A GENERAL WAY AND LET THE PROBLEM OF WHETHER A HEALING OR A DELIVERANCE IS NEEDED TO GOD?

Prayer is a very serious and important activity and one which should be approached intelligently. The least God can ask of us is that we make an effort to discuss the person's need before coming to Him in prayer.

Also, the source of healing is God, while the power of deliverance has been given to the Christian himself in Jesus' name. The person asks God to heal but he does not ask God to remove satanic influences, for that is the person's own power in the name of Jesus.

Those experienced in healing and deliverance have found the two to be quite different and the need to discern very important.

Chapter Nine

The Gifts of Faith and Miracles

*Through the Spirit
one receives faith...
and still another
miraculous powers.*
(1 Cor. 12:9-10)

INTRODUCTION

PROBABLY NO CHARISMATIC MINISTRIES ARE SO OVER-
looked as faith and miracles. The word-gifts of tongues,
interpretation and prophecy are part of the weekly prayer
meetings. Healing and discernment of spirits have become
almost cliches, even in normal Church life, as well as wisdom and knowledge. Yet faith and miracles are often
overlooked, probably for directly opposite reasons. Faith
seems such an ordinary ministry, while miracles seems far
too extraordinary for the average person to bother to
study it.

Yet Paul lists these two as regular charismatic ministries to be known, studied and sought. As regular, and
therefore normative, powers of a local Church, their absence signals a lack in the power of the Body to help its
members and to add to its numbers.

This chapter attempts to show that the charismatic gift
of faith is not that ordinary, distinguishing it from the
virtue and the fruit, also called faith. It also tries to show
that miracles are not that extraordinary, at least not as
far removed from normal Church life as many Catholics
believe. In fact, many devout Catholics can usually re-
count a number of stories in which God's intervention
seemed to happen in a miraculous way.

These two are power gifts, seemingly stronger than,
but not as prevalent as, the healing ministry. Since they
seem to be associated with an advanced charismatic and
devout life, probably the time of great faith and miracles
is still in the future of Charismatic Renewal.

Although in the future, let us prepare now by a study
of these gifts and await the divine anointing when charismatic faith will permeate every prayer and the gift of
miracles will be bestowed in abundance on all who follow
the Lord.

THE GIFTS OF FAITH AND MIRACLES

A) *Understanding the Gift of Faith*

1. WHAT IS THE CHARISMATIC GIFT OF FAITH?

It is a manifestation of the Spirit making God's power present here and now within the person; whereby he is enabled, without human reasoning or any sense of doubt on any level, to ask or to speak in the name of Jesus in such a way that what he says or asks must come to pass. God, who inspires the person with this faith, will necessarily grant what he asks.

2. WHAT IS THE DIFFERENCE BETWEEN THE THEOLOGICAL VIRTUE OF FAITH AND THE CHARISMATIC GIFT CALLED "FAITH"?

The virtue of faith is a power which Christians have all the time. It is the dynamism within them by which they assent to Christian truths and even act upon them in a usual way (as attending mass). This faith is brought about by listening to God's Word and is the salvific faith necessary for salvation.

The charismatic gift is a passing power by which God moves the person to pray or to act with certitude. By charismatic faith, God manifests His power through a person. Christ described charismatic faith as capable of moving mountains.

It can be said that the theological virtue is "our" faith, given to us permanently (as long as we do not sin against faith). The charismatic gift is "God's" faith which flows through us at a given moment when God wishes to act. Obviously, this gift is closely connected with healing and miracles.

3. WHAT IS THE DIFFERENCE BETWEEN THE CHARISMATIC GIFT OF FAITH AND BELIEF?

Belief is a condition of mind whereby a person is ready to lend credence or give assent to what is said or happens. Thus, upon hearing a story about a healing taking place, the person might have belief, given the credibility of the one recounting the event.

The *charismatic gift of faith* is not a condition of the mind, nor is it even a state of mind that the person himself can arrive at. It is a divine gift, bestowed at a given mo-

ment to which the person *yields*. It is *this faith,* and none
other, which never fails to bring about results.

4. WHAT IS THE DIFFERENCE BETWEEN THE CHARIS-
MATIC GIFT OF FAITH AND THE FAITH LISTED AS A
FRUIT OF THE HOLY SPIRIT?

Faith as a fruit of the Spirit:
a) Grows with time.
b) Is a quasi-permanent state.
c) Results from our abiding in the Vine which is Christ.
d) Aids our own sanctification.

The charismatic gift of faith:
a) Is complete within a given circumstance.
b) Is a passing manifestation.
c) Results from the action of God's Spirit within us.
d) Is directed primarily to others, either an individual
or the community.

The fruit of faith is the necessary precondition for the
exercise of all the charismatic gifts.

B) *Scriptural Basis for this Gift*

5. WHAT ARE EXAMPLES FROM THE OLD TESTAMENT
OF THE GIFT OF FAITH?

The list has a number of outstanding examples of faith:
a) Noah believed God's Word and with great assur-
ance built the ark (Gen. 6).
b) Abraham's faith is praised by St. Paul in Romans 4
as the needed condition for him to be made the father of all believers.

Many examples of faith are linked to the Exodus and
to Moses' actions:
c) Parting the Red Sea (Exod. 14).
d) Obtaining water from the rock (even though Moses
struck it twice) (Exod. 17).
e) Gaining victory over Amalek through Moses' prayer
(Exod. 17).
f) The prayer of atonement (Exod. 32).

Another famous Old Testament act of faith is recounted

in I Kings 18 as Elijah confounds the prophets of Baal by his prayer for fire upon his sacrifice as a divine sign.

6. WHAT EXAMPLES OF FAITH ARE GIVEN IN THE NEW TESTAMENT?

Christ's ministry was filled with the power of faith. His prayer at the raising of Lazarus from the dead is filled with confidence: "Father, I thank you for having heard me. I know that you always hear me" (John 11:41-42).

Sometimes others in the gospel stories exercise the gift of faith—such as the Centurion (Matt. 8:10) and the Canaanite woman (Matt. 15:22).

In Acts 3, Peter heals the crippled man and later attributes the healing to the power of faith in Jesus' name (Verse 16).

C) *Using the Gift*

7. HOW IS THE GIFT OF FAITH MANIFESTED?

The following would be manifestations of the gift of faith:

a) A person being faithful to God, even in difficult circumstances, knowing that God will not abandon him. Every martyr needed the help of this charismatic gift to stand firm.

b) Leaders making a decision under the power of this gift, which brings many blessings to the community when, at the time, a "more prudent" way of acting seemed called for.

c) A person saying a prayer of deliverance must be anointed with this faith.

d) Using this gift in prayers of petition, especially in those areas where divine assistance is absolutely necessary, since other means have been exhausted.

e) Sometimes, deciding not to do anything about a situation comes from the gift of faith, since the person is led to trust that God will remedy the problem.

8. WHEN CHRIST DEMANDED FAITH FROM THE PERSON BEFORE A HEALING, WAS THIS CHARISMATIC FAITH?

Normally, the person being prayed for needed only "normal" faith, that is, an openness to God's activity. In these cases, the charismatic gift was being exercised by Christ, for His humanity was the instrument of God's power.

Thus, the person with the ministry of charismatic faith is the instrument of divine activity. Others accept this activity and benefit from it by removing any obstacles of disbelief. They need not exercise the charismatic gift.

9. DOES THE PERSON AFFECTED BY GOD'S POWER EVER HAVE TO YIELD TO, OR EXERCISE, CHARISMATIC FAITH?

There are times when God prompts or moves a person to yield to the charismatic gift for his own benefit. This "yielding" to faith is usually a gentle attraction, a prompting, that continues to come, and is released by a "letting go," or by allowing the prompting to remove any attitudes of uncertainty.

10. WHEN PEOPLE SAY, "IF ONLY YOU HAD ENOUGH FAITH, YOU WOULD BE HEALED," ARE THEY SPEAKING ABOUT THE CHARISMATIC GIFT?

First, the saying itself is dangerous and can lead to great emotional and spiritual turmoil.

Secondly, it betrays a great misunderstanding about charismatic faith. This gift is not something the person has, or can even merit, or "work himself up to"—it is a gentle, passing manifestation of God's power. There is a divine sovereignty about the gift and no one can presuppose its presence in every case where a physical healing is needed.

D) *Yielding to This Gift*

11. HOW DOES A PERSON YIELD TO THIS GIFT?

Certain conditions seem to favor the presence and exercise of this gift:

   a) A living faith, in which daily decisions, choices and motives are guided to a high degree by the theologi-

cal virtue of faith and the sanctifying gifts of wisdom, knowledge and understanding.
b) A committal to God's work and the spreading of His Kingdom.
c) A daily life of prayer and reading of Scripture.
d) A sensitivity to God's inspirations, allowing Him to break down thought and activity patterns that are not rooted in His Spirit.

12. As the person fulfills these conditions, what begins to occur?

First, it should be noted that these conditions have to be persevered in for a period of time and the foundations of Christian living firmly established before the following usually occur:
a) God begins to intervene in a very definite way, not only in the person's own life, but in the lives of others with whom he is associated.
b) The faith relationships that have been persevered in tend to become more powerful and more charismatic.
c) The powerful gift of intercessory prayer emerges and the person, together with others, grows extremely sensitive to this power.
d) Moments then occur when the person, or the group, comes to a definite certitude that God wishes to grant certain petitions or to bless certain decisions. At this moment, all he needs to do is yield to God's promptings.

13. Should the gift of faith be exercised by an individual acting alone or with a group?

The charismatic ministries are best exercised in a community, for the group is the best safeguard in the use of the gifts, and also seems to be the most powerful means. In practice, most yield to the gift of faith in a prayer group, through the encouragement and prayers of others. A person who purposely withdraws from the group or from those faith relationships which God seems to intend is running a great risk.

However, in some cases, the person does find himself

alone in the exercise of this gift. In this case, he should just proceed as he feels moved by God.

E) *Growth in the Gift*

    14. WHAT IS MEANT BY "GROWTH IN THE CHARIS-MATIC GIFT OF FAITH"?

First, a growth in this gift is different than growth in the virtue of faith or in the fruit of faith. Growth means a sensitivity to God's unceasing action, whereby, especially, the needs of persons and of the group are more and more fulfilled by intercessory prayer and decisions are made with greater trust in God's action.

    15. ARE THERE ANY SECRETS TO GROWTH IN THIS GIFT?

Those groups of persons tend to grow quickest in this gift, who:
  a) Place all of their confidence in God's activity.
  b) Are not afraid to act in faith.
  c) Are committed, individually, and as a group, to God's work.

    16. ARE THERE ANY DANGERS INVOLVED IN YIELDING TO THIS GIFT?

As with all charismatic manifestations, dangers have to be recognized and avoided as far as possible.
The possible dangers with this gift are:
  a) Refusal to use available human means, and adopting instead a "God will provide" mentality.
  b) Mistaking a human motivation for God's movement to certitude.
  c) Making decisions that are utterly irresponsible and not really "in faith."
  d) Making "have faith" a panacea for all problems and difficulties, refusing to look for more proximate solutions, or using it as an excuse for delaying action.

THE GIFT OF MIRACLES

A) *Understanding the Gift*

17. WHAT IS THE GIFT OF MIRACLES?

It is a passing manifestation of God's power whereby some obstacle is removed or some opportunity is seized in a very special way, so that the effect must come from God's intervention into human affairs. The gift is a sign of God's presence and power and, therefore, often a source of belief to many.

18. WHAT EVENTS WOULD BE CONSIDERED MIRACLES?

The following could be classified as miracles:
a) An instant healing of a serious disease.
b) A complete change of mind or heart by a person in authority.
c) The sudden conversion of an enemy of the Church.
d) The movement of physical objects, e.g., so that they could be found.
e) Sudden removal or the sudden arrival of persons under obvious divine influence, so that problems are solved or opportunities are taken.

The list could be extended, as also the question of whether a given event was from a special divine intervention or merely a coincidence. For official purposes, the Church is very slow to state definitely that a miracle has occurred.

19. IF IT IS OFTEN DIFFICULT TO SAY WHETHER OR NOT A MIRACLE HAS OCCURRED, OF WHAT VALUE IS KNOWLEDGE OF THIS GIFT?

It is important to know and to believe that God does intervene in miraculous ways so that if He is prompting a person to pray for a miracle, the person or group will know how to cooperate with His promptings.

20. WHAT IS THE PURPOSE OF A MIRACLE?

Usually, there are three purposes:
a) To correct the situation—which cannot be done by natural means.
b) To support and increase the faith of those concerned.
c) To place God's approval on a preaching ministry.
Certainly man has brought about many modern "mira-

cles" in medicine and technology which witness to man's power. However, these do not beget faith in God as much as wonder at the powers of man. A miracle, however, should lead people to awe and wonder of God's power.

21. ARE MIRACLES EVIDENT IN CHARISMATIC RENEWAL?

Every prayer group would have a number of stories that would seem to be miraculous. Although not every story should be given credence, it does seem that God has intervened a number of times. The openness of the groups to prayer and God's charismatic activity is the needed condition for God's power.

Since miracles is an extremely powerful gift, it seems that the emergence of the ministry of miracles is still ahead, as people continue to grow in the life of the Spirit.

22. IF MIRACLES ARE EXTRAORDINARY, WHY WOULD ST. PAUL LIST IT AS ONE OF THE REGULAR CHARISMS?

There are times, both in the life of a prayer group and in the life of an individual, that a true miracle of grace is needed to gain goals that God seems to want. Therefore, although an extraordinary help from God, its need arises in every group and in every individual's life.

Since St. Paul does list miracles, along with other charisms which are obviously present in Charismatic Renewal, then people should believe miracles will become a regular part of Christian life.

23. WOULD NOT THE PRESENCE OF MIRACLES AS A REGULAR PART OF CHRISTIAN LIFE BE TOO EXTRAORDINARY?

Miracles were certainly a regular part of the New Testament Church, and yet life for the Early Christians was also very ordinary. In most circumstances, miracles did not occur nor were they seen as something to be counted on. They were, rather, extraordinary interventions in the face of extraordinary needs. The people seemed to continue a normal life, yet believed in certain situations that God would intervene to save them.

B) *Scriptural Basis for Miracles*

24. WHAT IS THE OLD TESTAMENT ATTITUDE TO MIRA-
CLES?

It is difficult to say what the Old Testament's attitude to
miracles was, since nature was not seen as having fixed
laws and no word for miracles exists in Hebrew.

Certain Old Testament figures had miraculous powers
(such as Moses and Elijah), yet it is difficult to say just
what historically happened. Even the miraculous events of
the Exodus were written more in wonder at Yahweh's
power than in accurate description of what took place.

Therefore, without denying God's power and presence
among His people, it is difficult to point to historical events
in the Old Testament as a Scriptural basis for the charismatic gift of miracles.

25. WHAT BASIS DO THE GOSPELS GIVE FOR THE GIFT
OF MIRACLES?

The gospels use the word "power" to designate miracles,
and picture the power of God entering the world in a special way in the person of Jesus. This power is sometimes
portrayed very graphically, such as when Our Lord felt
power flowing out from Him (Mark 5:30; Luke 8:46).
Luke records Jesus' promise that His Church would be
clothed with the power from on high (24:49).

26. WHAT TEXTS IN THE NEW TESTAMENT TESTIFY
TO THE APOSTLES' POWER OF MIRACLES?

The following are clear evidence of the powers present
in the early Church:
a) Deaths of Ananias and Sapphina (Acts 5:1-10).
b) Miracles of Philip in Samarita (Acts 8:6).
c) Raising of Dorcas from the dead (Acts 9:36-43).
d) The blinding of Elymas (Acts 13:11).
e) Raising of Eutychus from the dead (Acts 20:10).
f) Paul's safety, even after being bitten by a snake
(Acts 28:5).
Paul in Galatians writes: "Is it because you observe the
law or because you have faith in what you heard that God

lavishes the Spirit on you and works wonders in your
midst?" (3:5).

C) *The Gift of Miracles and Other Charismatic Gifts*

27. HOW DOES THE GIFT OF MIRACLES DIFFER FROM
THE GIFT OF HEALING?

It differs mainly in two ways. First, the category of
miracles covers more situations and is not limited to a
healing process. Secondly, miracles are more powerful and
more obviously a sign of God's presence than healings.
For example, an instantaneous and great healing would
be considered a miracle, while normally a healing manifests itself slowly over a period of time.

28. HOW ARE THE GIFT OF MIRACLES AND THE CHARIS-
MATIC GIFT OF FAITH RELATED?

The two gifts are very closely connected in the sense
that, by both of them, God raises the power of intercession
to a new level. Also, the gift of faith seems to be operative in a miracle.

The difference seems to be that the gift of miracles has
some external, verifiable effect and, therefore, is an extraordinary sign of God's power and protection. Paul used
the phrase "workings of power" to refer to miracles. The
gift of faith need not have this external, verifiable sign.
Even the person himself might not be aware of the power
of his prayer of faith.

29. HOW IS THE GIFT OF MIRACLES AND THE WORD
OF WISDOM RELATED?

Both seem to be operative in important or dangerous
situations. The Word of Wisdom is God acting more in a
spiritual or intellectual way so that people are moved by
the power of the words.

Miracles solve the situation by God's power, and possibly no words are spoken.

D) *Yielding to this Gift*

30. WHEN DO MIRACLES USUALLY OCCUR?

Sometimes God is willing to work a miracle even for those who are running away from Him. This would be attributed to the prayers of others.

Often, in the beginning of a person's turning to Him, God works a miracle as an unforgettable sign to the person of God's power and fidelity. However, the regular presence of miracles is not usual at the beginning of a spiritual life.

Since miracles is a power gift, its presence naturally increases as the person or the group allows God to deepen His work within them.

31. HOW DOES A PERSON YIELD TO THIS GIFT?

Since the gift of miracles is very similar to the gift of faith, yielding to the power of miracles is also very similar. It means extreme sensitivity to God's promptings and a yielding to His miraculous power when that is discerned.

Miracles demand an active faith and a love for the brethren that moves the person to continue to cry out to God and not to let off prayers of intercession. Miracles, since frequently dealing with more extraordinary occasions, also necessitate a deeper yielding to divine power.

E) *Growth in the Gift*

32. ARE THERE ANY CONDITIONS THAT FOSTER THE GROWTH OF THIS GIFT?

The following are such conditions:

a) Since miracles are often God's confirmation of preaching, they are present most when God's word is preached and lived.

b) Since miracles are meant to remove obstacles to God's will, they are most present when the persons are totally committed to His Will and the spread of the Kingdom.

c) As with all the gifts, miracles are most present among those who have matured in the Life of the Spirit.

33. IS IT NOT PRESUMPTUOUS TO SPEAK OF A GROWTH
    IN THE GIFT OF MIRACLES?

Although it seems presumptuous even to speak of miracles, let alone a growth in the gift of miracles, that "presumption" is based upon the following:

   a) St. Paul lists miracles as a ministry given regularly
      to Christian communities (1 Cor. 12:10).

   b) Ministries, formerly accorded only to saints or the
      saintly, are becoming more abundant for the good of
      the Church, such as the gift of tongues, prophecy,
      and healing of hearts. These gifts now seem abun-
      dant in the charismatic communities.

If God is making some charismatic ministries prevalent
in His Church, it would not seem presumptuous that He
would restore all the ministries listed by St. Paul to His
Church.

   c) There seems to be a growth in all of the gifts—a
      growth in frequency and in power. This is in accord
      with traditional spiritual teaching and the prac-
      tice of the lives of the saints.

F) *Practical Application of the Gift of Miracles*

34. HAS NOT THE AGE OF MIRACLES PASSED, NOW THAT
    MAN HAS UNCOVERED "MIRACLE DRUGS" AND
    OTHER MEANS TO CHANGE LIFE?

Although God will not do for man what man can do for
himself, certainly the age of miracles is more dawning
than fading because:

   a) With the complexity of modern life, man is faced
      with many more problems than ever before.

   b) With all his powers, man seems helpless in the face
      of his difficulties.

   c) Man's powers themselves (modern warfare, etc.)
      are the cause of many of the problems.

35. WHAT ATTITUDE SHOULD A PERSON TAKE TOWARD
    MIRACLES?

The following summarizes a balanced outlook on miracles:

a) Miracles occur only when human means have failed or are not present.

b) Man should not look to God's miraculous powers as normal, to-be-counted-on means, but rather see them as extraordinary interventions of God's love. No one should, therefore, go around looking for miracles.

c) On the other hand, man should not limit God's action by preconceived ideas of what God won't do.

d) The individual should commit himself totally to God's will and the spread of the Kingdom, using every gift of prudence and discernment, yet realizing that when extraordinary obstacles are present, he can look in faith to God for the extraordinary help of miracles.

Note: The Scriptural background for the gift of miracles relies heavily on the scholarship of Rev. John L. McKenzie in the article on miracles in *Dictionary of the Bible* (Bruce, 1965, page 578).

Chapter Ten

The Gift of Discernment of Spirits

*To another
power to distinguish
one spirit from another.
(1 Cor. 12:10)*

INTRODUCTION

"DISCERNMENT," LIKE THE WORD "CHARISMATIC," IS widely used today. Unfortunately, the widespread use has obscured or overshadowed the technical definition of the charismatic gift listed by Paul.

Discernment of Spirits is not a capacity for criticism nor even a keen ability to judge human nature. The gift has to do with spirits—and the naming of the source of man's actions and inspirations—God's Spirit, man's spirit or evil spirits.

Before charismatic discernment can be explained, certain other notions have to be understood and believed. These would include:

a) A God who inspires man, intervening in his life by divine actions that are a normal part of Christian life.

b) A world of evil that interrupts and confuses man, cleverly leading him down a road that moves him quickly away from the divine will.

c) A world of nature, that strains for and is open to God, but needs grace to actually enter into divine life and activity.

The charismatic gift is not present unless there exists an established pattern of daily experiencing God's activity, of constantly attempting to yield to God's power and to be united to His will. Paul wrote, "The natural man does not accept what is taught by the Spirit of God. For him, that is absurdity. He cannot come to know such teaching because it must be appraised in a spiritual way. The spiritual man, on the other hand, can appraise everything, though he himself can be appraised by no one" (1 Cor. 2:14-15).

"Testing the Spirits" is meant to provide the judgment needed when a great flow of ideas and impulses arises from religious enthusiasm. Discernment, therefore, presupposes Church life that is filled with supernatural powers and manifestations of God's presence. The very richness of divine activity forces evil to the surface and also is the atmosphere for misguided religious activity.

Discernment is the watchful mother who at once delights in the activities of her children and yet watches carefully that nothing they do leads them into harm. It is the power to see through the outward aspects of this activity, to the very heart of the matter, naming the source either God, man or evil.

Discernment is not meant only to be the constant "naysayer," the perennial source of disillusionment. It is also meant to be the source of joy and of religious activity, at times peeking through the darkness and saying with John, "It is the Lord" (John 21:7).

DISCERNMENT OF SPIRITS

A) *Understanding the Gift*

1. WHAT IS MEANT BY "DISCERNMENT OF SPIRITS"?

Discernment is an illumination by God which enables the person to see through the outward appearance of an action or inspiration in order to judge its source. Inspirations or actions can come from three sources (or "spirits") —from God, from the person or from the devil. Having correctly discerned the source, the person can then proceed in the situation with more wisdom.

2. COULD THESE THREE SOURCES BE MORE FULLY EXPLAINED?

When a person has an inspiration or is moved to activity, there is some basic power for this attraction. The sources could be:

a) The person himself—since man has drives, desires, hopes, fears and many other feelings which lead him into activity.

b) God—who is always attempting to speak to man, to motivate and guide him to happiness.

c) The fallen angels—who retain their relationship to creation, even though fallen from grace, and who now are negative, harmful and destructive.

3. HOW DOES DISCERNMENT OF SPIRITS DIFFER FROM
PRUDENCE, GOOD JUDGMENT OR OTHER QUALITIES
USUALLY ASSOCIATED WITH AN INTELLIGENT PER-
SON, GOOD COUNSELOR OR OUTSTANDING LEADER?

Discernment differs in a number of ways:

a) It is always used to find God's will in a situation,
while the others are often used for other purposes.

b) It answers only one question—the source of an action or impulse, while the others deal with many
questions in a given situation.

c) Discernment normally presupposes these other qualities, but goes beyond them and at times might entirely bypass these natural qualities. Thus, a simple
person, unskilled in many ways but deeply united to
God, might possess a high degree of discernment.

d) Discernment presupposes a certain level of daily
prayer, a condition not demanded for exercising the
natural qualities mentioned.

B) *Applying Discernment*

4. WHAT SHOULD A PERSON DO IF HE DISCOVERS THAT
AN INSPIRATION IS FROM GOD?

The person should not act immediately, but should try
to discern exactly what God is calling or urging him to do
or say, when this should occur and what would be the most
appropriate way to carry this out in the given situation.

5. WHAT IF THE PERSON DISCERNS THAT THE INSPIRA-
TION ARISES FROM HUMAN NATURE?

Although an inspiration might be from human nature,
it could also be in conformity with God's will—such as a
desire to study, or to enjoy human friendship or even
something physically pleasant. In these cases, the person
should try to purify his motives, so that his intention in all
of these things is God's glory (1 Cor. 10:31).

If the inspiration arising from human nature is not in
conformity with God's will—e.g., would go against the

commandments or would be done for merely human vainglory, then the inspiration should be rejected.

6. WHAT IF THE PERSON DISCERNS THAT THE INSPIRATION ARISES FROM THE EVIL SPIRIT?

Then it should be rejected immediately and the person should ask that God protect him and keep him from any such influence.

7. IS NOT ALL OF THIS SOMEWHAT COMPLEX AND CONFUSING, LEADING THE PERSON TO BECOME OVERLY INTROSPECTIVE.

A number of things should be mentioned here:

a) Small decisions should be discerned quickly and the person should not be overly concerned. Here, the discernment would be that human life and feelings should flow in a joyful and outgoing way.

b) Rules on discernment are always more complex than the act of discernment itself, since many of these things are done naturally anyway.

c) The person gets more adept at discernment and, instead of rules, a sense of discernment (or divine intuition) grows.

d) If the decision is an important one, the person should be somewhat introspective and not proceed too quickly, thus avoiding a wrong or naive decision.

C) *Various Uses of Discernment*

8. HOW MANY KINDS OF DISCERNMENT ARE THERE?

Although there is just one gift, the situations and the ways in which it is exercised can be many. Discernment is used regarding charismatic manifestations, individual promptings and group decisions. Discernment can be personal or communal. The prayerful person, seeking God's will, would use discernment frequently each day.

9. WHAT IS THE BASIC PURPOSE OF DISCERNMENT FOR THE INDIVIDUAL?

Discernment enables the person to sort out the many promptings and impulses of each day so that his will is better able to be united to God's will. As a person begins "to walk in the Spirit," God shows him that many of his impulses and activities come from a selfish nature and must be brought into line with the divine plan. On the other hand, discernment also helps the person not to go overboard spiritually, but to maintain the needed balance so that singularity or practices far beyond the person's strength are avoided.

10. WHAT IS THE FUNCTION OF DISCERNMENT FOR THOSE CALLED UPON TO GUIDE OTHERS?

For those involved in giving guidance, discernment helps them to see through to the source of what is motivating the person, that is, from what source the various impulses come. When these have been discerned, then the guide can use the other natural and charismatic gifts of knowledge and wisdom so that God's will is ascertained, at least in a general way.

11. WHAT IS THE ROLE OF DISCERNMENT FOR LEADERS IN A PRAYER GROUP?

Leaders would need to discern whether charismatic manifestations are truly from God.

Leaders would use discernment regarding every aspect of the prayer group—the use of charismatic gifts, the quality of prayer, the various suggestions made by the members. They use this gift, therefore, to guide the group into God's will.

D) *Scriptural Basis for Gift of Discernment*

12. WHAT EXAMPLES OF DISCERNMENT ARE PROVIDED BY THE OLD TESTAMENT?

Since discernment is God's understanding, His insight into the heart of man, the following are Old Testament texts of God's discernment:

a) Psalm 139:1—"O Lord, you have probed me and you know me."

b) Jeremiah 17:10—"I, the Lord, alone probe the mind and test the hearts."

c) 1 Chronicles 28:9—"the Lord searches all hearts and understands all the mind's thoughts."

The following are Old Testament texts of the power of discernment given to men:

a) 1 Kings 3:9—when Solomon prays, "Give your servant, therefore, an understanding heart to judge your people and to distinguish right from wrong."

b) Lamentations 2:14—Jeremiah discerns, "Your prophets had for you false and specious visions and they beheld for you in vision false and misleading portents."

c) 1 Kings 22:23—Micah discerns evil spirits—"So now, the Lord has put a lying spirit in the mouths of all these prophets of yours."

13. WHAT EXAMPLES ARE GIVEN IN THE GOSPELS OF CHRIST DISCERNING SPIRITS?

The following are outstanding examples:

a) John 1:47—Jesus, in speaking of Nathaniel, states, "This man is a true Israelite. There is no guile in him."

b) Matthew 16:17—Jesus discerns the Father's action in Peter, "No mere man has revealed this to you, but my heavenly Father."

c) Matthew 16:23—Jesus discerns activity in Peter that is not from God, "Get out of my sight, you satan!... You are not judging by God's standards but by man's."

d) Mark 9:33—Jesus discerned the human spirit in the apostles as they sought to be first.

e) John 2:25—praises Christ's discernment, "He needed no one to give him testimony about human nature. He was well aware of what was in man's heart."

14. WHAT EXAMPLES DOES THE NEW TESTAMENT GIVE TO SHOW THE DISCERNMENT OF THE APOSTLES?

The following can be listed:

a) Acts 5:1-11—Peter discerns the lying spirit in Ananias and Sapphira.
b) Acts 8:20-24—Peter discerns the evil in Simon Magus.
c) Acts 13:9-10—Paul discerns the fraud in Elymas.
d) Acts 16:16-18—Paul discerns the evil spirit in the slave girl, even though her words are true.

Paul contrasts various sources of "wisdom" in 1 Cor. 2:6-7: "There is, to be sure, a certain wisdom which we express among the spiritually mature. It is not a wisdom of this age, however, nor of the rulers of this age, who are men headed for destruction. No, what we utter is God's wisdom, a mysterious, a hidden wisdom. God planned it before all ages for our glory."

E) *Theological and Traditional Basis for Discernment*

15. ON WHAT DOCTRINES IS THE GIFT OF DISCERNMENT BASED?

Two basic doctrinal tenets support the gift of discernment:

a) That God is all-knowing, which extends to knowing what is in man's mind and what moves him.
b) That God is provident, sharing this knowledge with those to whom He has given a care for and a ministry within His Church.

Paul, listing discernment as a regular ministry in the Church, shows that God actually does share this knowledge through the charismatic gift.

16. CAN A PERSON DISCERN WITHOUT GOD'S HELP?

If discernment is used in the wide sense, such as making naturally sound judgments or even deep insights into human nature, then a person can do this without a special help from God.

However, discernment in the strict sense of seeing through the exterior to name the inner source does demand God's help by means of the charismatic gift.

17. IS NOT DISCERNMENT EXERCISED BY MANY NOT IN-
    VOLVED IN CHARISMATIC RENEWAL?

God's action through charismatic gifts occurs in every
phase of the Church's life, and many Catholics (especially
those deeply immersed in prayer), use charismatic gifts of
which they are unaware.

Therefore, to teach that all discernment of spirits is a
charismatic gift in no way means that those not involved
in the charismatic movement are not using the gift.

18. WHAT IS THE TRADITION OF THE CATHOLIC
    CHURCH ON DISCERNMENT?

The Church, in its spiritual authors, has a long tradition on discerning the sources. This tradition was made
extremely practical in the Spiritual Exercises of St. Ignatius, who distinguished various good and evil sources
and provided rules for discernment.

F) *Role of Discernment for the Individual*

19. WHY IS DISCERNMENT OF SPIRITS SO NECESSARY
    FOR AN INDIVIDUAL WHO HAS EXPERIENCED THE
    BAPTISM OF THE SPIRIT?

The Baptism of the Spirit lifts the person from a merely human, or even a sinful level, to a spiritual level whereby Jesus, the Lord, becomes the center of all activity. Extremely important to this new life in the Spirit are God's
inspirations within the person and God's activity in the
events of his life. Discernment is necessary so the person
can distinguish those inspirations that are from God and
those movements that come from evil elements or the selfish parts of human nature.

Growth in the Spirit demands an ever-increasing sensitivity to God, and is usually accompanied by temptations
that are increasingly subtle.

20. CANNOT A PERSON TELL WITH EASE WHETHER AN
    INSPIRATION IS FROM GOD, FROM HIMSELF OF FROM

THE DEVIL WITHOUT THE SPECIAL CHARISMATIC
GIFT OF DISCERNMENT?

Often it is not easy, and the person very much needs
this gift at every stage of his life in the Spirit. Established patterns of religious life, such as a seminary or a
novitiate or the new reality of the prayer group, are a
great help in learning discernment, for someone just beginning to experience God's action.

Even the advanced person needs discernment, since
temptations become more subtle as he progresses. As
Christ put it, the wolf gets dressed in sheep's clothing to
deceive even the elect.

21. WHAT ARE SOME CONCRETE EXAMPLES OF INSPIRA-
TIONS THAT MIGHT DECEIVE A PERSON?

The following, although seemingly good, are listed by St.
Ignatius as not from God's Spirit.

a) To seek perfection inconsistent with the duties of
state of life.

b) To practice showy virtues and become singular.

c) To have a contempt for small fidelities and want to
be sanctified in a grand way.

d) To reflect complacently on deeds, desiring to be held
in esteem for virtues.

e) To complain and lose heart in the midst of trials.

Many other examples can be added. It is important for
the person to realize that certain inspirations are beyond
his capability, or not in keeping with his state of life or
his emotional and spiritual state. These inspirations would
move the person far beyond God's grace and result in dis-
couragement or spiritual illusion.

22. ARE THERE ANY "SIGNS" THAT THE PERSON CAN
RECOGNIZE IN ORDER TO DISCERN THAT INSPIRA-
TIONS ARE NOT FROM GOD?

There are a number of signs which indicate that promptings are not from God:

a) Peace of soul is lost without any objective reason
(i.e., no evident fall from grace).

  b) Anxiety sets in over not following God's promptings.
  c) Sadness begins and the source cannot be detected.
  d) The person is tempted to turn back from the spiritual life and to abandon this life in the Spirit as too difficult.
  e) Fears, unknown before this, arise. Perhaps scrupulosity or preoccupation with always doing the right thing is manifested.

23. WHAT SHOULD THE PERSON DO WHEN HE RECOGNIZES THESE SIGNS?

The person should:
  a) Ask God for discernment, and judge inspirations ahead of time before accepting them or putting them into practice.
  b) Learn from past mistakes. God often uses these early mistakes so that bigger mistakes will be recognized in the future.
  c) Seek the guidance of a spiritual director and present to him the problems that are being experienced.

G) *Importance of Discernment in Maintaining Peace of Soul*

24. WHAT IS THE RELATIONSHIP OF DISCERNMENT TO PEACE OF SOUL?

Discernment is the safeguard to peace of soul by helping the person:
  a) Understand the various impulses and inspirations within himself so that he does not blindly follow every impulse before discerning.
  b) Detect those factors that have already caused a possible loss of peace.

When a person is clear about the sources of inspirations, he avoids much confusion and can remove any confusion that has already occurred.

25. IN JUST WHAT WAY DOES DISCERNMENT HELP WITH PEACE?

Peace results from a union of the person's will with

God's will. Discernment uncovers God's activity within
and also reveals activity that would easily seem like God's
but is not. Discernment helps the person understand himself by enabling him to identify the sources of inspirations,
to realize those factors which destroy his peace and what
specific temptations he faces from his human nature and
the devil.

When a person is sincerely striving to serve God and yet
is torn by anxiety or finds himself deluged with responsibilities that he cannot handle, often discernment will point
out the sources of these problems.

26. WHY IS PEACE OF SOUL SO IMPORTANT?

Only in an atmosphere of peace does the soul grow in
God's life. Even in the midst of trials permitted by God, a
deep inner peace should still remain. Since the road to
God is a long one, many would turn back if peace were not
a normal condition of the journey. Many, unfortunately,
do turn back, having lost peace of soul due to a lack of
discernment.

H) *Importance of Discernment for the Prayer Group*

27. WHAT ROLE DOES DISCERNMENT PLAY IN A PRAYER GROUP?

As the actions within an individual spring from God,
the human self or the devil, so the actions and decisions of
a prayer group can also spring from these three. Also,
just as the individual in opening himself up to God's Spirit
also opens himself up to new and subtle temptations, so a
prayer community, in being open to God, also is open to
various trials and temptations from the evil one.

Leadership in a prayer group has to discern the sources
of inspirations or else God's designs for that group will
be ruined.

28. WHAT ARE SOME EXAMPLES FOR THE NEED OF DIS- CERNMENT BY LEADERS?

The following examples could be given:

a) Someone might want the group to take on a certain

work or move in a certain direction, e.g., toward
more living in common or toward a covenant community.
b) People present themselves or are presented for
leadership positions.
c) New factors begin entering into the prayer meeting, such as specific prophecies or new teachings.
d) Certain people become more prominent in the prayer
group.

These and a host of other questions have to be discerned
by leadership—whether God is speaking to them or whether these events spring from the human spirit or even from
the evil one.

29. WHY IS DISCERNMENT IMPORTANT IN THESE AND OTHER DECISIONS?

Upon this discernment is based the response of leadership. Since the response commits the community to a certain path, if it is God's will, then the community will
prosper. If it is not God's will, then much will have to be
undone to get the group back where it belongs (if it is
not already too late).

I) Method and Criteria of Discernment

30. IS DISCERNMENT BEST DONE BY AN INDIVIDUAL OR A GROUP?

Obviously group discernment, especially in matters
affecting the group, is much safer. This group discernment takes two forms—a decision by the leaders, or an
informal gaining of a consensus of all the members. Sometimes the decision has to be made by the leaders alone. At
other times, it is best to seek the discernment of all.

It is best, whenever possible, for leadership within a
community to be shared by a team, with the members of
the team having various backgrounds and temperaments.

31. HOW MUCH TIME AND EFFORT SHOULD BE GIVEN TO DISCERNMENT?

That varies with the seriousness of the question. Some

ideas are so slight that it is best just to try them out to see if they work. Other decisions, however, are serious to a group and experimentation without prior discernment of spirits should not be engaged in. Many problems should be avoided by discernment before commitment.

J) Objective Guidelines to Discernment

32. IS DISCERNMENT "SUBJECTIVE" OR "OBJECTIVE"?

Just as knowledge is a combination of an "objective" world and a subjective "knower," so discernment is a combination of subjective and objective criteria. The charismatic gift is obviously "subjective," operating within the individual.

However, there are "objective" standards by which to judge if the discernment is true.

33. WHAT "OBJECTIVE GUIDELINES" ARE AVAILABLE TO AID DISCERNMENT?

The following can be listed:

a) Scripture. Any inspiration which goes against a clear teaching of Scripture must be disregarded. Obvious examples would be adultery, murder, lying.

b) The Teachings of the Catholic Church. To go against infallible pronouncements would certainly not be of Christ's Spirit. Other teachings of the Church would also act as criteria, depending on what is commonly called the "theological note" or weight of the teaching.

c) Duties of one's state of life. Inspirations have to be dovetailed with obvious responsibilities of daily life.

d) Obedience to Authority. Certainly legitimate authority must be obeyed. If God wills something, He will change the minds of those in authority who might oppose His will.

These objective criteria are based on the principle that God does not contradict Himself. God does not speak in one way through Scripture, the Church, or other legitimate authority and quite a different way in the heart of the person.

K) *Growth in the Gift of Discernment*

34. WHAT DOES IT MEAN "TO GROW IN THE GIFT OF DISCERNMENT OF SPIRITS"?

Although the basic purpose of this charismatic gift is simple, to help the person to know the source of an inspiration or action, the circumstances in which this question of source is presented becomes more and more subtle.

A person experienced in discernment has little or no trouble discerning the problems of beginners, yet might have great difficulty or even wrongly discern in the circumstances of his own spiritual life. Because God's action becomes continually more sensitive as the person comes closer to Him, the gift of discernment must also increase if the person is to distinguish God's promptings from those arising from other sources.

35. HOW DOES A PERSON GROW IN THE GIFT OF DISCERNMENT?

To grow in the gift the person must:

a) Lead a deep life of prayer.

b) Sincerely attempt to seek and be united with God's will.

c) Believe that God will aid him in discerning.

d) Realize the need for discernment and accept the very real possibility of deception and mistake in decisions.

e) Seek the advice of others, especially those likely to disagree or see the question differently.

f) Study the Church's teaching on the spiritual life.

g) Learn from those involved longer in the spiritual life and, if possible, have a spiritual guide.

Chapter Eleven

The Gifts of the Word of Wisdom and Knowledge

*To one the Spirit
gives wisdom in discourse,
to another the power
to express knowledge.
(1 Cor. 12:8)*

INTRODUCTION

SAINT PAUL, IN HIS CORINTHIAN TEXT ON CHARISMATIC gifts, presupposes a daily experience in these divine manifestations. Those who experience a Church life in which charismatic manifestations are not as abundant as at Corinth, often find a difficulty trying to piece together what he was referring to by the phrases "wisdom in discourse" and "power to express knowledge."

This chapter examines each of these gifts under what seems to be their main power for Church life. The Word of Wisdom is seen as practical, directive words for a given situation, words which open the listener (individual or group), to God's grace or protect them from evil. The Word of Knowledge is studied under the aspect of inspired preaching and teaching.

A few things should be noted:

The main power of each gift stressed in this chapter does not exclude other aspects not touched upon.

The gifts flow from the same Spirit, which means that charismatic manifestations tend to blend into one another and even overlap. For example, inspired preaching or counseling often seems to merge into revelational gifts, such as reading hearts. Obviously, much charismatic activity cannot be exactly categorized.

Because these two gifts are so closely related to natural human powers—such as prudent judgment, solid teaching, or powerful preaching, they are often overlooked by many. The other gifts seem so much more divine—the mystery of tongues, the power of prophecy, the effects of healing—while Wisdom and Knowledge seem so commonplace.

However, their tremendous importance for Church life can be seen from the following:

First, the Kingdom depends on faith and faith upon preaching: "And how can they believe unless they have heard of him? And how can they hear unless there is someone to preach?" (Rom. 10:14).

Secondly, a great number of words flow from everyone's lips each day. There are words in the human spirit—flattering words, self-serving words, idle words. There are words in the critical spirit—unkind words, demeaning words, words that hurt and wound.

How different all would be if words flowed mainly from the Spirit—words of service that came from renewed minds (Rom. 12:2). Without "watering down" the gift, is not a Word of Wisdom connected with speech that uplifts, consoles, places in a good mood, and provides divine humor. Should not the Word of Knowledge be present frequently on the lips of parents as they speak of God to their children, and of religion teachers to their students.

These gifts, therefore, spread into many areas of the body, and are able to uplift and sanctify the most difficult faculty of all, the human tongue: "If a person is without fault in speech, he is a man in the fullest sense, because he can control his entire body" (James 3:2).

THE WORD OF WISDOM AND THE WORD OF KNOWLEDGE

A) *Understanding These Two Gifts*

1. WHY ARE THESE TWO GIFTS TREATED IN THE SAME CHAPTER?

These are treated together because so many aspects are similar: They are both charismatic knowledge and are manifested in spoken words. Also, they are best understood when contrasted with each other.

2. WHAT ASPECTS OF THESE GIFTS ARE SIMILAR?

They are ways whereby God first enlightens the person's intellect with understanding and then helps him to formulate that intuition into words which will be a source of grace to the listener. Both gifts, therefore, have two parts —first, an enlightenment, and secondly, an apt expression of this understanding in words designed especially for the one listening.

Both gifts involve natural knowledge, raised to a level

beyond the speaker's normal capacity and put forth in words that build up or protect or guide the community or an individual.

3. WHY ARE THESE GIFTS CALLED "THE WORD OF" AND NOT JUST WISDOM AND KNOWLEDGE?

The expression, "the word of," is used to show:

a) That the gift is not completely yielded to unless words are spoken. The charismatic elements contain not only an enlightening but also an expression of this enlightment into apt words.

b) That the gift does not comprehend all knowledge and wisdom but only that segment which the listener needs to hear.

c) That the charismatic gifts are distinct from the personal gifts of wisdom and knowledge since these latter refer only to the inner enlightenment sanctifying the soul in which it is received.

B) Relation of Personal Gifts to Charismatic Gifts of Wisdom and Knowledge

4. ARE THERE NOT OTHER GIFTS OF THE HOLY SPIRIT CALLED WISDOM AND KNOWLEDGE? WHAT IS THEIR RELATION TO THESE CHARISMATIC GIFTS?

There are two sets of "gifts of the Holy Spirit"; one is personal, sanctifying the individual, and the other is charismatic, meant for the good of the community.

The personal gifts of wisdom and knowledge help the person himself to grasp doctrinal truths and see their application for life. The charismatic gifts are spoken words which help others come to God.

5. WHAT ROLE DO THESE PERSONAL, INTELLECTUAL GIFTS PLAY IN THE CHARISMATIC MANIFESTATIONS OF THE WORD OF KNOWLEDGE AND OF WISDOM?

Since the charismatic gifts of the Word of Wisdom and the Word of Knowledge are inspirations from God directing the person to speak in a definite manner, a person who regularly acts under the influence of the personal gifts of the Holy Spirit is more ready to yield to God's charismatic promptings.

C) *Understanding the Word of Wisdom*
6. WHAT IS THE WORD OF WISDOM?

The Word of Wisdom is a passing touch by God so that the person is enabled to give active, directive or practical teaching which is an instrument of God for the hearers. This teaching applies natural knowledge and the truths of faith to the situation. Its purpose is to open the hearers to God's wisdom in handling or reacting to a situation, or to silence an opponent. It is the right word in times of opportunity or emergency.

7. WHAT WOULD BE SOME PRACTICAL USES OF THE WORD OF WISDOM?

The following would be situations in which the gift operates:

a) In times of decisions (whether of an individual, a prayer group, a family, or a parish). When the decisions are made under the influence of the charismatic gift, then the person or the group is opening itself up to God's help. When the decisions are made away from God's guidance by this gift, then the person or the group is closed in some way to God's help.

b) In times of counseling—as the person places before another all the facts, asking for help in resolving a difficulty. The counselor must truly seek God's wisdom and His will. Usually, if there is prayer before and after the counseling, some solution will emerge. The Word of Wisdom is not dictated, but gradually emerges, with the counselor using this gift a number of times, as God leads him into certain questioning or probing. The person also should seek the Word of Wisdom to know what facts to present.

By this gift a new dimension is introduced into

counseling, not just the inner dynamism of the person reaching out for happiness but the Provident love of the Father reaching out for His children.

c) In moments of trial, when God's work, either within an individual or in a group, is threatened, a word of Wisdom in the situation removes the threat.

d) In moments of opportunity—the right words can open a person to God's Spirit or be the needed climax to a long series of graces, or a long period of personal searching.

e) In moments of crisis—whether personal crisis or the crisis of a group, the words given by God heal the situation or provide needed guidance.

8. How does the Word of Wisdom help in decisions?

This gift helps us to know God's will by giving us some grasp of His plan. God has a plan for His people—a very definite plan. There are certain activities, either directly involved in Charismatic Renewal (days of renewal, talks, new groups formed, etc.), or directly involved in the institutional Church (such as teaching C.C.D.), or just daily obligations (such as works of charity), which He wills us to carry out.

There are other activities which seem good but which He does not want us to carry out, either because they are beyond our resources, or they come from human ambition, or they would distract us from the main works He has in store for us.

By the Word of Wisdom the person or group sees that part of God's plan which they need to know to follow His plan.

D) *Scriptural Basis For the Word of Wisdom*

9. What is an example of the Word of Wisdom in the Old Testament?

In the Old Testament, the most famous Word of Wisdom was spoken by Solomon when called upon to solve the dis-

pute between the two women fighting over the one child
(I Kings 3:16-28).

10. WHEN DID CHRIST USE THE WORD OF WISDOM?

Some examples of Christ using this power are:

a) His practical directive (to the rich young man) that
he should sell all that he had to join the Kingdom
(Luke 18:22).

b) His silencing of opponents in Matthew 22:21 (pay-
ing to Caesar what was owed) and in Matthew
21:25 (asking the chief priests what they thought of
the baptism of John).

c) His defining of His ministry in Luke 12:14—
("Friend, who has set me up as your judge or
arbiter?").

On many occasions, Christ promised his disciples these
special words from His Spirit: (Luke 12:11-12) "When
they bring you before synagogues, rulers and authorities,
do not worry about how to defend yourselves or what to
say. The Holy Spirit will teach you at that moment all
that should be said" (*cf.* Matt. 10:19; Mark 13:11).

11. PLEASE LIST SOME OCCASIONS WHEN THE APOSTLES
USED THIS WORD OF WISDOM.

The following are the main examples of the disciples'
use:

a) At the Council of Jerusalem, in deciding the question
of the Gentile converts and the prescriptions of the
Mosaic law, the group not only used the Word of
Wisdom in settling the controversy, but were consciously aware of using the special gift promised to
them: "It is the decision of the Holy Spirit and ours
too, not to lay on you any burden beyond that which
is strictly necessary, namely, to abstain from meat
sacrificed to idols, from blood, from the meat of
strangled animals, and from illicit sexual union.
You will be well advised to avoid these things.
Farewell" (Acts 15:28-29).

b) Peter and John used the gift before the Jewish
leaders, answering, "Judge for yourselves whether

it is right in God's sight for us to obey you rather than God. Surely we cannot help speaking of what we have heard and seen" (Acts 4:19-20).

c) The gift was used in solving the problem of the Hellenists against the Hebrews by the ordaining of deacons. "Look around among your own number, brothers, for seven men acknowledged to be deeply spiritual and prudent, and we shall appoint them to this task. This will permit us to concentrate on prayer and the ministry of the word" (Acts 6:3-4).

12. ARE THERE ANY OTHER TEXTS IN SCRIPTURE THAT SHOW AN AWARENESS OF THIS CHARISMATIC GIFT ON THE PART OF THE DISCIPLES?

Paul shows an explicit awareness of the Gift of Wisdom:

He states clearly that his preaching was in this gift—"As for myself, brothers, when I came to you I did not come proclaiming God's testimony with any particular eloquence or 'wisdom.' My message and my preaching had none of the persuasive force of 'wise' argumentation, but the convincing power of the Spirit" (1 Cor. 2:1 and 4).

E) *Understanding the Word of Knowledge*

13. WHAT IS THE WORD OF KNOWLEDGE?

The Word of Knowledge is a passing manifestation of God's presence whereby a person is enabled to explain divine truths with clarity and unction. The person is able to apply the traditional teaching to a new context or to use natural examples to explain the mysteries of faith. This gift helps the hearer to understand God and His activity among men.

14. WHAT WOULD BE SOME PRACTICAL USES OF THIS GIFT?

This gift is used primarily in preaching and teaching, raising the natural powers to a new level of faith. This is extremely important, for God's Kingdom is built primarily by preaching and teaching that can beget faith.

This gift helps the person to enter into God's mind to speak with His understanding and to touch hearts by His power. Various aspects of its use in preaching would be the following:

a) In selecting subject matters, so that the speaker is led by God to those parts of Christian teaching that the group needed to hear.

b) In presenting the message in a convincing way, according to the culture, the hopes, problems and needs of the group. The Spirit "custom-tailors" each message even though the theme is the same.

c) In providing power that moves the will to faith. Faith always and everywhere remains a free gift from God which He and no one else (not even the most naturally-gifted preacher) can bestow. This power accompanies preaching in which God is active by His gifts.

d) In moving the feelings (as to tears). The disciples going to Emmaus witnessed to this power in Christ's teaching, that their hearts burned within them (Luke 24:32). Preaching should not only move to faith but also touch the feelings—not in the false emotions of a crowd that is whipped-up but in the true movements of an experience of God's presence and power. This true experience cannot be programmed by clever people but can easily be brought about by a speaker open to these charismatic gifts.

F) *Scriptural Basis for the Word of Knowledge*

15. WHAT ARE THE OUTSTANDING EXAMPLES OF THE WORD OF KNOWLEDGE IN THE OLD TESTAMENT?

The Old Testament begins with a very definite Word of Knowledge in the creation account. In this simple story, a great number of doctrinal teachings are made clear:

a) The true God is not the moon, nor the sun, nor the stars, since He had created all of these.

   b) He is not man, either, although man has a unique
      place in the creation and a special likeness to His
      creator.
   c) Man is now estranged from God because of his will
      and not God's original plan.

Many other truths about God and man are cleverly
brought out by the Genesis account which is an excellent
example of the Word of Knowledge used to give doctrinal
teaching.

The gift of this word to the Jewish people, through
their leaders and writers, led them to a much higher understanding of God and His ways than the knowledge of
the neighboring peoples even though they were more advanced than the Jews in other knowledge. This is especially true of key doctrines—the oneness of God, His
transcendence, His care for man and His sovereign power
over all creation.

16. WHAT ARE SOME NEW TESTAMENT EXAMPLES OF THE WORD OF KNOWLEDGE?

All of the parables used by Christ would be examples of
the Word of Knowledge—the apt words to convey the doctrinal or moral teaching.

The sermon on the mount (Matt. 5:1-12) and the
restored teaching on divorce (Matt. 19:1-9) are examples of a renewed understanding of God's demands and
of the new Christian life.

Each of the gospel accounts relies heavily on the Word
of Knowledge, as the authors attempt to explain Christ
to a given audience or culture. John, especially, in using
the Greek concept of the "Logos" to describe Christ was
helping the message to be effective in a new environment.

17. WHAT EXAMPLES DOES THE ACTS OF THE APOSTLES PROVIDE OF THE APOSTLES USING THE WORD OF KNOWLEDGE?

The following are outstanding:

   a) Peter's discourse on Pentecost as he outlined God's
      plan in Jewish history and interpreted for the audi-

ence the recent events of Christ's death, resurrection and sending of the Spirit (Acts 2).

b) His discourse at the healing of the cripple, again interpreting the events and Sacred Scripture (Acts 3).

c) Stephen was aware that his teaching was under the power of the Spirit (Acts 7:51).

18. WHAT ARE OTHER EXAMPLES OF THE WORD OF KNOWLEDGE IN THE NEW TESTAMENT?

There are so many examples of the Apostles attributing their preaching to the Spirit that it is impossible to list them all. Paul, in Ephesians, outlines his use of this gift.

a) He states clearly that a Word of Knowledge was given to him about what he should preach. "That is why to me, Paul, a prisoner for Christ Jesus on behalf of you Gentiles, God's secret plan as I have briefly described it was revealed" (3:2-3).

b) This secret plan concerned the Gentiles: "It is no less than this: In Christ Jesus the Gentiles are now co-heirs with the Jews, members of the same body and sharers of the promise through the preaching of the gospel" (3:6).

c) He attributes his whole ministry to this gift: "Through the gift God in his goodness bestowed on me by the exercises of his powers I became a minister of the gospel" (3:7).

d) This power to enlighten extended to every part of his preaching: "To enlighten all men on the mysterious design which for ages was hidden in God, the Creator of all" (3:9).

e) Paul asks the people to pray for him for this gift: "Pray for me that God may put His word on my lips, that I may courageously make known the mystery of the gospel" (6:19).

G) *Wisdom and Knowledge as Primarily "Understanding" and "Teaching" Gifts*

19. WHAT IS THE DIFFERENCE BETWEEN PROPHECY
AND THE WORDS OF WISDOM AND KNOWLEDGE?

Both are messages to the community or to an individual, given under God's prompting. The differences between prophecy and the other two gifts are:
Prophecy:

a) Is a more powerful gift.
b) Is able to enter into God's mind.
c) Can deal with matter totally unknown to the person using the gift.
d) Gains its power from being a message from God.

The other two gifts:

a) Do not possess the same power as prophecy.
b) Do not presume to enter into God's mind.
c) Present a message from material that is known naturally.
d) Possess their power from the clarity, the unction, or the presentation that goes beyond the natural powers of the speaker.

20. DO THESE GIFTS HAVE ANYTHING TO DO WITH
KNOWLEDGE THAT IS NOT NATURALLY ACQUIRED,
SUCH AS REVEALING PARTS OF A PERSON'S LIFE,
EITHER PAST OR FUTURE?

These gifts do not directly touch on unknown things, since, strictly speaking, that is the role of the prophetic gift. These, rather, are explaining and teaching gifts. The charismatic element in the gifts is that this natural knowledge is used in a way that is above the speaker's normal power.

A person, for example, is led to a clear and powerful explanation of a simple truth (such as in teaching "Life in the Spirit") or is led to preach about something he was not going to speak on. In these, and in other cases, the element of God's charismatic outpouring is in the clarity, the unctions, the simplicity, the choice of subject matter of the teaching or counseling.

However, these gifts do not involve "direct revelation" in the sense of knowing things by God's activity which are not known by natural knowledge. Rather, the person is led by this gift to say things which he already knows. The charismatic element is that the person says those words at a certain time in a definite situation, in a specific way. Sometimes the person realizes only later how God was using him.

Some do use the phrase "Word of Knowledge" to refer to a discernment of God's activity that is not known by natural means, such as in a healing ministry. Since all the gifts arise from the same Spirit, it is difficult to categorize the exact type of divine activity. It seems, though, that the "revelational" aspects of charisms are part of the prophetic gift.

21. WHAT IS THE RELATIONSHIP OF THESE GIFTS TO SO-CALLED "NORMAL TEACHING" IN THE CHURCH?

Certainly, the Church needs basic teaching in Christian truths and values, and therefore devotes many resources to training priests, religious and laity to "teach all nations" in the normal way of communicating the truths of a given body of doctrine.

These charismatic teaching gifts build upon and go further than the regular way of teaching. Through them God acts upon the speaker so that light, understanding and motivation are communicated to the listener, leading him to faith, conversion or to reach out to God.

A basic Catholic principle asserts that God reserves to Himself the communication of grace. It is God's activity in the teaching that contains the power to move hearts.

22. ARE THERE SCRIPTURAL EXAMPLES OF THESE EFFECTS?

Our Lord's own teaching is the chief example, for the gospels frequently record the reaction of the hearers:

a) The apostles saying that Christ no longer spoke in parables but clearly (John 16:29).

b) The person in the crowd who was led to proclaim "Blessed are the breasts that nursed you" (Luke 11:27).

c) The crowds who saw Christ as one speaking with

authority and not as the Scribes and Pharisees
(Matt. 7:29).

d) The disciples on the road to Emmaus whose hearts
burned within them as the Lord spoke (Luke 24:32).

H) *Yielding and Growing in These Gifts*

23. HOW DOES A PERSON PREPARE FOR THESE GIFTS?

There are a number of fundamental dispositions which
prepare the person for this type of ministry:

a) A deep life of personal prayer—especially the prayer
of simplicity whereby the person listens to God in
a childlike way.

b) An habitual faith that God wants to reveal His will
and guide our decisions, sometimes in extraordinary
ways.

c) A desire to serve others, free from efforts to control
people or the ambitious desire to be listened to in
decisions.

24. HOW DOES A PERSON YIELD TO THESE GIFTS?

First, the person has to be willing to submit his human
thoughts and talents to God. If someone is too attached to
his own ideas or prides himself on powers of preaching,
counseling, or decision-making, he might not be willing to
submit these powers so God can teach him wisdom that
can only be obtained in prayer.

Secondly, the person must be looking for God's will in
every situation. This sincere desire forces the other faculties of intellect, imagination and memory to seek enlightenment and apt words.

Thirdly, the charismatic touch of God comes as a sort
of final stage, after the human cooperation has been complete (charismatic gifts are not a ticket to laziness).

25. WHAT IS MEANT BY GROWTH IN THESE GIFTS?

Growth in the Word of Knowledge results in the teaching becoming:

a) More unified, as the parts of the Christian message
are seen in closer relation to one another.

b) More simple, relying more on God's power than on human powers.

c) More powerful, able to move even those who are hardened.

Growth in the Word of Wisdom results in:

a) A deeper belief in and following of God's guidance.

b) A quicker recognition of human motives and plans.

c) A deeper grasp of divine activity in one's own life and in the life of others and of the community.

Often, charismatics use the words "The Lord showed us" or "The Lord is teaching us." In most cases, they are referring to the Word of Wisdom or Knowledge, those powerful gifts of the teaching Lord among us.

26. How does a person grow in these gifts?

The following conditions are necessary:

a) Place no limit to what the Lord will do among His people.

b) Continue to trust divine wisdom and refuse to return to former ways of solving problems (such as unchristian attitudes).

c) Be patient, knowing that divine wisdom brings forth lasting fruit.

d) Believe that only God's word can build the house or be of service to the Kingdom.

Chapter Twelve

Understanding Charismatic Prayer Groups

*The body is one
and has many members,
but all the members,
many though they are,
are one body;
and so it is with Christ.*
(1 Cor. 12:12)

INTRODUCTION

To COME TOGETHER AND PRAY IN A SPONTANEOUS WAY of free praise and worship has never been part of Catholic practice, at least not in the memory of most. Therefore, the sudden appearance of more than a thousand charismatic prayer groups in the United States Catholic Church has surprised everyone.

To Catholics, involvement in Church life means primarily participation in a Sunday parish Eucharist. On the other hand, involvement in Charismatic Renewal means primarily participation in the charismatic prayer group. Most charismatic Catholics seem to share easily in both groups, finding no contradiction between the two communities, but rather a complementarity.

The prayer group is the heart of Charismatic Renewal. This latest outpouring of the Spirit could easily have been wasted, "gone down the drain" so to speak, except that those who experienced the charisms and the power of the Baptism of the Spirit were led to come together in a group establishing a model for those who came later.

Two distinct terms are used for this regular coming together—"groups" and "communities." The latter indicates a greater degree of sharing and commitment than the former even though, in both, the heart of the coming together is the "prayer meeting."

This chapter attempts only to describe the prayer group for three reasons. First, the greater majority are involved in prayer "groups" rather than "communities" (even though the terms are often used interchangeably). Secondly, the author's experience in the renewal has mainly been with prayer groups and not communities. Thirdly, communities usually possess all that is present in a prayer group so that what is written about groups can be applied also to communities.

UNDERSTANDING CHARISMATIC PRAYER GROUPS

A) *Nature of a Charismatic Prayer Group*

1. WHAT IS A PRAYER GROUP?

It is a number of people meeting regularly, usually at least once a week, varying in size from a handful to hundreds. They do not come together to discuss theology, nor to study Scripture, nor to be involved in the Church's social action programs—although the members might be involved in one or more of these activities at some other time. Rather, the people come together to praise God, to ask forgiveness for their sins, to present to God their petitions, to hear God's word in Scripture and to raise their voices in holy song.

2. WHAT IS A CHARISMATIC PRAYER GROUP?

A charismatic prayer group stresses the Baptism of the Holy Spirit and regularly uses charismatic gifts, both in the weekly prayer meeting and in private prayer.

3. WHY ARE THESE GROUPS SPRINGING UP?

The groups are springing up because of the reappearance on a vast scale of the Baptism of the Spirit and of the charismatic gifts. Since continuing in prayerfulness is vital if the full effects of this Baptism of the Holy Spirit and of the gifts are to be reaped, the prayer group has become a necessity for thousands. It is also the instrument of communicating this infilling of the Spirit and His gifts to still more people—thousands upon thousands more.

B) *Scriptural Basis of a Prayer Group*

4. IS THERE ANY SCRIPTURAL BASIS FOR A PRAYER GROUP?

Strictly speaking, there would be no firm Scriptural basis for prayer groups. The Scriptural proofs offered below apply to the Church. Thus, a given prayer group cannot claim for itself Scriptural texts that apply only to the total ecclesial community.

However, the Church community has always recognized that its work is done effectively in groups and deliberately establishes religious communities. It also fosters other groups needed by the faithful for their devotional life.

The Scriptural texts, therefore, are not so much a proof for the theological necessity of prayer groups but an insight into God's plan in sanctifying us.

5. WHAT INSIGHT INTO GOD'S PLAN IS OFFERED BY THE OLD TESTAMENT?

God's work in the Old Testament centered upon the formation of a people committed to Him. His care for them extends to:

a) The care of Moses (Exod. 3).
b) His care for them in the Exodus, the central event of the Old Testament (Exod. 12 and on).
c) The giving of the covenant (Deut. 5).
d) The raising up of the Judges (Book of Judges and 1 Sam.).
e) The permitting of Kings (1 and 2 Kings).
f) The sending of the prophets.

God's care forged the Israelites into a people. This history provides an insight into God's pastoral plan—namely, that individuals come to Him by becoming a part of a community.

6. WHAT INSIGHT INTO GOD'S PLAN IS PROVIDED BY THE GOSPELS?

Jesus formed various communities:

a) He called the twelve, setting them apart for a distinct role (Matt. 10:2; Mark 3:14; Luke 6:13).
b) He chose the seventy-two (Luke 10:1).
c) He gathered the Holy Women (Luke 8:2).

Besides forming these groups, He also lamented that other shepherds were not available to care for the formation of all the people.

Within these communities, Jesus formed the group and taught them to pray. The members of each group shared experiences with one another and with Jesus. From time to time, Jesus sent them outside of the community to witness to those who had not yet heard (Luke 10; Mark 3: 14).

7. WHAT BASIS FOR GROUPS IS OFFERED BY THE ACTS

OF THE APOSTLES?

Following in the tradition of God's care for the Jewish people and Christ's example of forming a Christian community, the early Christians clearly understood God's pastoral plan—namely, that they should come together in Christian community, developing all the internal and external activities that Jesus had taught them.

The key text is from Acts 2:42-47:

"They devoted themselves to the apostles' instruction and the communal life, to the breaking of bread and the prayers. A reverent fear overtook them all, for many wonders and signs were performed by the apostles. Those who believed shared all things in common. They would sell their property and goods, dividing everything on the basis of each one's need. They went to the temple area together every day, while in their homes they broke bread. With exultant and sincere hearts they took their meals in common, praising God and winning the approval of all the people. Day by day the Lord added to their number those who were being saved."

8. WHAT INSIGHT IS OFFERED BY THIS TEXT?

The early Christians understood the following pattern:
a) They came together for instruction, the breaking of bread and prayer (Verse 42).
b) They shared all things in common (Verse 43).
c) They did many things together—going to the temple, taking meals and praising God (Verses 46-47).

By these means the following apostolic results occurred:
a) God blessed the community with signs and wonders (Verse 43).
b) New members were added daily (Verse 47).

9. SHOULD THESE ASPECTS BE VERIFIED IN EVERY PRAYER GROUP?

The above qualities of the early Christian Church are basic to the Church and to all those communities and groups which are formed to foster its work.

How, and to what degree, each of these is fulfilled in

each community or group would vary. What is important is to realize that God's pastoral activity is very much connected with calling people together in groups. Unless this plan of God is understood, His action through the Spirit is curtailed.

C) *Theological Background for a Prayer Group*

10. IS THERE ANY DOCTRINAL BASIS FOR A PRAYER GROUP?

Just as the Scriptural basis for a prayer group refers primarily to the total ecclesial community and only indirectly to a prayer group, so the doctrinal foundations apply directly and totally to the whole Church, and only indirectly and partially to those groups encouraged by the Church as means of sanctification.

11. WHAT THEOLOGICAL DOCTRINES CAN BE APPLIED INDIRECTLY TO PRAYER GROUPS?

Two doctrines are central to the Church as God's community: the doctrines of the Mystical Body and of the Eucharist (the presence of Christ's physical, glorified Body among us). These doctrines are the underpinning to the Christian concept of the Church, and also support the charismatic prayer groups since these are not isolated, but participate in the life, albeit unofficial, of the Church.

12. WHAT IS THE THEOLOGICAL DOCTRINE OF THE MYSTICAL BODY?

The following is a short outline of that doctrine:

a) In St. Paul, the notion of the "Body of Christ" means the actual, risen, personal body of Christ.

b) As the term "Body of Christ" is applied to the Church, it means that body which gathers, by means of the Spirit, the whole assembly of the faithful.

c) This union comes about by the fellowship in faith professed at Baptism, and is perfected through the Eucharist.

Basically, this doctrine stresses that Baptism does not

just unite us to God but incorporates us into Christ's Body as members.

13. HOW IS THIS DOCTRINE A THEOLOGICAL BASIS FOR PRAYER GROUPS?

As mentioned previously, the doctrine can be applied directly and totally only to the entire ecclesial community. However, the coming together, even in unofficial and informal ways, such as in a prayer group, manifests the power of the Spirit in joining members of the Body.

A prayer group is the concrete and powerful manifestation of what the Spirit has done in an invisible way, uniting the members by faith, Baptism and the Eucharist.

On many occasions, Paul pointed out that we were members of one body. "The body is one and has many members, but all the members, many though they are, are one body; and so it is with Christ" (1 Cor. 12:12; see also Romans 12:14; 1 Cor. 10:17; 1 Cor. 12:26; Col. 3:15).

14. HOW IS THE EUCHARIST A THEOLOGICAL BASIS FOR THE PRAYER GROUPS?

Besides being spiritual food, the Eucharist is also the most powerful act of the Church, as Christ becomes really, truly and substantially present among the members. The sacrament manifests and makes concrete the unity already existing among the members.

A prayer group even when the Eucharist is not celebrated:

a) Manifests and makes concrete the unity that exists.

b) Prepares the members for a more fruitful reception of the Eucharist.

Paul, in 1 Corinthians, Chapter 10, brings together the doctrines of the Mystical Body and the Eucharist:

"Is not the cup of blessing we bless a sharing in the blood of Christ? And is not the bread we break a sharing in the Body of Christ? Because the loaf of bread is one, we, many though we are, are one body, for we all partake of the one loaf" (Verses 16-17).

15. WHAT DO THE CHARISMATIC GROUPS OFFER TO TOTAL CHURCH LIFE?

The prayer group fulfills so many purposes that its power for the modern Church has only begun. It provides the following, so needed in the Church today:

a) An atmosphere in which people can give more time to devotional practices.

b) An atmosphere in which people can bring other people to the Lord.

c) An atmosphere in which people want to spend long periods of time praying, sharing and learning about spirituality.

d) The support of Christian relationships needed to withstand the pressures of the modern world.

e) An opportunity to get deeper teaching, personalized instruction and spiritual guidance.

Many other helps could be listed which are sorely needed by the Church and the faithful.

16. IS THIS IDEA OF PRAYER GROUPS AND CHRISTIAN COMMUNITY NEW?

The prayer group in the Catholic Church is new, although much thought in recent years has been given to methods of bringing people together in dynamic and powerful faith relationships.

Only with the understanding of the Baptism of the Holy Spirit, the emergence of charismatic gifts, and other elements within charismatic groups, has the existence of these faith relationships been realized on such a widespread scale.

17. WHAT DO THE CHARISMATIC PRAYER GROUPS OFFER TO THE CATHOLIC ACT OF WORSHIP AT MASS?

The charismatic groups offers the following helps to Catholic worship:

a) As people know each other, pray together and talk about the Lord among themselves and to others, the communal aspects of the Eucharist can be realized. Presently this central act of worship loses much of its effect because many who are assisting at mass share little else during the week.

b) The liturgical renewal of the mass is lifted to a new

level as the power of the charismatic gifts, of free praise and other elements of a prayer meeting are blended with the Liturgy of the Word and of the Eucharist.

c) The homily of the mass is more powerful as the people are *experiencing* the communitarian aspects of the prayer group.

Many feel that Charismatic Renewal offers the Church some powerful elements which will revivify Church life, not destroying what is already present but bringing everything to life again. The stress on community, the patterns of prayer communities that have emerged, and the power of the Baptism of the Spirit in drawing people together are very important dynamic elements offered to the Church by this renewal.

D) *Importance of the Prayer Groups to Charismatic Renewal*

18. WHY IS THE PRAYER GROUP ESSENTIAL TO CHARISMATIC RENEWAL?

The prayer group plays so many roles in Charismatic Renewal that it would be impossible to conceive of any large scale Catholic Pentecostal Movement without the prayer group. The vast majority of those now involved in the Movement came into the Baptism of the Spirit and charismatic gifts through the prayer group.

19. WHY HAVE SO MANY ACCEPTED RATHER QUICKLY THIS RELATIVELY NEW IDEA OF "BELONGING TO PRAYER GROUPS"?

A number of reasons exist:

First, for many years now books on renewing Church life have stressed Christian community.

Secondly, people find many wonderful experiences and opportunities within the prayer group.

Thirdly, the power and fruits of Charismatic Renewal, for the present at least, are happening within the prayer groups.

Fourthly, in the concrete, belonging to Charismatic Renewal, in most cases, means being a member of a charismatic group.

20. WHAT ARE THE PRINCIPLES BEHIND THE IDEA OF BELONGING TO THE PRAYER GROUP?

The following principles underlie the power of prayer groups:

a) When two or three come together, Christ is present in a new way.

b) When together, Christians can be used in ministries to one another.

c) When together, Christians are a sign and help to others.

As previously explained, the power possessed by the Early Church seems directly linked with its following Jesus' plan of Christians coming together (Acts 2:42-47). This Scriptural model, according to people's state of life, is being reproduced in the prayer groups and, hopefully, in the near future, in every parish.

21. WHAT ROLES DO THE PRAYER GROUPS FULFILL IN THIS MOVEMENT?

The prayer group has the following vital roles:

a) Through the prayer group, God introduces most people to Charismatic Renewal, as described in the Acts, "Day by day the Lord added to their number, those who were being saved" (Chapter 2, Verse 47).

b) Introduces the members to the Baptism of the Spirit and is used by God, in most instances, as an instrument, in His conferring this power.

c) Explains the various charismatic gifts and teaches the members how to yield to them.

d) Provides all members with an indispensable help in continuing to "walk in the Spirit." Regular participation in a prayer group seems absolutely essential to spiritual growth.

e) Within the prayer group, various ministries evolve and individuals frequently discover their mission and apostolate for the Church.

E) *Accomplishing the Goals of the Prayer Group*

22. HOW DOES THE PRAYER GROUP INTRODUCE ITS MEMBERS TO THE "BAPTISM OF THE SPIRIT"?

As mentioned earlier, the Baptism of the Holy Spirit is not a sacrament but basically a very important prayer experience. Although a gratuitous gift from Jesus, certain conditions favor its bestowal. These conditions include:

a) Having faith in this action of Jesus.

b) Fostering a prayerful spirit.

c) Seeking from God this Baptism of the Holy Spirit and giving to God a total committal of life.

The prayer group provides an atmosphere and teaching which helps the person be open to this gift. Thus, the prayer group makes it possible for most, if not all, to come into the full power contained in the Baptism of the Spirit.

23. HOW DOES THE PRAYER GROUP HELP ITS MEMBERS TO GROW IN THE CHARISMATIC GIFTS?

The prayer group provides the following in fostering charismatic gifts:

a) Teaches Catholics about the charisms, overcoming the almost total ignorance of these important and powerful manifestations.

b) Helps its members to actually yield to, use, and grow in the gifts.

c) Attracts other members who need the help of charismatic ministries.

24. WHY IS THE PRAYER GROUP INDISPENSABLE TO CONTINUED GROWTH IN THIS NEW RELATIONSHIP TO THE HOLY SPIRIT?

The following reasons can be given:

a) Especially in the modern world, people tend to forget prayer, or at least they find it difficult, to "get themselves down to praying." A commitment to a prayer group overcomes this usual neglect of prayer. Even religious, already aided by a daily schedule, receive help in prayer from the groups.

b) The members need help from one another to grow
spiritually. This help includes receiving counsel,
avoiding spiritual pitfalls, getting over moods, experiencing the faith and good example of others who
are also "walking in the Spirit."

c) The charismatic gifts seem to be most operative
when prayer is shared by others who also use the
gifts. When charismatic gifts are used well by some
in the prayer group, this frequently releases or
touches off the gifts in many of the members.

d) By their nature, the gifts are given for the building
up of the group. Without a group, the regular use
of and growth in the gifts usually will not occur.

F) *Renewing the Church through Ministries*

25. WHAT DOES "FINDING A MINISTRY" WITHIN THE
PRAYER GROUP MEAN?

A "ministry" serves the needs of those people who are
trying to grow into the fullness of the Christian life. In
trying to serve God, people need help from the various
ministries, such as discernment, words of wisdom, psychological and spiritual healing or prophecy.

Because a ministry is exercised mainly within a group,
these various ministries are coming forth as people gather
together in a group. "Finding a ministry," therefore,
means to discover the way or ways a person serves the
members of the prayer group.

26. DOES THIS REPRESENT "REAPPEARANCE OF MINIS-
TRIES"?

There is a reappearance of the ministries mentioned in
1 Cor. 12 (*cf.* also Ephesians 4, and Romans 12). Unfortunately, many of these ministries, vital to Christian
power, were not present in the daily life of the Church.
Their reemergence is an important part of Charismatic
Renewal.

27. WHAT IS THE CHURCH'S ATTITUDE TO THESE MIN-
ISTRIES?

In recent years, the Church has been very open to a variety of ministries. Vatican II states, "He distributes special graces among the faithful of every rank. By these gifts He makes them fit and ready to undertake the various tasks and offices which contribute toward the renewal and building up of the Church, according to the words of the Apostles, 'The manifestation of the Spirit is given to everyone for profit!' " (Chapter 2, #12—*Constitution on the Church*).

G) *Problems with Prayer Groups*

28. ARE THERE ANY DANGERS INVOLVED IN THIS SUDDEN APPEARANCE OF HUNDREDS OF PRAYER GROUPS?

Obviously, when a movement of such size exists, proportionate dangers exist. The following could be listed:

a) The rich tradition of the Church in prayer be overlooked in favor of only charismatic teaching.
b) The guidance given to members of the groups not be sound.
c) The leaders confront established Church authorities.
d) The distinction between charismatic and hierarchical Church be overlooked.
e) The groups move away from the mainstream of Church life.

29. HOW WOULD THESE DANGERS BE AVOIDED?

The following are safeguards:
a) Priests be involved with the groups.
b) Parishes open their facilities so that the groups can meet as a parish organization.
c) The ministries of the Spirit be rightfully acknowledged.

In truth, much of this has occurred and, in most dioceses, Charismatic Renewal is at home in the established Church.

30. CANNOT THIS SETTING UP OF CHARISMATIC PRAYER

GROUPS LEAD TO AN "ELITE" FEELING AMONG THOSE WHO BELONG?

If the prayer groups were open only to the initiated, as gnostic groups tend to be, then the danger of "elitism" would be present. However, the groups welcome everyone, actively seek the presence and guidance of the Church's ordained priests, and offer themselves for inspection by the American hierarchy. In practice, previous hostility toward the Church and toward other Catholics is removed from a person as his involvement in a charismatic group continues.

H) *Future of Charismatic Groups*

31. WILL PRAYER GROUPS CONTINUE TO EXIST?

Since large numbers have acquired a new appreciation for prayer, and for the importance of communal, charismatic prayer, it seems that these prayer groups will continue for some time.

Hopefully (and it seems to be occurring already), the effects of this renewal will be present in the total Church and will touch many who might never attend a prayer group.

32. SOMETIMES A CONTRAST IS MADE BETWEEN A CHARISMATIC MOVEMENT AND A CHARISMATIC CHURCH. WHAT IS THE DIFFERENCE?

A movement consists of a certain group within a larger group that has specially defined goals and definite means to attain them.

At present, Charismatic Renewal is a movement with some members of the Church participating and others not participating. The goals of these groups are quite definite and limited, not extending to every area of Church life.

Perhaps, someday, the Church will be charismatic in the sense that the goals and means of this renewal are so accepted into the Church that every member of the Church experiences the life of the Spirit as now occurs within the groups.

Chapter Thirteen

Understanding
a Prayer Meeting

When you assemble, one has a psalm,
another some instruction to give,
still another a revelation to share;
one speaks in a tongue,
another interprets.
All is well and good,
so long as everything
is done with a constructive purpose.
(1 Cor. 14:26)

INTRODUCTION

CATHOLICS ARE ACQUAINTED WITH VARIOUS STRUCTURED prayer forms of worship—the mass, common recitation of the rosary, novenas, etc., and are used to having individual spontaneity in prayer left to the individual's private prayer, such as meditation or a visit to the Blessed Sacrament. Only recently has communal free praise and worship entered into modern Catholic life.

Even though the idea is new, however, United States Catholics in over a thousand places gather weekly to praise God in a prayer meeting. Many are finding in the meeting a tremendous help in fulfilling the duty of prayer.

The prayer meeting provides a setting for prayer, the good example of others, solid teaching on prayer, and a number of other helps that have become a weekly spiritual nourishment to thousands of Catholics. Many, who never prayed before or who found great difficulty with private prayer, witness to the spirit of prayer present in a room filled with people praising God.

Even before Charismatic Renewal, many sought new forms of prayer and realized that people should be coming together to pray. At that time, the phenomenon of "shared prayer" emerged—priests saying the breviary together, religious or members of Cursillo groups trying to share some common, spontaneous prayer. Yet "shared prayer" never became the tremendous force in the Church that the charismatic prayer meeting has developed into.

What factors are present in making the Charismatic prayer meetings such a source of spiritual help?

This chapter attempts to analyze and outline the answers to that question. Since worship is the very heart of the Church, any movement that can enhance the power and vitality of Church worship certainly has something to offer. A movement that continues to grow and has attracted so many, so quickly, leading them to deep public and personal lives of worship, seemingly has many things to offer the Church.

It is not yet clear just how and when the charismatic prayer meeting will affect the Sunday liturgy of the normal Catholic parish, and it would be wrong to approach the charismatic prayer meeting as a panacea for any problems of parish Sunday liturgy, or even to feel that all that is needed is a transplant, moving the prayer meeting to Sunday and joining it to mass. The integration of the two will probably be more subtle than that, and in God's own way, it will be much more powerful than what we ourselves could design.

At present, the charismatic prayer meeting is held apart from Sunday mass, attracting those who are so motivated, being allowed to keep to its own goals and to develop its own style.

This chapter is dedicated to understanding the dynamics of a prayer meeting so that the meeting itself can be effective and, so when the average parish begins to integrate prayer meeting and Sunday mass, the dynamism of the former would be understood and not lost or swallowed up in the union.

CHARISMATIC PRAYER MEETING

A) *Understanding a Charismatic Prayer Meeting*

1. WHAT IS A PRAYER MEETING?

A prayer meeting is a group of people, of any size, coming together to pray. In recent years, even before the Catholic Pentecostal Movement, many groups held "prayer meetings" under the name of "shared prayer." This trend was prevalent in the Cursillo Movement and among women religious.

2. WHAT IS THE DIFFERENCE BETWEEN A "CHARISMATIC PRAYER MEETING" AND "SHARED PRAYER"?

As contrasted with shared prayer, the charismatic prayer meeting would:

  a) Provide deeper teaching on the action of the Holy Spirit and how the people yield to that power.

  b) Use freely the charismatic gifts—especially prayer tongues and the word gifts.

    c) Stress more the prayers of praise and thanksgiving, while being free and more open in praise (as the Word of Praise).

    d) Take advantage of a wealth of hymns that have evolved from the movement.

    3. IS THERE ANY "FIXED FORM" TO A CHARISMATIC PRAYER MEETING?

There is no pre-formed pattern to the prayer meeting in any way similar to the prescribed liturgy of the Mass. However, certain *stable* elements seem to be present in all the meetings. These elements would be:

    a) Prayer of praise—one person prays aloud in English while the others are quiet (or the entire group praises God aloud together).

    b) Scripture readings—usually spontaneous from members of the group.

    c) Hymns.

    d) Prayer in tongues.

    e) The gift of tongues followed by an interpretation.

    f) Prophecy or inspired teaching.

    g) Periods of recollection, or "Waiting on the Lord."

    h) Witnessing.

    i) Instruction (sometimes prepared, and at other times given as a spontaneous "Word of Wisdom").

How these elements are blended together, the way they are used, the stress placed on each, varies with each prayer group and can be called the "style" of the group's prayer meeting.

B) *Charismatic Elements of a Prayer Meeting*

    4. ARE THE CHARISMATIC GIFTS REALLY THAT IMPORTANT TO A PRAYER MEETING?

They are extremely important and only as the gifts become widespread has the phenomenon of people coming together for spontaneous prayers also spread.

To prohibit the gifts or to shun the gifts and force "charismatic" prayers to be limited to "shared prayers" would effectively cripple God's activity in this movement.

5. HOW DO THE CHARISMATIC GIFTS AFFECT "REGULAR OR SHARED PRAYER"?

The gifts fulfill the following purposes:

a) Allow God's Spirit greater freedom of movement, thus limiting much of the "human spirit" that harms "shared prayers."

b) Provide a sense of unity so that even large crowds or gigantic gatherings feel of one spirit.

c) Touch people directly since the gifts are used by one member for the good of others.

d) Offer a reason for coming together.

e) Provide a sense of God's presence that is missing when the gifts are not used.

6. HOW DOES THE USE OF THE GIFTS ALLOW GOD'S SPIRIT MORE FREEDOM OF ACTIVITY IN A PRAYER MEETING?

As a person understands the Spirit's activity through the gifts, when he comes to prayer he is more attentive to how the Spirit wishes to pray within him.

Prayer is not seen as something important that the person tells God, but as something the person is led by the Spirit to say to God or to others.

Charismatic prayer meetings possess a whole dimension of prayer that is not present in many other parts of the Church, namely, a sensitivity to the Spirit and a yielding to His action in prayer.

Even those involved in prayer meetings for many years are constantly "getting better" at praying together.

7. HOW DO THE GIFTS PROVIDE A "SENSE OF UNITY" IN A PRAYER MEETING?

The unity is bestowed by:

a) The group praying and singing together in prayer tongues, especially as all the voices blend into a beautiful harmony.

b) The group listening to God's word in prophecy.

c) The group united in a charismatic prayer of praise or listening to a Scripture reading.

d) The group stirred by the power of charismatic

preaching as the person is led by God to delineate His activity among them.

8. HOW ARE PEOPLE TOUCHED DIRECTLY BY THE GIFTS AT A PRAYER MEETING?

Often the use of prayer tongues provides a sense of God's presence in the group. Also, there is a beauty and a peace in listening to someone use the gift of tongues, especially as sung.

Prophecy frequently is the bearer of very special graces for the group or the individual. Inspired teaching will treat the very topic the members need to hear.

The gifts, therefore, are meant to touch the individual, lifting him up from his burdens, freeing him from difficulties and bestowing on him a sense of God's presence.

9. HOW DO THE GIFTS OFFER A REASON FOR COMING TOGETHER?

All of the benefits listed above are, naturally, reasons offered by the gifts for people to come together. The nature of the gifts is to serve others, and people can only be served as they come together.

Paul, in speaking of the gifts, always relates them to the community. He ranks prophecy as first because it, most of all, builds up the Church, and he speaks of using the gifts "when you assemble" (1 Cor. 14:26).

In practice, the charismatic gifts attract people, not because they are spectacular (for the fad quickly passes), but because people are helped and served by them.

C) *Scriptural Basis for a Prayer Meeting*

10. IS NOT THE SCRIPTURAL ADMONITION THAT A PERSON, WHEN PRAYING, SHOULD GO TO HIS ROOM ALONE SO ONLY THE FATHER CAN SEE HIM?

A number of things should be said of that text, since many use it as an objection to public prayer meetings.

First, the admonition was given against the problem of performing acts to be seen by men, not as a condemnation of temple worship.

Secondly, much personal prayer in the solitude of a room should and does take place in Charismatic Renewal.

Thirdly, this text is frequently quoted by sincere people who are confused and do not know how to react to the sudden appearance of prayer meetings.

Fourthly, the evidence for coming together to pray is present throughout Scripture.

11. WHAT IS THE SCRIPTURAL BASIS FOR A PRAYER MEETING?

Throughout the Old Testament, God's activity was primarily collective, in and through a people, especially a people who praised Him. Much emphasis was placed on the Temple, able to be constructed only in Solomon's time.

"You know that my father David, because of the enemies surrounding him on all sides, could not build a temple in honor of the Lord, His God, until such a time as the Lord, should put these enemies under the soles of his feet. But now the Lord, my God, has given me peace on all sides (1 Kings 5:17-18).

In the New Testament arises the prominence of the concept of Church, a word used originally by the Jews to signify local religious assemblies outside of Jerusalem. It was later applied to the Church by the Christians of Jerusalem and then to each local assembly of the faithful.

Therefore, the Old Testament concepts of God's people and the temple, together with the New Testament's idea of the Church, indicate that as individuals come to God they should also come together.

A prayer meeting, therefore, is one aspect of the Church which is God's people coming together.

The Book of Revelation frequently lists groups collectively praising the Risen Lamb as a preview that eternity will be a never-ending prayer meeting (*cf.* Rev. 4, 5, 14, 19).

D) *The Prayer Meeting and Official Worship*

12. WHAT IS THE CATHOLIC CHURCH'S ATTITUDE TO-WARD PRAYER MEETINGS?

The following would be the Church's approach:

a) The center of all public worship is the Sacrifice of the Mass, for which nothing can substitute.

b) Other forms of public worship are authorized by the Church and form part of Her official praise of God, extending throughout the day the praise of the mass. This would be primarily the Liturgy of the Hours.

c) Other collective forms of worship are encouraged so that the devotional life of the faithful is nourished.

13. WILL PARTS OF THE PRAYER MEETING EVER BECOME PART OF MASS?

Certainly, the prayer meeting provides many elements helpful in renewing Church worship and eventually will probably become integrated into the mass. This already occurs within charismatic groups.

It is not yet clear how the power present in charismatic prayer meetings is meant to become part of the Church's official worship or what steps should be taken.

14. IF THE LITURGY IS THE CENTRAL ACT OF WORSHIP, WHY DOES NOT EVERY PRAYER MEETING INCLUDE THE EUCHARIST?

A number of reasons exists:

a) A priest might not be present regularly.

b) Accomplishing some of the goals of a prayer meeting, namely to help people to pray, to use charismatic gifts and to praise God in a spontaneous way, demands a certain amount of time. The weekly meeting could become too long if there were added to this the time needed to celebrate mass devoutly for a large group.

c) Mass is regularly available at other times. Attendance at charismatic prayer meetings usually increases a person's attendance at mass.

d) Most groups do have mass as part of the prayer meeting from time to time (perhaps monthly).

E) *Importance of the Prayer Meeting*

15. CANNOT THE DUTY AND GOALS OF PRAYER BE AC-
COMPLISHED IN PRIVATE PRAYER? WHY DOES THE
PERSON NEED TO ATTEND A WEEKLY PRAYER MEET-
ING?

The idea of attending a weekly prayer meeting is new to
most Catholics and, therefore, they logically question the
need for such a committal. However, practice has shown
that a weekly prayer meeting is indispensable for any
growth in the Spirit over the extended period.

The following reasons can be given:

a) The weekly committal to a prayer group overcomes
the human tendency to postpone prayer.

b) The good example of others who pray deeply is a
much needed inspiration.

c) The charismatic gifts are more abundant and actively used by people when they pray with others who
are also charismatic.

d) The problem of delusions in prayer, of spiritual
pride, and a whole host of other dangers listed by
spiritual writers are lessened by sharing in a prayer
group rather than by "going it alone."

e) A prayer meeting provides a lay person with a help
long available to religious, i.e., others who share the
ideal of an inner life of prayer.

16. IS THERE ANY OTHER ROLE FOR THE PRAYER MEET-
ING?

An important role of the prayer meeting is to witness to
God's action in the midst of a modern world. As the whole
group gathers to praise God devoutly and to share the
effects of the Spirit upon them, a great witness to God's
activity in the modern world results. People can see that
not just one or a few but *many* have been touched by God's
action. This unique type of witnessing occurs only as people come together.

F) *Judging a Prayer Meeting*

17. IS THERE ANYTHING LIKE A "GOOD" AND A "NOT
SO GOOD" PRAYER MEETING?

Although all prayer is good and no human being can judge whether one prayer is better than another, certain judgments have to be made by leadership about whether the prayer meeting was "good" or "not so good" and why. Otherwise, mistakes cannot be corrected.

18. WHAT WOULD BE THE CHARACTERISTICS OF A GOOD CHARISMATIC PRAYER MEETING?

In general, those characteristics would be:
a) A large part of the prayer meeting is spent in prayer of praise and thanksgiving to God.
b) These prayers are made *simply*, like a little child and not *forced* or *displayed*.
c) Many participate and the time is not monopolized by a few.
d) The charismatic gifts are used openly and freely.
e) A sense of God's presence is experienced and could be easily recognized even by newcomers.

19. WHAT WOULD BE THE CHARACTERISTICS OF A PRAYER MEETING THAT WAS NOT SO GOOD?

The following could be listed:
a) The meeting becomes a weekly songfest.
b) Teaching or sharing predominates over prayer.
c) The word gifts are hardly used.
d) The periods of silence are not productive but deadening.
e) Few are really refreshed by a sense of God's presence or power.

20. WHAT SHOULD LEADERSHIP DO IF IT JUDGES THAT THE PRAYER MEETINGS ARE NOT GOING WELL?

There are a number of steps they should take:
First, they should discuss this calmly among themselves, attempting to analyze the problems and the solutions.
Secondly, the steps decided upon should be taken, even if it means saying some hard things to some people who might be causing the difficulties.
Thirdly, if leadership cannot solve the problem, then leaders from other prayer groups should be asked for help.

G) *Dos and Don'ts at a Prayer Meeting*

21. WHAT SHOULD BE AVOIDED IN A PRAYER MEETING?

The members of the group:

a) Should not seek publicity for the prayer meeting. If the prayer meeting is vital and a true spiritual help to those who participate, they themselves will witness to others about it. Publicity often attracts curiosity seekers and betrays an anxiety for large numbers, rather than a desire to do God's will. There are times, however, such as for conferences or special days, when publicity would be according to God's will.

b) Should not speak too much of the devil.

c) Should not be anxious over normal periods of quiet. People growing anxious because "nothing is happening" are often obstacles to some of the Spirit's deeper actions.

d) Should not impose quiet unless it is discerned as God's will.

22. WHAT ARE SOME POSITIVE HINTS FOR A PRAYER MEETING?

This set of hints will be of two kinds—outside of the prayer meeting and during the prayer meeting:

A) Outside of the prayer meetings there should be:

a) Deep, personal prayer and reading of Scripture during the week on everybody's part.

b) A small prayer group meeting at some other time during the week in which members can grow in prayer. Some personal mortification for the success of the larger prayer meeting should be made.

B) During the prayer meeting there should be:

a) Moderators, who are carefully chosen. They should have tact in handling people and sensitivity to the Spirit.

b) An understanding by mature members of the group how they can support the moderator.

c) Solid teaching and instruction on the use of the gifts, on the prayer traditions of the Church, and

on every aspect of Christian living.
d) An atmosphere of love for the brethren even when abuses have to be corrected. The all too human critical spirit has to give way to God's Spirit.

H) *Leadership in a Prayer Meeting*

23. WHAT IS THE ROLE OF LEADERSHIP AT A PRAYER MEETING?

Leadership must see that God's purpose in the prayer meeting is fulfilled. Basically, this means that God is praised and that all experience a sense of prayer. When the prayer meeting is small, this can usually be accomplished by small teachings on prayer and using the gifts.

As the prayer meeting grows in numbers, the role of leadership becomes more complex. In these cases, it is important that everyone know clearly who the leaders are, so that the members can manifest their satisfaction or their difficulties with the meeting, and needed corrections can be made.

24. WHAT JUDGMENTS MUST LEADERSHIP MAKE?

Leadership has to strike a balance between freedom and the needed control of the group so that the prayer meeting will be responsive to the Spirit.

If leadership imposes too much control by unnecessary restrictions, then the Spirit cannot operate and is preempted, in a sense, as the primary moderator.

If, however, leadership imposes no control, then elements which disrupt the prayerfulness of the group inevitably begin to manifest themselves, leaving many disheartened and dismayed.

25. WHAT WOULD BE AN EXAMPLE OF "TOO MUCH CONTROL"?

The following could be listed:
a) Leaders imposing their ideas on a prayer meeting rather than waiting to see what the Spirit intends.
b) Leaders being anxious about moments of silence, not knowing how to "wait on the Lord,"

c) Leaders dominating a meeting too much, interrupting the flow of prayer by constant "teachings."
d) Leaders restricting the use of the gifts, overanxious about "improper" use.

26. WHAT WOULD BE EXAMPLES OF "NOT ENOUGH CONTROL"?

The following could be listed:
a) Allowing the meeting to become too superficial.
b) Not fostering, or being aware of, the presence of prophecy or interpretation among the members.
c) Allowing people to disrupt the prayer meeting by assuming roles normally reserved to leadership.
d) Allowing emotionally unstable people to dominate the prayer meeting.

In all things, leaders have to keep in mind the good of the group which is in their care, realizing that correction sometimes is needed for the common good.

I) *Newcomers to a Prayer Meeting*

27. IS THERE ANY PROBLEM WITH "NEWCOMERS" TO A PRAYER MEETING?

Two problems are obvious:
a) Usually they do not know what is involved in a prayer meeting.
b) It is difficult to have a "prayerful" prayer meeting if too many newcomers are present at once.

The obstacles are usually overcome by introductory talks and the formation of a smaller prayer group through the Life in the Spirit seminars. In this way a smooth integration of newcomers into the prayer meeting takes place.

28. DO MANY NEWCOMERS FIND THIS PRACTICE OF PRAYING OUT LOUD, WHETHER ALONE OR TOGETHER, DIFFICULT TO ACCEPT?

Often the newcomer is quite attracted by the spontaneity and simplicity of the prayer group, even if somewhat

startled by this new practice. Most get used to this and
other new aspects of a prayer meeting rather quickly.

As the prayer group tries to welcome newcomers and
explain what is happening, the new people are willing to
put up with the discomfort of trying to feel at home.

29. HOW DO NEWCOMERS REACT TO PRAYING IN TONGUES?

There are varied reactions. Some find themselves very
attracted by this gift, while others find it an obstacle to
the movement. Still others take the phenomenon in stride,
neither attracted nor dismayed by its presence.

30. WHAT IS THE NORMAL PROGRAM FOR NEWCOMERS?

Most prayer communities have introductory talks, explaining the history of charismatic renewal and answering
questions about the gifts and the prayer meeting. Following this introductory talk, the newcomer is invited to begin the Life in the Spirit seminars which open the person
to the action of the Spirit, including prayer in tongues and
charismatic gfts.

J) *Other Questions about Prayer Meetings*

31. WHERE DO THE FRUITS OF THE SPIRIT FIT INTO THE PRAYER MEETINGS?

The following fruits of the Spirit should be evident:

a) Fraternal charity manifested by a "love for the
   brethren" and concern for one another is the primary sign to newcomers (even more than praying
   in tongues) that God's Spirit is at work.

b) Joyfulness rooted in a lively hope and manifested
   by the enthusiasm and the discipline of the members
   during the prayer meeting.

c) Peace—manifested in the mutual forbearance of
   the members with each other's faults and in the absence of anxiety.

32. WHAT IS THE RELATIONSHIP OF THE PRAYER MEETING TO APOSTOLIC WORKS?

This varies greatly and depends on the nature of the

prayer group. Eventually a prayer life should lead to apostolic works. Sometimes, however, the prayer group has such diverse membership that any attempt to "force" apostolic works would be damaging. In this instance, such works must be left to the individual within the circumstances of his own life.

At other times, the prayer group might be homogeneous, or even precommitted to a given apostolate (such as a religious community). In this case, prayer meetings would naturally offer light and power to further these apostolic works.

Sometimes overlooked in the rush to apostolic works is that the greatest deed done for anyone is to help that person come to know the Lord. A great deal of truly apostolic work is done within the prayer meeting especially through the teachings and sharing.

33. SHOULD THERE BE MANY "PRAYER MEETINGS" IN AN AREA, OR ONE LARGE ONE?

The most "natural" (and, therefore, best) setting for any prayer meeting is the "natural" community. The prayer meeting is just the "weekly expression" of a truly "prayer-filled" community.

Ideally, every parish should naturally be a center for a prayer meeting and, in large parishes, the group could be broken down even further. When Charismatic Renewal ceases to be a movement and there exists instead a charismatic Catholic Church, then every parish and every other Church grouping will be a charismatic community.

In the beginning, however, until this ideal is reached and especially until a large enough group of leaders emerge, it seems best to have Catholic Pentecostal prayer groups as they now exist, i.e., one group serving a given area which usually encompasses many parishes.

Chapter Fourteen

Understanding Leadership in a Prayer Group

*I have a solemn charge to
give you, Timothy, my child.*
(1 Tim. 1:18)

INTRODUCTION

PEOPLE OFTEN CONTRAST AUTHORITY-LED GROUPS WITH spirit-led communities and are somewhat surprised to discover the important role of leaders in charismatic groups. Paul's version, however, was that leadership ministries were a very much needed charism.

Scripture pictures how carefully God picked those who would lead His people. The apostles sought community discernment in selecting deacons (Acts 6). Paul reminded Timothy how he was established as the head (1 Tim. 1:18).

Leadership in the charismatic group is extremely difficult, often taxing every aspect of personal strength and wisdom. Even priests and religious, somewhat skilled in leadership, find a greater need for sensitivity in charismatic leadership than in more traditional roles.

A successful prayer group has many aspects—a deep prayer, correct and extensive teaching, discernment of ministries, growth in the gifts, order yet fervor at the prayer meetings. All of these develop under good leadership, and atrophy when it is not present.

This chapter does not treat the question of lay or clerical leadership, although a later chapter touches on the importance of priests in Charismatic Renewal. Many lay leaders have performed remarkably, especially considering that many were thrust into leadership after only a short time and with no formal background in theology or pastoral care. Priests, by their training and ordination, seemed to be called, both in theory and in practice, to leadership roles in prayer groups.

Two final thoughts are put forth:

First, the call to leadership should be discerned in prayer, and those called to such leadership should respond for the good of others.

Secondly, it is extremely important to keep those people out of leadership who are really not called to it. Volumes could be written about the problems arising from poor leadership.

This chapter is dedicated to the many leaders of

charismatic prayer groups who have undertaken the burdens of others, with no other motive than serving the Lord and the brethren.

LEADERSHIP IN A PRAYER GROUP

Since many roles of leadership have been described in other chapters, these questions are limited to a general discussion.

A) *Understanding Leadership*

1. WHAT IS LEADERSHIP?

Leadership is the power to help a group gain its goals by means of direction, guidance, admonition and motivation. These goals are usually gained by each member co-operating and by fitting into the role which best serves the group and which most corresponds to the person's talents. Leadership also demands the authority to carry out its decision.

2. WHY DOES THE CHARISMATIC MOVEMENT PLACE SUCH EMPHASIS ON LEADERSHIP?

As mentioned elsewhere (chapter on prayer groups), the charismatic group is an indispensable part of this renewal. A great deal of God's action and a tremendous source of His grace is present there. A group without effective leadership will either cease to exist as an effective instrument, or worse still, will be a positive source of spiritual danger.

Many have gone to groups with poor or ineffective leadership and have become "turned off" by Charismatic Renewal, not realizing that other groups, with good leadership, would have been a tremendous help for them.

For this reason, St. Paul places the leadership ministries as first in the Church.

B) *Scriptural Basis for Leadership*

3. WHAT IS THE SCRIPTURAL BASIS FOR LEADERSHIP?

Scripture emphasizes, in both the Old and New Testament, that God's plan for salvation involves "calling His people together."

In forming a people, Scripture notes how God carefully selects those He places in charge. The following examples are outstanding:

a) The call of Abraham as the Father of many nations (Gen. 17).
b) The call of Moses to lead the Chosen People (Exod. 3).
c) The call of David to be king (1 Sam. 16).

NEW TESTAMENT

a) The call of the Twelve (Matt. 10).
b) The call of Peter (Matt. 16).
c) The call of Paul (Acts 9).

This establishing of leadership continues in the pastoral epistles to Timothy and Titus.

"I have a solemn charge to give you, Timothy, my child. This charge is in accordance with the prophecies made in your regard, and I give it to you so that under the inspiration of these prophecies you may fight the good fight" (1 Tim. 1:18).

4. WHAT EXAMPLES DOES SCRIPTURE GIVE OF GOOD AND BAD LEADERSHIP?

In the Old Testament, strong leadership brought the Chosen People through many problems (Moses in the Exodus) and into great benefits (David and his Kingdom). Poor leadership led them into turmoil (Saul with his false gods) or into total ruin (Kings after David).

In the New Testament, Christ spoke of the importance of the shepherd and what would happen to the sheep if he were only a hireling (John 10:12).

Paul often was explicit on the qualities demanded of Church leaders (cf. 1 Tim. 3; Titus 1:5-9).

5. CAN THESE SCRIPTURAL TEXTS BE APPLIED TO LEADERS IN CHARISMATIC GROUPS?

The texts, naturally, apply primarily to the total Church community and directly to the established office of hierarchy in the Church. But God raises up a variety of leaders and of ministries of His Church, and at every level He is concerned that those whom He has called and chosen be discerned.

C) *Types of Leadership*

6. ARE THERE VARIOUS KINDS OF LEADERSHIP WITHIN THE SAME GROUP?

Leadership is either total or partial. In total leadership the person has total and ultimate responsibility for every phase of the group's life. In partial leadership, the person has responsibility for a given phase of the group's life (as teaching, arrangements, etc.) and is held accountable to those exercising the ultimate responsibility.

7. IS LEADERSHIP DIFFERENT IN VARIOUS PRAYER GROUPS?

Since prayer groups vary in size, form and degree of sharing, leadership within them will also vary.

Leadership in a prayer group, gathering one night a week to pray, differs greatly from leadership in a prayer community, in which people share much more and are more extensively committed.

D) *Roles of Leadership*

8. IN PRACTICE, WHAT IS THE ROLE OF TOTAL LEADERSHIP IN A PRAYER GROUP?

Considering the simplest and most widespread example of prayer groups (the weekly prayer meeting supplemented by auxiliary structures), and not touching upon leadership in the more advanced prayer communities, the following roles can be listed:

a) To see that the prayer meeting is well conducted. Leaders should make sure that the gifts are rightly used, that prayers of praise are frequent, that as many people as possible participate, that the music is done well and that order is present.

b) To care that all, both newcomers and those who have been with the group for a while, are receiving good teaching, adequate to their needs.

c) To make sure that people who have talents for the community are being used accordingly.

d) To provide growth groups—i.e., auxiliary structures besides the weekly prayer meeting to help people to grow in the Spirit.

e) To exclude people with personal or emotional difficulties from leadership positions (such as teaching), which would be detrimental to all concerned.

f) To admonish those who disrupt the community, either at the prayer meetings or at other times.

Many other duties can be added to total leadership.

9. WHAT ARE SOME ROLES OF PARTIAL LEADERSHIP?

The following seem to be present in most communities:

a) Teaching—providing programs for newcomers and for continued growth of the members.

b) Books and tapes ministry—assuring a supply of suitable books and tapes.

c) Welcoming—greeting people on arrival.

d) Follow-up ministry—contacting people who persevered for a time and now no longer attend—not to cajole them back into coming but to help if some difficulty is present.

e) Physical arrangements—being responsible for chairs and for cleaning up.

f) Hospitality—providing refreshments if that is part of the weekly meeting. Also, having a list of homes where strangers might stay for the night.

Many other ministries, helpful to the group, could be added.

E) Qualities of Leaders

10. WHAT QUALITIES SHOULD CHARACTERIZE A LEADER?

Although the list could be very long, the qualities given

here are the more obvious.

On the *natural level* the person should:

a) Be emotionally balanced, not given over to excessive moods or unbridled enthusiasm.

b) Possess good judgment, knowing when and how to correct a given situation or when not to interfere.

c) Have no serious difficulties in his personal or family life. St. Paul asked, "If a man does not know how to manage his own house, how can he take care of the church of God?" (1 Tim. 3:5).

d) Be responsible by keeping his word and promises.

e) Be able to aid others in developing their natural potentialities and charismatic gifts.

On the *supernatural level*, the person should:

a) Manifest the fruits of the Spirit.

b) Have a correct attitude toward the charismatic gifts, neither being carried away by charismania nor despising the gifts.

c) Be committed to a life of daily prayer.

d) Possess a developed gift of discernment.

11. WHO, THEN, SHOULD BE EXCLUDED FROM LEADER-SHIP?

Besides anyone seriously lacking the above-mentioned qualities, the following should be excluded:

a) Someone who pushes himself into leadership—at least until this all too human spirit has been corrected.

b) Emotionally unstable individuals, such as those who invite arguments or seek religious experiences out of emotional need.

c) Those who lose their sense of reason with the gifts (as using charismatic gifts to give direction when simple prudence suffices).

d) Those who have trouble with normal human relationships.

e) Anyone who is not truly prayerful or who exercises poor discernment.

F) *Judgments and Problems of Leaders*

12. WHAT JUDGMENTS MUST LEADERSHIP MAKE?

Judgments would extend to every part of the prayer community. The following are common questions:

Concerning the prayer meetings:

a) Is the quality of the group's prayer good? Are the gifts used, and if so, are they used correctly? Is everyone sharing in the prayer? Is the meeting truly prayerful, given over to prayers of praise and not merely a songfest or a teachathon?

Concerning teaching:

b) Is the teaching for newcomers adequate? What could be done to improve the program? Are newcomers ministered to in a personal way, so that any problems or questions can be answered? Are the regular members provided with teaching or spiritual growth?

Concerning goals:

c) Is the community growing at least in depth or is the prayer community in a rut? Or worse still, is it off the track, somehow missing its purpose?

13. WHAT PROBLEMS DO LEADERS USUALLY HAVE TO FACE?

Even with good leadership, the following problems might occur:

a) False and disruptive prophecy—usually given by disturbed people who put a great stock on charismatic manifestations.

b) Dull prayer meetings—when people do not respond to the Spirit urging them to praise God and use his charismatic gifts.

c) Misunderstandings regarding God's activity—people wondering why God does not help them more or seems to abandon them or allows things to get worse.

d) Satanic activity—manifested openly by disruptive actions or manifested quietly within the heart of one of the members who is being led astray (*cf.* discernment).

e) Inability of individuals to integrate this new action of God's Spirit in their lives with the duties of their state of life.

f) Human relationship difficulties—a clash of personalties (perhaps among the leaders themselves), an emotional involvement, jealousy over abilities or service roles.

Problems are inevitable. If leadership is not creating them and is attempting to solve those that do arise, most prayer group members will be patient, realizing that the movement is not problem-free.

G) *Relationship of Leaders to One Another, the Church and the Parish*

14. WHAT SHOULD CHARACTERIZE THE RELATIONSHIP AMONG THE LEADERS THEMSELVES?

The relationship among the leaders should be characterized by the following:

a) The ability to pray deeply together.

b) Love for one another, accepting personality differences, ministries to one another (perhaps even by an admonition) and being able to accept the role assigned on the team.

e) Total commitment—especially the keeping of promises, and an equal share of the burden.

d) Honesty—being able to speak openly and not be forced to hold back feelings.

e) Trust and acceptance—as each leader feels enough at home not to fear mistakes, knowing that the others will accept him as he is, and in loving discernment, help him to grow.

15. WHAT SHOULD BE THE RELATIONSHIP OF LEADERSHIP IN A PRAYER GROUP TO CHURCH AUTHORITY?

The relationship should be a close one, and regional leadership should establish a liaison with diocesan authority.

Leadership should also:

a) Adhere to Church regulations, such as liturgical norms. Violating these norms invites criticism and fosters prejudices against Charismatic Renewal.

b) Advise local Church authorities of places and times of charismatic prayer meetings, and extending an open invitation to attend. They should also make known the names of the leaders and of the priests who are involved.

c) Avoid theological debates (such as birth control, role of the Church in the peace movement, necessity of auricular confession, clerical celibacy, the future of religious life). Leadership should stick to presenting gospel teaching as clearly and as simply as possible.

16. WHAT SHOULD CHARACTERIZE THE RELATIONSHIP OF LEADERS IN THE PRAYER GROUP TO THE PARISH?

Whether the group is based in the parish itself or not, the relationship should include:

a) Some involvement in other phases of normal parochial life (lectors, parish council, C.C.D. teachers) not using this involvement to in any way "take over" the parish but to be truly of service.

b) Maintaining the parochial and social relationships that were present before involvement in the charismatic prayer group.

Relationships and service activities within a prayer group are often very satisfying. A temptation is often present to withdraw from other non-charismatic relationships in favor of only charismatic ties and activities.

Chapter Fifteen

Chapter Fifteen

Charismatic Renewal and the Kingdom of Darkness

Our battle is not against human forces but against the principalities and powers,
the rulers of this world of darkness,
the evil spirits in regions above.
(Ephes. 6:12)

INTRODUCTION

A FEW YEARS AGO, MOST "ENLIGHTENED" PEOPLE DID not believe in the existence of devils. Now, priests are asked to give talks on the all but forgotten rite of Church exorcism, and surveys show that some people believe in devils who don't even believe in God.

Because belief in devils was rejected, modern man felt very free to delve into the occult world, knowing little about its dangers and ignoring the usual Christian prohibitions. As a result, there has developed an insatiable appetite for strange powers and people who formerly were seen as somewhat "freakish" are now viewed as "experts" in the coming world of psychic phenomena.

Concerning the kingdom of darkness, Charismatic Renewal follows the Church's traditional teaching that evil comes from many sources—the effects of original sin, bad habits, the example of others, the world system and the devil. Therefore, not every problem can be attributed to devils. Yet, sometimes it is evident that some are directly caused by them, or at least aggravated by them.

Understanding the kingdom of darkness, and psychic phenomena, discerning the true sources of difficulties, and delivering people from occult bondage are important aspects of Charismatic Renewal. For years now, leaders in this movement have read carefully the traditional teachings of the Church, have learned from the deliverance ministries of Protestant Pentecostals, and have gathered much wisdom from their own experience.

The Church teaches (Roman Ritual on "Exorcism") that the power to remove Satan's bondage was a highly prized charismatic gift among the early Christians. It is also meant to be an extremely important power for the modern Church. Only as the Church is renewed in the power of deliverance which it has over Satan will it be able to stem the tide of the kingdom of darkness and handle the growing problems of bondage.

This chapter is an outline of the victory of Christ over this kingdom and includes a description of the occult world, bondage, discernment, and deliverance. The following questions are an attempt to open up to the total Church the power and wisdom found in Charismatic Renewal teachings. Hopefully, the ministry of deliverance (and in very special cases, of exorcism) will be totally restored to the Church, so that Jesus, the Victor over all bondage, can continue to bring every Christian into the freedom of the sons of God.

Note: *A special word of gratitude to Hobart E. Freeman, author of* Angels of Light, *who has granted permission for the use of various lists of occult practices and problems found in this chapter.*

CHARISMATIC RENEWAL AND THE KINGDOM OF DARKNESS

A) *Understanding This Kingdom*

1. WHAT IS MEANT BY THE KINGDOM OF DARKNESS?

It is a general term referring to the existence of personal, rational non-human beings who have fallen away from their original goal but continue a relationship to creation. Now, however, that relationship is negative and destructive.

2. IS THIS DEFINITION ACCEPTED BY ALL?

Obviously, people who do not believe in the world of devils would not accept this definition. They would attribute various phenomena to unknown powers of man or of nature. Even many who believe in devils are unaware of the extent or influence of the kingdom of darkness.

B) *Traditional Teaching of the Catholic Church on the Kingdom of Darkness*

3. WOULD THE CATHOLIC CHURCH ACCEPT THIS TEACHING?

The Church accepts and teaches the existence and influence of this kingdom. Theologians, however, would not call this teaching "infallible," since certain aspects could be open to further development.

4. WHAT IS THE COMMON TEACHING OF THE CATHOLIC CHURCH CONCERNING DEMONS?

The following are the essential teachings:
a) Devils are created, personal, but non-human beings, having all the natural attributes of angels.
b) There is a plurality of these demonic powers.
c) These powers have an essential, natural, personal relationship to the world, to nature and to the history of salvation.
d) These beings were originally oriented to supernatural fulfillment, but have renounced that goal.
e) They have culpably shut themselves off from their own fulfillment in a definitive way.
f) Christ is the victor over the power of evil spirits, but their opposition to the Church will continue until they are cast definitively into hell. (See *Sacramentum Mundi*, Volume 2, Article entitled "Devil.")

5. WHAT DOES THE CHURCH'S RITUAL SAY ABOUT MAN'S PROBLEMS WITH DEMONS?

The teachings of the Roman Ritual are clear and nearly complete, pointing out the following:
a) That a world of demons exists is part of Judeo-Christian teaching.
b) Christ overcame this kingdom of darkness so man could be delivered from occult power.
c) This kingdom has both an ordinary and an extraordinary influence over man.
d) The ordinary power is called "obsession" and the extraordinary power is called "possession."
e) The early Christians frequently used the charismatic gifts of healing and of driving out devils in applying Christ's victory.
f) Sometimes, even the extreme case of "possession" is not due to any fault of the person involved.

C) *Scriptual Basis for This Teaching*

6. WHAT EVIDENCE DOES SCRIPTURE GIVE FOR THE EXISTENCE OF THE KINGDOM OF DARKNESS?

References to Satan and his kingdom abound in Scripture. The first book pictures Satan in the guise of a serpent (Gen. 3). The final book tells of his downfall (Rev. 20:10).

The Old Testament has references to sacrifices to the kingdom of darkness: "No longer shall they offer their sacrifices to the satyrs" (Lev. 17:7). Deuteronomy (32:17) says: "They offered sacrifices to demons, to "no gods."

In the New Testament, when Jesus was accused of using Beelzebub's power, He in no way denied the existence of Beelzebub or his kingdom, but proved that He Himself was not acting in the power of that kingdom (Matt. 12:22-28).

In fact, Jesus gave powers over unclean spirits (Mark 6:7).

Paul wrote clearly about "the rulers of this world of darkness" and "the evil spirits in regions above" (Eph. 6:12).

7. WHAT EVIDENCE DO THE GOSPELS GIVE FOR SAYING THAT SATAN EXERCISES POWER OVER MAN?

The gospels frequently attribute difficulties experienced by man to the kingdom of darkness:

a) "A possessed man who was brought to him was blind and mute. He cured the man so that he could speak and see" (Matt. 12:22).

b) "Jesus, on seeing a crowd rapidly gathering, reprimanded the unclean spirit by saying to him, "Mute and deaf spirit, I command you: Get out of him and never enter him again'" (Mark 9:25).

c) "There was a woman there who for eighteen years had been possessed by a spirit which drained her strength. She was badly stooped—quite incapable of standing erect" (Luke 13:11).

Also Christ discerned the action of Satan upon Peter (Matt. 16:23), and St. John attributes Judas' betrayal of Christ to the power of the devil: "The devil had already induced Judas, son of Simon Iscariot, to hand him over" (John 13:2).

8. WHAT OTHER EVIDENCE FOR THE POWER OF THIS KINGDOM IS OFFERED BY THE NEW TESTAMENT?

a) Peter discerned the influence of evil spirits in Simon Magus (Acts 8:9-24).

b) Paul frequently writes about man's problem with Satan. In 2 Thessalonians (2:12), he describes the final days when the wicked one will appear, opposing all things and even claiming to be God, being overcome, however, by the Lord Jesus.

c) Paul wrote to Timothy: "The Spirit distinctly says that in later times some will turn away from the faith and will heed deceitful spirits and things taught by demons" (1 Tim. 4:1).

d) In Ephesians (6:10-12), Paul issued the famous battle cry to spiritual warfare: "Put on the armor of God so that you may be able to stand firm against the tactics of the devil. Our battle is not against human forces but against the principalities and powers, the rulers of this world of darkness, the evil spirits in regions above."

e) St. Peter also wrote in his first epistle, "Your opponent the devil is prowling like a roaring lion looking for someone to devour" (5:8).

9. DO THE GOSPELS GIVE ANY BASIS FOR THE IDEA OF DEVILS SEEKING REST BY CONTACT WITH MAN?

The gospels picture the demons as having no rest and seeking it in a material body, preferably human.

Our Lord warns: "When an evil spirit goes out of a man, it travels over dry country looking for a *place to rest*. If it can't find one, it says to itself, 'I will go back to my house which I left.' Then it goes out and brings along seven other spirits even worse than itself and they come in and live there'" (Matt. 12:43-45).

Three of the gospels narrate the story of the devils begging to be given some place to rest as Christ drove them out of the man named "Legion" (Matt. 8:23-32; Mark 5:11-13; Luke 8:32-33).

10. WHAT IS THE SCRIPTURAL BASIS FOR BELIEVING THAT CHRIST'S POWERS OVER THIS KINGDOM WERE GIVEN TO THE CHURCH?

Just as the other powers of Jesus were passed on to the disciples, so this power over the Evil One continued after Pentecost. The Acts of the Apostles lists the following examples:

Philip in Samaria: "There were many who had unclean spirits, which came out shrieking loudly. Many others were paralytics or cripples and these were cured" (8:7).

Paul in Ephesus: "Meanwhile God worked extraordinary miracles at the hands of Paul. When handkerchiefs or cloths which had touched his skin were applied to the sick, their diseases were cured and evil spirits departed from them" (19:11-12).

D) *Awareness of the Kingdom of Darkness*

11. ARE MANY IN THE CATHOLIC CHURCH AWARE OF THE PROBLEM WITH THIS KINGDOM?

Unfortunately, even with the very solid traditional teaching, most Catholics are unaware of practical problems or solutions. They would not be able to discern the influence of this kingdom, know how to pray for deliverance, or be able to recognize satanic teachings. With the upsurge, however, in occult phenomenon, many are awakening to the situation and are looking to the traditional wisdom of the Church for guidance.

12. IS THERE ANY SIGNIFICANCE THAT CHARISMATIC RENEWAL IS TAKING PLACE IN THE CATHOLIC CHURCH JUST AS THE OCCULT WORLD BECOMES MORE WIDESPREAD?

A tremendous significance exists between the two phenomena, i.e., the growth of charismatic power in the Church and the increase of occult powers in the world. The following could be listed:

a) A complete knowledge of the occult, a fear of its in-
    fluence and a warning against involvement is pres-
    ent in the Charismatic Renewal movement and
    seemingly nowhere else in the Church. Knowledge
    of this kingdom is woefully lacking even among
    priests and religious. Catholic colleges even get in-
    volved in studying psychic phenomena, and other
    avenues into the occult, with little realization of
    what is involved.
b) The charismatic powers—especially the gift of dis-
    cernment of spirits and the power of deliverance—
    deal directly with the occult. The Early Christians
    prized these powers of liberation given to them by
    Christ.
c) The spiritual renewal through the Baptism of the
    Holy Spirit is strengthening the Church for the
    warfare ahead: It is significant that Christ (follow-
    ing His Baptism by John and the external sign of
    the Spirit's infilling) immediately began to make
    war on these powers.

E) *Understanding Demonic Influence*

13. WHAT IS "DEMONIC INFLUENCE"?

This term means that in some way the person has come
under the power of the kingdom of darkness. This influence varies from a slight problem to a very grave difficulty.
The Roman Ritual uses the term "obsession" for the
slight problem and "possession" when the person's faculties (bodily organs and lower spiritual faculties) are under the control of the demonic world.

14. WHAT IS MEANT BY "OBSESSION"?

It means that the kingdom of darkness oppresses a
person in that area of his personality which is vulnerable
to such an influence. Since personalities vary, the influence is different in each. For some, this influence is one
of the seven capital sins. For another, it might be a personality difficulty such as depression, fear, or sorrow.

Sometimes the connection between obsession and its

cause is easily detected. Many times, however, the relationship is hidden, and discovered only by spiritual discernment.

15. HOW DOES "OBSESSION" DIFFER FROM "POSSESSION?"

It differs in a number of ways:

a) Obsession is much more common and could be termed a "normal" problem in the Christian life. In a sense, everyone at some time has been the subject of obsession.

b) It is not as disturbing to a normal way of life, nor even to leading a Christian life.

c) It afflicts only a certain portion or area of life, or is manifested only in certain situations.

d) It is relieved by prayers of deliverance, said by the person himself or by another.

Possession, on the other hand, is experienced rarely, can totally disturb the person, and is relieved by the extraordinary means of exorcism, said (in the Catholic Church) only by a priest duly authorized by a bishop.

16. HOW DOES A PERSON BECOME SUBJECT TO OBSESSION?

A person can become subject to this power:

a) By yielding to a sin in such an extraordinary way as to lose all control, allowing himself to be totally swept away by the problem. Examples of this would be totally blasphemous language, unnatural sexual practices, drugs, alcoholism, or gambling. This total giving of oneself to these sinful actions seems to open the person up to satanic influence.

b) By direct involvement in the occult world. Avenues into the occult will be listed and explained later in this chapter.

c) By other openings into bondage, some of which are not even the person's fault—such as the occult involvement of parents or personality wounds inflicted by others.

Whatever the cause, it is important that the connection

be discerned, so that God's power can be used for deliverance.

17. IS OBSESSION ALWAYS SERIOUS?

The degree of difficulty with obsession varies from very slight—such as a continual emotional annoyance, slight temptations that will not go away, a recurring personality problem—up to very serious problems of bondage that constantly bind the person in habits of sin or result in psychic phenomena.

18. CATHOLICS HAVE A PHRASE, "THE STATE OF GRACE," WHICH MEANS THE PRESENCE OF GOD WITHIN THE SOUL. CAN THE PERSON BE IN THE "STATE OF GRACE" AND STILL EXPERIENCE BONDAGE?

Yes, the two frequently can and do coincide, especially with the lighter cases of obsession. This is an important distinction for Catholics, since in no way should it be implied that problems with "occult" bondage are incompatible with being God's child. A total surrender to Christ's Spirit, however, would eventually lead to a removal of these problems.

F) *Problems Arising from Demonic Influence*

19. DO MANY PROBLEMS ARISE FROM DEMONIC INFLUENCE?

The problems which can arise from this influence are as legion as the devils themselves. It is always a sensitive subject to list these manifestations, because some of them could well have their source in something else—as physical indisposition, chemical imbalance in the body, or in other scientifically explainable areas. These other possibilities should be explored first, before attributing these difficulties to the kingdom of darkness.

20. SPECIFICALLY WHAT ARE SOME PROBLEMS THAT MIGHT BE DUE TO DEMONIC INFLUENCE?

They can be divided into the following groups:

    a) Mental and emotional problems.
    b) Spiritual problems.
    c) Physical difficulties.
    d) Social and domestic problems.

21. WHAT ARE SOME MENTAL AND EMOTIONAL DIFFI-
CULTIES WHICH MIGHT BE DUE TO THIS INFLU-
ENCE?

As mentioned previously, careful discernment is needed
since the problems might have natural causes rather than
supernatural ones. The following, however, seem to be
aggravated by the demonic world, if not caused by it:
    a) Extreme irritability and impatience.
    b) Compulsive thought and behavior.
    c) Extreme morbidity and moroseness.
These examples could be expanded. The common trait
among them is the person's lack of control. The individual
senses that he is under an influence beyond his own
powers.

22. WHAT ARE SOME SPIRITUAL PROBLEMS DUE TO
DEMONIC INFLUENCE?

Again, the true source of these problems has to be
rightly discerned. However, the following frequently are
rooted in or aggravated by demonic influence:
    a) Indifference to spiritual things.
    b) Serious doubts of faith and disbelief.
    c) Religious aberrations such as heresy, etc.
    d) Inability to receive the full gift of the Baptism of
the Spirit.
    e) Resistance to teaching against the occult.
    f) Inability to pray or to believe in Christ.
    g) Enslavement to drugs, drink, gambling, or abnor-
mal sexual activity.

23. WHAT WOULD BE THE SOCIAL OR DOMESTIC DIFFI-
CULTIES ARISING FROM DEMONIC INFLUENCE?

These difficulties arise in various relationships—problems such as serious marital disputes, parental discords,
or persistent financial mistakes. This is epecially true
when there seems to be little or no objective cause for the

difficulty, or the problem seems insoluble or out of control.
Within Charismatic Renewal itself, problems can arise
among the leaders of a prayer community, which can only
be discerned as the devil's action—his attempting to sow
discord within the group.

G) *Deliverance from Demonic Influence*

24. HOW IS A PERSON FREED FROM DEMONIC INFLU-
ENCE?

If the problem is so serious that "possession" is present,
then the person or the place would have to be exorcised.
This can be done in the Catholic Church only with the permission of the bishop, which is given usually to a priest
whose life and learning equip him to handle the situation.

If the problem is the less serious difficulty of "obsession," then the person is prayed with by a prayer of deliverance.

25. WHAT IS A PRAYER OF DELIVERANCE?

This prayer is a command in the power and in the name
of Jesus that evil influences leave the person or the place.

This could be an informal prayer, that is, one said in a
general way, or it could be a formal prayer in which the
person mentions specifically those areas of life which seem
totally out of his control (fears, hatred, depression, abnor-
mal sexuality, drugs, etc.).

26. WHEN SHOULD A PRAYER OF DELIVERANCE BE
SAID?

This prayer can and should be said at various times.
General and informal prayers of deliverance are said, as
a matter of course, before praying for the Batpism of the
Holy Spirit and before a prayer meeting. This prayer
might also be said privately and quietly by leadership if
they discern demonic influence during a prayer meeting.

Prayers of deliverance are said at other times when it
is discerned that a person is under the power of obsession.
Generally, difficulties with the occult are brought out
during the Life in the Spirit seminars. If the person

has a problem with obsession, and especially if effects are evident in his life (psychic phenomena, inability to pray, other serious psychological and moral problems), then mature members could discern the need for prayers of deliverance. Also, the person should be urged to use sacramental confession.

H) *Praying for Deliverance*

27. CAN ANYONE SAY A "PRAYER OF DELIVERANCE"?

General or informal prayers of deliverance, as said before praying for the Baptism of the Spirit or before a prayer meeting, would be said by whoever is leading the prayers.

However, specific prayers of deliverance should be said only by mature members who are able to handle the situation. The deliverance ministry is difficult, demanding much experience, discernment and holiness of life.

28. SHOULD A PRIEST BE INVOLVED IN DELIVERANCE PRAYERS?

Since the priest has the special graces of ordination, he should be involved in these prayers. If he is not available, then those who have the background in a deliverance ministry should pray. If an occult problem is presented to an inexperienced member, the person involved should be referred to leadership.

29. DOES A DELIVERANCE ALWAYS OCCUR IF THE PRAYER IS SAID?

Definitely not. In the gospels even the apostles had difficulties. Frequently the freeing from bondage occurs only over a period of time.

Sometimes there is a partial deliverance whereby some of the evil influence is removed. Here, the nature of the problems might require that deliverance occur in stages, as the causes and nature of the occult bondage surface or as the person gains self-knowledge concerning his attachment to sin or his need for deliverance.

30. WHY DOES DELIVERANCE SOMETIMES NOT OCCUR?

The reasons are many:

a) The person might refuse to admit that he needs deliverance. No one can be delivered from occult bondage until he agrees that he needs and wants such freedom (although sometimes this desire need only be in a general way).

b) The discernment of spirits was not correct, and the prayer did not touch the core of the problem.

c) The person praying for deliverance either did not have great faith in prayer or deliverance, or was not sufficiently abiding in Christ to draw upon the power of His name.

I) Conditions for Deliverance

31. WHAT IS NEEDED ON THE PERSON'S PART FOR DELIVERANCE FROM OCCULT INVOLVEMENT?

The following is needed:

a) Profession of faith in Christ.

b) Confession of faults (at least *interior* recognition and acceptance of wrongdoing).

c) Renunciation of Satan and his works in the person's life.

d) Being helped in this renunciation of Satan by the prayers of others, especially by priests in the Sacrament of Penance.

e) Taking future safeguards.

32. WHAT ARE THE FUTURE SAFEGUARDS FROM INVOLVEMENT?

The person must avoid the following:

a) Any future contact with the occult.

b) Giving credence to any belief that is not in harmony with the Scriptures or the Church's teachings.

c) Having occult objects in the house.

The person must practice the following:

a) Daily personal prayer and reading of Scriptures.

b) Continued sharing in the prayer community.

c) Continued resistance to satanic attacks.

J) *Judging the Effects of the Deliverance Prayer*

33. HOW DOES THE PERSON KNOW THAT DELIVERENCE HAS OCCURRED?

There is a total psychological and physical sense of well-being. What was formerly uncontrollable is now within the normal control of self-discipline.

These good fruits are not the result of newly-formed habits but of a quick and immediate release from the problem. Deliverance is marked by a lifting of a burden, a new freedom in thinking and feeling, a release from captivity that was previously seen as a personal problem or as a personality defect.

34. HOW DOES A PERSON KNOW THAT DELIVERANCE HAS NOT OCCURRED?

It has not occurred if this release from the problem does not happen. The people involved should fast and pray privately and then come together again to pray with more faith in Jesus' power.

35. CAN A PERSON SAY A PRAYER OF DELIVERANCE FOR HIMSELF?

Since no one is free from occult problems, especially those who are trying to yield to Christ's Spirit, the person should say prayers of deliverance, even on a regular basis, asking to be guarded and protected by Christ's Precious Blood. Although more powerful and subtle attacks await everyone along the way, the Spirit will give the discernment and power needed to overcome the Evil One.

36. WHAT ARE THE DANGERS IN A DELIVERANCE MINISTRY OR IN PRAYERS FOR DELIVERANCE?

The dangers are many. A few of the more common are:
a) To attribute every problem to the devil and indiscriminately pray for deliverance.
b) To handle imprudently the teaching on deliverance, resulting in unnecessary fears and reactions by members of the community.
c) To pray openly for deliverance for someone, thus

communicating to all a discernment of the person's occult involvement.

d) To refuse to seek more natural and available remedies for problems wrongly discerned as occult, e.g., psychiatric or medical help.

Deliverance, perhaps more than any other area of Charismatic Renewal demands holiness of life, depth in the charismatic powers, and extreme prudence and judgment in every phase of this ministry.

K) *Understanding the Occult World*

(The following section explores one avenue of involvement in the kingdom of darkness. It is especially needed at the present time with the tremendous upsurge in psychic phenomena.)

37. WHAT IS MEANT BY THE "OCCULT WORLD"?

The "occult world" is a general term which refers to many practices, objects and phenomena whose source and power is the personal, evil world of devils.

38. WHAT IS MEANT BY THE PHRASE "WHOSE SOURCE AND POWER IS THE PERSONAL, EVIL WORLD OF DEVILS"?

The phrase means that the occult object, practice or phenomena is rooted in and participates in the power which the fallen angels continue to have over mankind and material creation.

39. WHAT PSYCHIC POWERS ARE DUE TO DEMONIC INFLUENCE?

The following psychic powers seem closely linked to the occult world:

Subjective psychic abnormalities are:

a) Clairvoyance—seeing things spontaneously beyond normal sight, as future death or misfortune ("second sight").

b) Clairaudience—hearing spirit voices (disguised as a dead relative or friend).

c) Precognition—knowing future events.

d) Telepathy—power to transfer thoughts from one mind to another.
e) Divination—using objects (cards, ouija boards, etc.) to foretell the future.
f) Psychometry—ability to tell the facts about an owner's object.
g) Radiesthesis—use of dowsing rod or pendulum to divine for water, oil, or minerals.
h) Magic practices—"white magic" (invokes powers for good ends), "black magic" (invokes powers for evil or destructive ends), and witchcraft.
i) Spiritism or medium powers:
   i) Self-induced powers.
   ii) Communicating with the dead (seances).
   iii) Automatic writing.
   vi) Telekinesis—objects moved mysteriously.
   v) Materialization—alleged dead spirits in visible form.
   vi) Parakinesis—to control objects by power of mind.

Objective psychic abnormalities are:
a) Poltergeist phenomena to which the person is subjected—such as flying objects, mysterious noises, or fires breaking out .
b) Apparitions and monstrous phantoms.

   40. ARE THERE ANY OTHER AVENUES INTO THE OC-
       CULT?

Besides the above, the following seem linked with the occult world:
a) Astrology.
b) ESP games.
c) Horoscopes.
d) Ouija boards.
e) Tarot cards.

Also, certain religions which, in effect, reduce God to nature, or whose tenets stress the power of mind (to heal, etc.), seem to participate in occult powers.

A great question exists about such things as "mind control," "concept therapy," and other methods which bring about effects that seem to lack sufficient explanatory cause.

41. IN THE ABOVE LIST, ARE NOT SOME PRACTICES MORE SERIOUS THAN OTHERS?

Probably what would be termed the more popular practices (such as horoscopes or ESP) are also less serious involvement. However, as the practices are taken seriously or get deeper into occult involvement, then the problem is more serious.

42. IS IT POSSIBLE FOR A PERSON TO BE INNOCENTLY INVOLVED IN SOME OF THESE OCCULT PRACTICES?

Probably everyone, at some time, has been involved with some of the lighter forms of the occult. This should not cause alarm, although these practices should be discontinued. If the involvement, although innocent, was prolonged and intense (i.e., the person became attached to these practices and even guided his daily decisions by them, such as the horoscope), then probably some occult influence might be present. The person should consciously renounce the involvement, and either himself or someone else should say a prayer of deliverance concerning the matter. For Catholics, it should be mentioned in sacramental confession.

L) *Scriptural Admonitions Forbidding the Occult*

43. WHERE DOES THE OLD TESTAMENT PROHIBIT OCCULT INVOLVEMENT?

The Old Testament contains many prohibitions against occult involvement: "You shall not let a sorceress live" (Exod. 22:17).

"A man or woman who acts as a medium or fortuneteller shall be put to death by stoning; they have no one but themselves to blame for their death" (Lev. 20:27).

44. WHAT EXAMPLES DOES THE NEW TESTAMENT OFFER OF PROHIBITIONS AGAINST OCCULT PRACTICES?

The following are expressly prohibited:

a) Clairvoyance—"It is while we were on our way out to the place of prayer that we met a slave girl who had a clairvoyant spirit" (Acts 16:16).

b) Magic—(Not necessarily the magic of professional entertainers). "They traveled over the whole island as far as Paphos, whence they come across a Jewish magician named Bar-Jesus" (later condemned by Paul) (Acts 13:6).

"A certain man named Simon had been practicing magic in the town and holding the Samaritans spellbound" (Acts 8:9).

c) Sorcery—"Neither did they repent of their ... sorcery" (Rev. 9:21). "The sorceress, the idol-worshipper and deceivers of every sort—their lot is the fiery pool of burning sulphur, the second death" (Rev. 21:8).

d) Idolatry—"It is obvious what proceeds from the flesh; idolatry, sorcery, and the like. Those who do such things will not inherit the kingdom" (Gal. 5:20). "I am telling you, whom I love, to shun the worship of idols" (1 Cor. 10:4).

SUMMARY

The following, then, are the essential points to be made about the kingdom of darkness:

a) The kingdom of darkness is composed of personal beings, fallen from their original goal of happiness, who retain a relationship to mankind which is now harmful and destructive.

b) Christ has given to His Church power over this kingdom.

c) Scripture explains this destructive influence, giving man various warnings and teachings.

d) Charismatic Renewal involve powers and teachings desperately needed by the Church at this time.

e) Demonic influence is either by "obsession" or "possession."

f) Problems on many levels can be discerned as rooted in the Kingdom of Darkness.

g) "Obsession" is handled by prayers of deliverance, while "possession" demands exorcism. The latter requires the permission of the bishop.
h) Knowledge and maturity are needed for a deliverance prayer.
i) The person must have certain dispositions to experience deliverance.
j) The prayer for deliverance is judged by the effects.
k) Occult practices represent a very special avenue into demonic influence, and should be shunned entirely.

Chapter Sixteen

Priest and Charismatic Renewal

> *In practice we recommend that bishops involve prudent priests to be associated with the movement. Such involvement and guidance would be welcomed by the Catholic Pentecostals.*
>
> *(Report of the American Bishops' Committee on Doctrine, November 14, 1969)*

INTRODUCTION

TWO THINGS CAN BE SAID ABOUT PRIESTS AND CHARIS-
matic Renewal. First, Charismatic Renewal needs
priests and, secondly, priests need Charismatic Renewal.
A variety of reasons keep priests out of this renewal.
The main ones offered by priests are:
   a) Just have not experienced the movement (even
      though having heard much about it).
   b) Don't feel the need for it.
   c) Don't like emotionalism.
   d) Can't stand prayer tongues.
   e) Feel it is good for some but is not meant for all.
Other underlying reasons might be that:
   Involvement often comes slowly for priests—a gradual
attraction, annoying curiosity, the witness of another
priest who is involved, or a sense of something lacking
in prayer or in the ministry. Even after some attendance
at charismatic groups, the priest might not particularly be
touched or moved to a committal. This book is written so
that priests might grasp the power and the wisdom in
what could easily be seen as a passing fad or just another
movement.
   It would be a terrible shame, as Charismatic Renewal
strengthens Church life, for priests in large numbers to
stand on the sidelines, unaware of what is involved.
   Charismatic Renewal offers the Roman Catholic priesthood an opportunity to reemerge as a powerful force in
the last part of this century—not in the sense of control-
ling or dominating this powerful renewal, but in offering
priests a chance to be among the people, serving and min-
istering to them. God's Spirit has brought many, even
those who had previously left the Church, into gifts of
prayer and ministries. These people are drawn to the sacraments and need a priest for teaching and guidance.
Others rejoice in having the chance to pray with the
priest, feeling secure that he is there.
   Certain qualities should mark a priest involved in this
renewal—namely, prayerfulness, detachment, ability to
allow the needed freedom in the Spirit, committal, fidelity

and a capacity to allow lay leaders to exercise various functions, both charismatic and administrative.

The full power of Jesus will be present in His Church only as every level and area of the Church is drawn into this life in the Spirit. It is the mixture and variety of members that insures success—the across-the-board response that makes for the fullness of the Body. Unless large numbers of priests become actively involved, immersing themselves in this new life and work in the Spirit, much of the power of the movement will be lost to the Church.

Many will not even hear about the movement except through the parish Church. Most Catholics will not join or persevere in groups unless priests are present. Even those who come and continue will be deprived of some blessings if the ordained priest is absent from their midst.

A priest should not be overwhelmed by laity exercising charismatic ministries, but allow them to develop and grow. At the same time, the priest must realize that he comes prepared in many non-charismatic ways for a role in leadership. He should take time to allow the charismatic spirituality to seep into his life, yielding to God's actions and learning about the gifts. Gradually, he will find his role and place in the group. Then, both he and the people will rejoice in this happy union of clergy and laity in His Spirit.

Although this chapter is written mainly for the priest, hopefully the lay reader will read, ponder and pray for priests. The laity are coming to realize, all too painfully, that priests are as human as the rest of mankind. Called to a divine ministry while still in the flesh, priests need the laity's simple living of the Spirit life as an example and inspiration so that Jesus will be their Lord also.

CHARISMATIC RENEWAL AND PRIESTS

A) *Investigating Charismatic Renewal*

1. WOULD A PRIEST HAVE AN OBLIGATION TO INVESTIGATE CHARISMATIC RENEWAL?

The following reasons are given for this obligation on
the part of priests:

   a) The American bishops have asked that priests be in-
      volved so that there would be correct teaching on the
      use of charismatic gifts.

   b) If the Roman Catholic Church is to be a truly power-
      ful force against the powers of evil in the decades
      immediately ahead, it will come about only through
      a more powerful life in the Spirit.

   c) The people should not be deprived of an opportunity
      for charismatic life. In practice, this will occur if
      priests refuse to learn about this Movement.

   d) If prayer experiences and charisms are supposed to
      be part of the Church's normal life of prayer, wor-
      ship, preaching and healing, then the priest should
      know about and be experiencing them.

   e) If this movement is from God and important for the
      effectiveness of the Church, then every priest should
      seriously investigate what is happening.

God does not want a charismatic movement in the
Church as much as a charismatically-renewed Church.
Without a large scale and serious involvement by priests,
a charismatic Church will never come about.

    2. ARE NOT PRIESTS DOING ENOUGH, IF THEY WAIT,
      LIKE GAMALIEL, TO SEE IF THE MOVEMENT IS FROM
      GOD?

Priests frequently feel that merely allowing the Movement to occur (or even to take place in their parish) is all
that God demands of them. The following should be said:

First, although assuming the stance of Gamaliel might
have been fitting when Charismatic Renewal was just beginning, to remain in that posture forever is certainly
not what God seeks.

Secondly, the very growth and power of the Movement
should lead many priests to realize that it is from God.

Thirdly, even though a Movement is from God, it will
not necessarily have all the effects upon the Church that
God intended it to have, unless priests take it seriously.

3. ARE MANY PRIESTS ACTUALLY INVOLVED IN CHARISMATIC RENEWAL?

Certainly the percentage of priests involved is small. Only as a much higher percentage of priests become involved will the full impact of this renewal occur. The full effects cannot occur until a much larger percentage of priests understand what is happening and dedicate themselves to this Second Pentecost.

4. WHY ARE PRIESTS SO IMPORTANT TO THIS MOVEMENT?

Priests are extremely important to this Movement for three reasons:

First, priests usually bring to the prayer groups sound teaching and can integrate new terms and practices (Baptism of the Spirit, charismatic gifts, etc.) into the Church's traditional teaching.

Secondly, as priests allow Church facilities to be used for the prayer groups, the people do not feel alienated from parish life, or forced to seek this prayer life in other denominations.

Thirdly, even with the spread of the lay apostolate, many Catholics are slow to accept anything in which the priest does not participate. Obviously, they are even slower to take part when the priest is actively opposed.

5. WHAT LEADS PRIESTS TO GET INVOLVED IN CHARISMATIC RENEWAL?

Although each priest's story of involvement is unique, certain general reasons emerge:

a) The priest sensed a need for more effectiveness in his ministry.

b) He was facing personal difficulties and realized that much was lacking in his spiritual life.

c) He was gently attracted by the good effects in the lives of those already involved.

d) He became involved by circumstances or events—such as laity asking him to help with a prayer group.

B) *Priest's Role in a Charismatic Group*

  6. WHAT DOES A PRIEST CONTRIBUTE TO A CHARISMATIC
     PRAYER GROUP?

The average priest could easily contribute the following:
  a) A background in theology which could integrate
     "Pentecostal" teachings with the Catholic faith.
  b) A background in the spiritual life and needed help
     as a confessor and guide.
  c) A general aptitude in pastoral care.
  d) The sacramental powers needed to complement the
     charismatic ministries.

  7. WHY IS THE PRIEST'S THEOLOGICAL AND SCRIPTURAL
     BACKGROUND IMPORTANT?

By means of this theology the priest is able to:
  a) Explain "Pentecostal elements" such as Baptism of
     the Spirit and charismatic ministries, in accord with
     Catholic dogma.
  b) Add the experiences and teaching on prayer and the
     spiritual life present in Church tradition.
  c) Integrate Pentecostal elements into the people's lives
     so that other helps given by God are not overlooked
     or shoved aside (sacraments, doctrinal teaching,
     moral guidance).
  d) Discern those elements of Protestant Pentecostal
     teaching which represent a denominational point of
     view, sometimes incompatible with Catholic doc-
     trine.
  e) Help the people avoid fundamentalism in scriptural
     interpretation.

  8. WHY IS HIS BACKGROUND IN THE SPIRITUAL LIFE
     IMPORTANT?

Through the Baptism of the Holy Spirit, many lay people have been launched into a very deep life of prayer and
spirituality. They need professional guidance to avoid the
pitfalls of being overzealous and imprudent. They need
spiritual and pastoral counseling.

The priest has to be acquainted with Tanquerey's *The
Spiritual Life*, with various authors on prayer and spir-

ituality (as St. Francis de Sales, Eugene Boylan, Edward Leen, Dom Marmion), and with the principles of pastoral counseling, especially in the field of personal psychology. Also, his years of seminary training should have provided him with some basic safeguards to sound spirituality. All of this, however, has to be complemented by the priest's own spiritual experiences and growth.

9. WHY IS IT IMPORTANT FOR A GROUP TO HAVE THE BENEFIT OF THE PRIEST'S SACRAMENTAL MINISTRY?

A number of reasons can be given:

a) Although prayer experiences and charismatic gifts are important for Church life, Catholics have been spiritually fed for centuries by the sacramental life. The place of these charismatic powers in the Church are not yet clear, even though certainly meant to be part of normal Church life.

b) The sacraments lend an objective element to the very subjective side of charismatic prayer and free praise and worship. Enthusiasm and fervor are sustained only by stable, dogmatically-certain, non-subjective rites.

c) The presence of the sacraments, so intimately connected with Holy Orders, insures that this charismatic outpouring will remain within and renew the institutional Church.

d) Prayer life should be helped not only by spontaneous and free worship but also by prepared and official prayers of the Church.

e) A sacramental ministry links the prayer group to the total Church, thus avoiding isolation.

C) *Effect Upon the Priest's Life and Ministry*

10. HOW DOES A PRIEST BENEFIT BY INVOLVEMENT IN CHARISMATIC RENEWAL?

The following benefits could be listed:

a) An improved life of prayer.

b) An increased faith in his work and ministry.

c) Deeper involvement in the priesthood because of relating more closely with the laity.

d) A fulfillment of many human needs by sharing in a prayer group.

11. HOW DOES INVOLVEMENT IN THIS MOVEMENT AFFECT THE PRIEST'S PRAYER LIFE?

The following effects are witnessed to by most priests:

a) A greater emphasis on prayer and more time devoted to it each day.

b) A greater faith in prayer, especially the priest's prayer of intercession for those entrusted to him.

c) A greater attraction for and understanding of Scripture.

d) Greater familiarity with God during prayer time.

12. HOW DOES INVOLVEMENT IN CHARISMATIC RENEWAL AFFECT THE PRIEST'S MINISTRY?

By participating in a prayer group, the priest should:

a) Grasp better God's plan for pastoral activity, realizing God's activity always forms a people.

b) Reevaluate his pastoral goals and practices, being willing to spend more time and energy in nurturing a Christian community.

c) Have more faith in his own preaching. The priest preaches Christ and the gospel message in a simpler and more powerful way, instead of using psychology or sociology as the dynamism of his talks.

d) Accept the role of working in a team, realizing that God has given others in the parish a definite ministry, albeit non-sacramental.

e) Have greater satisfaction in saying mass and greater joy and hope in distributing sacraments. The priest begins to appreciate the healing sacraments even more.

13. HOW DOES THE PRAYER GROUP BRING ABOUT DEEPER INVOLVEMENT IN HIS OWN PRIESTHOOD?

The following just naturally occurs from a priest's participation in a group:

a) His people see him regularly in a personal way.
b) By realizing his committal to prayer, they are more ready to present spiritual and personal problems to him.
c) Whether he is in leadership or not, he is often turned to for advice.
d) As he discovers difficulties, his own compassion and concern will force him to seek out those who would not approach him.

14. HOW DOES SHARING IN THE PRAYER GROUP HELP THE PRIEST TO PERSONAL FULFILLMENT?

Most people in a priest's life relate to him in a functional way. They need his help and call upon his services —either personal or sacramental. If a priest seeks personal fulfillment in human relationships, he usually does so away from his ministry.

In a prayer group, however, the priestly ministry and personal relationships are combined, as the priest prays with the people, shares, counsels, consoles and is consoled.

D) *Common Objections of Priests to Charistmatic Renewal*

15. WHAT OBJECTIONS DO PRIESTS USUALLY OFFER AGAINST CHARISMATIC RENEWAL?

The following are usually given:
a) Attracts unstable people and is a haven for those who are emotionally dependent.
b) Is too emotional, placing too much accent on feelings.
c) Goes against reason or sound theology.
d) Is naive in believing God intervenes directly, such as through healing or prophecy.

16. WHAT OTHER REASONS COULD BE GIVEN WHY MORE PRIESTS ARE NOT INVOLVED?

More priests are probably not involved because:
a) They have never had a real opportunity to experience a prayer group.

b) Even when an opportunity was present, they never felt moved to participate.

c) If they did participate, they did not find anything special about the group that would lead them to a regular committal.

d) They have never had the basic teachings of Pentecostalism explained or integrated into Catholic thought.

e) They saw only partial aspects of the movement, not realizing its importance for every phase of their life and ministry.

17. IS NOT THE PRIEST RIGHTLY CONCERNED ABOUT THE EMOTIONAL ASPECTS OF CHARISMATIC RENEWAL?

Since the emotional problem or question in Charismatic Renewal is such a great stumbling block for many priests, it would be well to treat it at length.

a) Attendance at a charismatic group would show much less emotion than outside observers think. Rather, there is a gentle, emotional freedom in expressing praise and worship.

b) Most charismatic groups allow expressions of joy or friendship which are not usually accepted in society. The relationships, however, in the prayer community are usually deep and beautiful ones, as contrasted with the often superficial friendships present elsewhere. Therefore, these expressions of friendly relationships might strike a priest as different at first sight, but truly represent a healthier expression of feeling than now exists in our very unhealthy American culture.

c) Priests cannot expect the laity to suddenly become seminarians or novices. God understands that many are moved only by some emotional experiences. Usually, after a time, the experience of prayer is more gentle and peaceful than striking and startling.

The young, especially, live in a very emotional world and God in His wisdom and kindness often touches them emotionally in prayer. However, close and long-term association with prayer groups shows that underneath the emotions God is building young people in very deep faith and that they continue to serve Him when the emotional elements are withdrawn.

18. DO NOT PRIESTS HAVE DIFFICULTIES WITH THE MANY STORIES OF HEALINGS THAT THEY HEAR FROM CHARISMATICS?

Priests, more than laity, do experience more difficulty with stories of divine intervention, probably because they rightly see themselves as discerners of true, valid, divine activity. Also some stories have been the result more of enthusiasm than objective facts. Yet the following should be stated:

a) Many healings—spiritual, psychological and physical—have occurred in Charismatic Renewal and probably these powers of healing will increase.

b) The Church officially prays for healings at the Eucharist. This renewal is merely restoring a belief in an overlooked power.

c) This movement has renewed people's faith in the healing power of the Sacrament of Penance and has restored that sacrament to general use.

d) The Church herself, in the new rite of the Anointing of the Sick, has stressed the power of the Spirit to heal in body and soul.

19. ARE NOT MANY PRIESTS AFFECTED BY RONALD KNOX'S "ENTHUSIASM," WHICH GAVE MUCH EMPHASIS TO THE PROBLEMS INHERENT IN ENTHUSIAST MOVEMENTS?

It is common for a priest to claim that he "can't buy" Charismatic Renewal because he was inoculated by Msgr. Knox. A full discussion of his book could not be undertaken here. Hopefully, however, the following points have been constantly stressed in the foregoing chapters:

a) Religious experiences represent only one phase of Church life and must be integrated with the sacra-

mental, doctrinal and moral aspects to effect a total
and balanced spiritual life.

b) Charismatic gifts are not "holiness" gifts but "service" powers to help the total Church.

c) Charisms are always subject to the discernment of
   spiritual office in the Church such as hierarchy.

d) Certain objective guides are above charismatic manifestations—Scripture, Church teaching, moral law.

e) Although all "enthusiast" movements (and Charismatic Renewal is such a movement) present dangers and problems, they also offer a new richness
   and fervor to Church life.

f) Leaders are well aware of problems encountered by
   such previous movements and do not wish to repeat
   past historical mistakes.

E) *Priests Getting Involved*

20. WHAT STEPS SHOULD BE TAKEN BY MEMBERS OF
    PRAYER GROUPS TO INCREASE THE PRIESTS' IN-
    VOLVEMENT IN THIS RENEWAL?

The following seem appropriate:

a) Pray for priests.

b) Make them aware of charismatic meetings and special events.

c) Priests already involved should exercise a quiet witness ministry.

d) Lay involvement in non-charismatic Church activity.

e) Requesting the priest to use his sacramental and
   pastoral gifts when he attends charismatic events.
   Especially in the beginning priests need a great deal
   of warm support since they are used to leading and
   guiding religious groups and not being just a
   learner again.

21. WHAT DANGERS SHOULD A PRIEST BE AWARE OF
    AS HE DOES GET INVOLVED?

A priest should keep the following in mind:

a) Although involved with the prayer group, his ministry must remain extended to all parts of the Church, charismatic and non-charismatic.

b) His performance in non-charismatic work should remain totally adequate so that people and other priests do not blame Charismatic Renewal for any inadequacies.

c) While enjoying the warmth of personal relationships in the prayer group, he should be aware of emotional involvement that would jeopardize his work or cause scandal. Generally, the laity in these groups are extremely broad-minded and in no way puritanical in outlook. However, a certain prudence should be present.

22. SHOULD THERE BE A "PRIEST PRAYER GROUP" OR SHOULD A PRIEST BELONG TO A REGULAR PRAYER COMMUNITY?

Probably both. A priest group is, in a sense, a natural community and in it the priest will find a teaching, an orientation, a support and a level of prayer that probably could not be found elsewhere. In practice, many priests feel more comfortable if initiated into Charismatic Renewal through a priest prayer group. After such an initial involvement, they frequently begin groups in their own parish or institution.

Also, priests directly involved with other prayer communities sense a need to come together and pray with other priests similarly involved.

In a large diocese, a priest prayer group seems indispensable if large numbers of priests are to be involved. As the priests get involved in other groups, they might move out of the priest prayer group, but the initial teaching and opportunity afforded by the priest group was necessary.

Chapter Seventeen

Problems in Charismatic Renewal

*Admittedly, there have been abuses,
but the cure is not a denial of their
existence but their proper use.*
(Report of the American Bishops'
Committee on Doctrine, November 14, 1969)

INTRODUCTION

IT WOULD BE IMPOSSIBLE FOR A MOVEMENT OF THIS SIZE, which has spread so rapidly, with so many aspects that are new, to be free of problems. Even excellent leadership cannot weed out all problems. In fact, good leadership learns to leave many problems alone, following the wisdom of the owner of the field who allowed the good and bad seed to grow together.

All types of problems do exist—charismatic problems, emotional problems, relationship problems, leadership problems, ecumenical problems. There are problems with prophecy, with healings, with poor discernment and, often, general misunderstanding of what Pentecostalism is all about.

Yet, in another sense, this movement has been amazingly free of problems, although the years just ahead will determine whether that state perdures. It has continued to attract thousands, has gained in acceptance by Church leaders, enjoys national and local leaders seen by all as God's servants, has not been the subject of any major scandal, and maintains a remarkable unity and charity. Any of the above constitutes a major accomplishment.

In a sense, this is a hidden movement, not yet exposed to the public scrutiny of normal Church life. As such, it has also been allowed to work out its own problems, and has assumed direct responsibility in doing so.

This chapter does not claim to discuss every, or even most, of the problems connected with this movement. It could easily be entitled "warnings to charismatic leaders" rather than "problems inherent in Charismatic Renewal."

It hopes only to be a small "Word of Wisdom," that partial insight which opens the group to God's grace and protects them from the Evil One.

PROBLEMS INHERENT IN CHARISMATIC RENEWAL

An honest approach to what the Spirit is doing among

us must include a just evaluation of difficulties. However, certain points should be noted:

  a) Prayer groups vary greatly from one another, even if geographically close.
  b) Prayer groups in different areas of the country naturally can vary to an even greater degree.
  c) In trying to present the problems honestly, the wrong impression could be given that Charismatic Renewal is just filled with all kinds of difficulties.
  d) Since people have problems and Charismatic Renewal is filled with people, many problems might exist that are not due to, yet are blamed upon, the movement.

A) *Theological Problems*

  1. MANY OBJECT THAT CHARISMATIC RENEWAL EX-ALTS THE HOLY SPIRIT TO SUCH A POINT THAT CHRIST IS OVERLOOKED.

First, the Holy Spirit is a member of the Trinity and it is theologically impossible to overexalt Him.

Secondly, those involved in Charismatic Renewal seek, and find to some degree, a personal relationship with all the members of the Trinity—the loving, provident Father, Jesus as Lord and the Spirit, Jesus' gift to us.

Thirdly, the main result of the Baptism of the Spirit is to bestow a deep personal knowledge and love for Christ.

Fourthly, by the charismatic gifts, Christians can share in the ministry of Christ, Who wants His Church to be equipped with His powers—"will do the works I do and greater far than these" (John 14:12).

  2. DOES NOT THIS MOVEMENT CENTER ON CERTAIN TRUTHS, SUCH AS THE BAPTISM OF THE SPIRIT AND CHARISMS, SO THAT ITS TEACHING IS OUT OF BAL-ANCE?

Certainly the movement stresses certain truths, but the following explanation can be given:

  a) The Charismatic Movement is not the whole Church but is a renewal of certain aspects of Church life.

(In fact, leadership has deliberately kept the movement out of many areas of Church concern.) It is legitimate, therefore, for the movement to attempt Church renewal in only those areas where it possesses experience.

b) The movement does not try to overturn, in an iconoclastic manner, other elements such as sacraments or doctrines, but hopes that the full life of the Spirit will renew all things in the Church.

c) As the movement continues, its teaching and experience broadens so that it does enter into many other concerns of the Church besides charismatic gifts.

d) This widening of horizons also happens to the people involved. The newcomer to a prayer group, naturally, is taken up by the charisms and the Baptism of the Spirit. As he continues, he realizes that the life in the Spirit touches every aspect of his life.

3. DOES NOT MUCH PENTECOSTAL TEACHING BORDER ON SCRIPTURAL FUNDAMENTALISM?

If Catholics get involved with fundamentalist groups, they will be affected by the teaching.

However, Catholic groups in general:

a) Read the Scriptures in a devout way, trying to accept the common-sense meaning of the texts.

b) Welcome scholarship and actively seek speakers to help their biblical understanding.

c) Integrate their reading of Scripture with the Church's dogmatic and sacramental theology.

B) *Charismatic Renewal and Modern Theology*

4. DO NOT PENTECOSTALS SET ASIDE MUCH MODERN THEOLOGY, AS ON THE CONSCIOUSNESS OF JESUS, OR THE VIRGIN BIRTH, OR THE EVOLUTION OF THE PRIESTLY POWERS, OR THE MANY OTHER TRUTHS THAT SCHOLARSHIP HAS BEEN LOOKING INTO?

Catholic Pentecostals, knowingly or unknowingly, live within the framework of certain fundamental truths. They use this set of truths as the helps needed to be guided daily by God's Spirit. Other questions being discussed by theologians are not averted to unless they touch upon or affect day-by-day yielding to the Spirit.

5. WHAT "SET OF TRUTHS" PROVIDES THIS THEOLOGICAL FRAMEWORK?

The following seem to be the theological basis for Catholic Pentecostalism:

a) God, although transcendental, has intervened in history, forming a Chosen People.

b) His most incisive intervention was the sending of His own Son, Jesus, Who is equal to the Father, the alpha and omega of all human existence, in Whom all are to be reconciled for all eternity.

c) Jesus has given His Spirit as His first gift, and through the Spirit continues to intervene in a saving action.

d) This saving action embraces many elements— Church teaching, sacraments, Scripture, charismatic ministries, help in prayer, and conversion experiences.

e) An aspect of that saving action is the special guidance given to the Catholic Church to preserve intact the fundamental truths of Christianity.

6. IN RECENT YEARS, CATECHETICS HAS RIGHTLY BROUGHT TO THE FOREGROUND THE ROLE OF THE CRITICAL, INTELLECTUAL FACULTIES, SO THAT MYTHS OR HALF-TRUTHS CONCERNING GOD'S ACTIVITY AMONG MEN ARE CORRECTED. DOES NOT CHARISMATIC RENEWAL WITH ITS INSISTENCE ON SIMPLE FAITH IN GOD'S ACTIVITY THREATEN TO UNDO THIS SCHOLARSHIP?

It would be easy to contrast Charismatic Renewal, with its insistence on expectant faith in God's activity, with modern theology and catechetics which seem so ready to demythologize divine interventions, and feel that the former, if followed, would sweep away the insights of catechetics.

The following should be said:
a) A valid life in the Spirit can be built only on truths, not by sweeping away opponents.
b) A healthy attitude exists in Catholic Pentecostals that the Spirit has been at work in many renewals in the Church—liturgical, Scriptural, catechetical—and the results have been welcomed.
c) All of these renewals are seen as releasing the power of the Spirit in the Church.
d) In every renewal, charismatic included, the discernment of spirits must be used so that changes are in God's will.

C) *Life in the Spirit Problems*

(Since problems arising with each charismatic gift were treated in the individual chapters, only some of the more general difficulties are taken up here.)

7. DO NOT CHARISMATICS TEND TO OVEREXALT THE ROLE OF THE BAPTISM OF THE SPIRIT, ALMOST BEING UNABLE TO SEE ANYTHING BUT A SPIRIT-FILLED LIFE AS TRULY CHRISTIAN?

On the positive side the following should be said:
a) The rediscovery of the Holy Spirit as a Person who is to be experienced, and a source of consolation, prayer experiences and charismatic powers, is a tremendous contribution, owed primarily to the Pentecostal Churches.
b) The belief in the release of the Spirit's power within us, and the understanding of how this is to occur, is central in renewing the pastoral practice of the Church.

However, these and all the other positive factors, summed up in the important term, "The Baptism of the Holy Spirit," should not hide the problems involved with the term and its application to Christian life.

8. WHAT DANGERS EXIST WITH THE TERM AND THE PRACTICE OF THE "BAPTISM OF THE SPIRIT"?

A great many problems are inherent unless the phenomenon is integrated into a correct theological and pastoral practice. The following problems could be noted:

a) Allowing the Baptism of the Spirit to become almost sacramental, both in its explanation and its practice.

b) To use this term to sharply distinguish between "Spirit-filled" and those not "Spirit-filled," leading to all kinds of unsound theological conclusions.

c) To overlook the fact that many do experience the Holy Spirit in their lives, even though they might not have received the Baptism of the Spirit.

d) To see the Baptism of the Spirit as so important that other means of sanctification (Sacraments, liturgical prayer, normal Church life) are overlooked or looked down upon.

e) To deny the objective help of sacraments because of overstressing the importance of subjective dispositions. This could lead, for example, to a belief in rebaptism.

9. WHAT DANGERS ARE PRESENT IN THE REEMERGENCE OF CHARISMATIC GIFTS?

Besides problems involved with each gift, the following problems are associated with the gifts:

a) To afford people who exercise striking charismatic gifts a larger role in Church life than God wills.

b) To confuse the presence of gifts with holiness, so that the gifts cover up the lack of even basic goodness.

c) To see God's action only in charismatic gifts, being unwilling to listen to other sources for direction, e.g., complaints of others, guidance of Church authorities.

d) To contrast too sharply the charismatic and non-charismatic Church leadership, and being willing to listen only to those who exercise gifts.

10. CANNOT THESE POWERS OF THE SPIRIT THREATEN OTHER ASPECTS OF CHURCH LIFE?

In general, gifts are a striking manifestation of God's

power and wisdom. As such, they present the danger of
setting apart those who exercise the gifts from those who
do not. In fact, all the Pentecostal elements (Baptism of
the Spirit, prayer tongues, charismatic ministries) can
erode the use of and belief in other elements of the Church,
especially Church leadership and sacramental life.
They also can introduce a new and different lack of bal-
ance. Just as stress was formerly placed on objective religious acts (such as reception of sacraments, attendance at
mass), so the stress could now swing over to subjective
religious acts—as prayer and charismatic manifestations.
The solution, of course, is an integration of the two into
a totally balanced and powerful Church life.

D) *Social Action Problems*

11. IS IT NOT TRUE THAT CATHOLICS INVOLVED IN SO-
    CIAL ACTION WITHDRAW FROM THEIR ATTEMPTS TO
    CORRECT INJUSTICES AS THEY BECOME INTERESTED
    IN CHARISMATIC RENEWAL?

There does seem to be some basis for that complaint.
However, the following could be said:

  a) Many others never involved in Charismatic Renewal
     have also withdrawn from social action.
  b) A great naivete about the social action role of the
     Church and what could be accomplished was preva-
     lent in the 1960s.
  c) Certainly the collapse of the War on Poverty cannot
     be blamed on Charismatic Renewal.
  d) Some withdrawal from these works resulted from
     an experience of their futility.

However, in spite of these reasons, a definite question
exists of balancing the stress placed by this renewal on the
spiritual life with the call of the Church to social action.

12. DOES NOT CHARISMATIC RENEWAL TURN PEOPLE
    AWAY FROM THE CALL TO SOCIAL ACTION THAT THE
    CHURCH HAS RECENTLY EMPHASIZED?

If Charismatic Renewal was deliberately turning the
Church away from social action and involvement in the

modern world, then it would be detrimental to Church life. However, a question could be raised about just how many Catholics were responding to their Church's insistence on social justice.

Concerning social action, Charismatic Renewal would say the following:

a) The primary work of the Church is to call people to the Father by a personal knowledge of Christ: "Eternal life is this: to know you, the only true God, and Him whom you have sent, Jesus Christ" (John 17:3).

b) Many social ills exist because men have wrongly oriented themselves and do not allow the basic principles of a Christian life to order their daily priorities.

c) People cannot apply the principles of Christ in social action unless they are helped to experience Christ by daily prayer.

d) Much social change will occur as people experience Christian relationships in a community and have a concrete idea of Christ's Kingdom.

e) Much more important than social change (new laws, new economic system, etc.) is social transformation (new outlooks, new sets of relationship among men). This latter is definitely occurring in charismatic prayer groups.

13. WHAT DOES CHARISMATIC RENEWAL OFFER TO THE SOCIAL ACTION OF THE CHURCH?

First, prolonged involvement in social action programs is impossible for large numbers of people unless they are nourished by religious convictions and fed by personal and community prayers.

Secondly, many who come to charismatic prayer groups find themselves much more oriented to their neighbors through these prayer groups and much social action takes place in a non-organized, person-to-person way.

Thirdly, Charismatic Renewal is certainly not expert in social action and it is not yet clear how this renewal will affect the social action movement in the Church.

Fourthly, leaders are aware of this just criticism concerning withdrawal from social action and are trying to remedy the problem without destroying the essential spiritual nature of the movement.

14. What is the Future of Charismatic Renewal and Social Action?

Christ is pouring forth His Spirit "To make all things new," including the Church's social action. It is true that the stress in the early stages of the movement (and in the early stages of each new prayer group) centers on "interior" concerns rather than exterior, or "social action" principles.

However, as time goes on, and God's action in the movement unfolds, Charismatic Renewal is being seen as a very complex phenomenon, carrying within itself the power to renew every phase of the Church's life. Hopefully this renewal will help social action in the Church according to its own dynamism, that is, a Christ-centered life and a stress on Christian Community.

E) *Ecumenical Problems*

15. What Ecumenical Opportunities are Offered by Charismatic Renewal?

The following could be listed:
a) Nowhere in the Church do Catholics and other Christians meet, share and pray together, as in this renewal.
b) Not only does this religious sharing occur, but a whole body of doctrine concerning the full life in the Spirit acts as a common belief and focal point of religious activity.
c) This common sharing and belief was extensive enough to form Pentecostal demoninations which continue to grow and have been termed "the third force" in Christianity.

16. What Problems are Present in Charismatic Renewal due to the Division of the Churches?

The outstanding difficulties are:

In theory:

a) Although united with other charismatics in the life of the Spirit, Catholics do not share all religious beliefs with them.

b) Although united with other Catholics in religious beliefs and doctrine, they do not share with them some aspects of religious practice—such as charismatic prayer.

In practice the following problems are present:

a) Those who are not Catholics must refrain from receiving the Eucharist, even though they have shared every other aspect of the group's worship.

b) Pressures arising from charity to remove Catholic practices and teachings from the prayer group to accommodate other Christians who attend.

17. IS THERE ANY SOLUTION TO THESE PROBLEMS?

No perfect solution exists until the radical division of the Churches themselves is healed by the Lord. Until then, every other solution has to be incomplete and not fully satisfying. The following guidelines could be followed:

a) Charity and thoughtfulness will always be blessed by God.

b) Ecumenical difficulties and religious differences should not be accented.

c) The religious divisions and diverse religious practices and beliefs must be faced honestly.

In fairness to all, a charismatic prayer group should be clear in its identity, whether it is Catholic, other-denominational or inter-denominational. In this way everyone understands the prayer and worship relationship they are entering into.

18. IF THE GROUP IS CLEARLY KNOWN AS A CATHOLIC GROUP, WHAT GUIDELINES CAN BE FOLLOWED?

If the group is Catholic, the following religious and cultural aspects can be present with no one able to take offense:

a) Mass is part of the prayer meeting whenever the leaders decide.

b) The Life in the Spirit seminars can be taught in Catholic terms, and draw upon Catholic traditions.

c) The general teaching can freely draw on Catholic tradition or even explain a Catholic practice (such as sacramental confession).

d) The group adheres to the diocesan guidelines and the Church's teaching on various issues.

A similar freedom is accorded to charismatic groups of other denominations.

19. IS NOT THE ABOVE ATTITUDE BUILDING "DENOMINA-
TIONAL WALLS" INSTEAD OF STRESSING THE ONE
LORD, ONE SPIRIT OUTLOOK?

The following should be noted:

a) Charismatic Renewal does not build denominational walls, but honestly admits that such walls exist due to historical divisions.

b) The denominational Churches seem to be taking honest steps toward unity.

c) Charismatic Renewal is not primarily an ecumenical movement and the heavy weight of ecumenism should not be thrust upon this still-young and, as yet, unformed movement. The burden of ecumenism rightly belongs with the denominational Churches themselves and not primarily upon a given movement in the Churches.

d) If Charismatic Renewal in the Catholic Church moves too quickly toward ecumenism, it will be totally unable to touch the millions of Catholics who have not yet experienced a full life in the Spirit.

e) The Catholic Church (and other denominations) contains many other elements of sanctification besides prayer experiences and charismatic gifts. Not to use these sanctifying elements because of ecumenism is to weaken this renewal seriously.

f) In the past, Charismatic Renewal has rightly refused to be an instrument for any cause, no matter how good (anti-war, pro-life, social action, liturgical renewal). This movement is not an instrument for any cause, except a full life in the Spirit for everyone.

g) Ecumenism means a belief that the Lord in his own time and in His own way will bring about a unity of all who confess Him as Lord.

F) *Other Problems in Charismatic Renewal*

20. DO NOT LEADERS ACT AND SPEAK AS IF THE CHURCH CANNOT DO WITHOUT THIS MOVEMENT?

It is true that most involved in this movement do feel that it contains power needed desperately by the Church.

Hopefully, this attitude does not seem haughty but manifests instead the simple joy of those who have found a pearl of great price, wanting to share this with all who will listen.

Certainly the Church will continue to exist until the end of time, even without Charismatic Renewal. The desperate need served by this renewal is in equipping the Church to deal with the modern world.

21. WHY DO MEMBERS OF CHARISMATIC PRAYER GROUPS LIFT THEIR HANDS AND ARMS WHILE PRAYING?

The raising of the hands or arms in prayer has a couple of effects:

First, it signifies the freedom of praise present in the group.

Secondly, and more importantly, it allows prayer to be part of the whole person—mind, heart, lips, body, arms, etc.—which is one of the many reawakened sources of spiritual life present in Charismatic Renewal.

22. DOES NOT THIS MOVEMENT THREATEN TO DIVIDE THE CATHOLIC CHURCH INTO PENTECOSTALS AND NON-PENTECOSTALS?

Obviously some dynamic is established when people within the Church are attracted to a certain way of prayer. However, certain attitudes within this renewal safeguard against the problem:

a) The very name "Pentecostals" is used less. Even the

phrase "Charismatic Renewal" is giving way to
phrases like "Catholics interested in a full life in
the Spirit."

b) The open acceptance of Charismatic Renewal by the
official Church removes the problem of "martyrdom"
or "martyr-complexes" that can be so unhealthy in
a misunderstood group.

c) The abundance of charismatic gifts, especially
"prayer tongues," removes pride or gnostic ten-
dencies.

d) A "holier-than-thou" attitude seems to have been
avoided in most groups, where joy and peace predominate.

23. IS THERE MUCH CHANCE THAT EARLIER ECCLESIAS-
TICAL HERESIES WHICH INVOLVED OTHER "ENTHU-
SIAST" GROUPS WILL BE AVOIDED?

These past heresies involved denying any authority
that was not charismatic, attributing sacramental powers
only to charismatic people, or splitting off from the non-
charismatic members of a Church.

The following reasons can be cited why these will not
occur:

a) Leaders are acutely aware of these heresies and see
as false any road leading in that direction.

b) The Church is basically in the hands of good bishops. There is not wide-scale corruption among the
hierarchy that needs to be scolded by a righteous,
charismatic group.

c) The level of education is much higher than at any
time in history, and "simplistic" or "fundamentalist" outlooks are seen as just that.

d) The dualistic heresies, denying the good of man's
body, are countered by the modern, widespread
knowledge of man's psychology and the Freudian insights into the subconscious. As a result, much self-
delusion present in other enthusiast movements
would now be spotted for what it was.

24. Does the Movement Have Sufficient Leadership?

No, and this book has been written to encourage involvement by those who have leadership talent. In a sense, though, lack of leadership witnesses to the fantastically quick spread of the movement and to the perseverance among the members. It also witnesses to the lack of background in so many things which should have been normal to Church life—charismatic gifts, power over the Evil One, diverse ministries in the Church, and the basic Christian community.

This book has been written with the intention of lending all Christians some basic instructions and guidance. *Praise the Lord.*

* * *

SELECTED BIBLIOGRAPHY

Since Charismatic Renewal Services and other sources of charismatic publications carry very lengthy lists of publications that are available, the following short bibliography is given listing those books which would provide deeper insights into the various aspects of the renewal. Two of the books, *Healing* by Father Francis MacNutt, O.P., and *Inner Healing* by Father Michael Scanlan, T.O.R., appeared after this book was already written. They are included because they represent an excellent and detailed explanation of the healing ministry.

BOOKS

The New American Bible. Camden, New Jersey: Thomas Nelson, Inc., 1971.
Bittlinger, Arnold. *Gifts and Graces.* Grand Rapids, Michigan: William B. Eerdman's Publishing Co., 1967.
Byrne, James. *Threshold of God's Promise.* Notre Dame, Indiana: Ave Maria Press, 1970.
Clark, Stephen B. *Life in the Spirit Seminars.* Notre Dame, Indiana: Charismatic Renewal Services, 1973.
————. *Where Are We Headed?* Notre Dame, Indiana: Charismatic Renewal Services, 1973.
Freeman, Hobart E. *Angels of Light.* Plainfield, New Jersey: Logos International, 1969.
Gee, Donald. *Concerning Spiritual Gifts.* Springfield, Missouri: Gospel Publishing House, 1972.

————. *Spiritual Gifts in the Word of the Ministry Today.* Springfield, Missouri: Gospel Publishing House, 1963.
Gelpi, Donald L., S.J. *Pentecostalism: A Theological Viewpoint.* Paramus, New Jersey: Paulist Press, 1971.
Harper, Michael. *Spiritual Warfare.* London: Hodder and Stoughtow, 1970.
Knox, R. A. *Enthusiasm.* New York: Oxford University Press, 1950.
MacNutt, Francis, O.P. *Healing.* Notre Dame, Indiana: Ave Maria Press, 1974.
McKenzie, John L., S.J. *Dictionary of the Bible.* London: Geoffrey-Chapman, 1965.
Martin, Ralph. *Unless the Lord Build the House.* Notre Dame, Indiana: Ave Maria Press, 1970.
O'Connor, Edward D., C.S.C. *The Pentecostal Movement in the Catholic Church.* Notre Dame, Indiana: Ave Maria Press, 1971.
Scanlan, Michael, T.O.R. *Inner Healing.* Paramus, New Jersey: Paulist Press, 1974.
————. *Power in Penance.* Notre Dame, Indiana: Ave Maria Press, 1972.
Tugwell, Simon. *Did You Receive the Spirit?* Paramus, New Jersey: Paulist Press, 1972.

ARTICLE

Wild, Robert. "Baptism in the Holy Spirit." In *Cross and Crown.* Oak Park, Illinois, 1973.

PUBLICATION

New Covenant Magazine. Ann Arbor, Michigan.

PAMPHLETS

Clark, Stephen B. *Spiritual Gifts.* Pecos, New Mexico: Dove Publications, 1969.
Cavnar, Jim. *Prayer Meetings.* Pecos, New Mexico: Dove Publications, 1969.

RESOURCES

Abbot, Walter M., S.J. *The Documents of Vatican II.* New York: America Press, 1966.
Denzinger-Schonometzer. *Enchiridin Symbolorum-Definitionum et Declarationum. (de rebus fidei et morum).* Barcelona, Spain: Herder, 1965. 33rd edition.
Rahner, Karl, ed. *Sacramentum Mundi.* New York: Herder and Herder, 1969. 6 vols.
Weller, Rev. Philip, ed. and translator. *The Roman Ritual.* Milwaukee, Wisconsin: Bruce Publishing Co., 1952.